Model Test Papers

ICSE Class 10

For Term 2

MATHEMATICS

Author:
Mr. Mohit Tripathi

Title	: Model Test Papers for class -X Mathematics
Author Name	: Mr. Mohit Tripathi
Published By	: EduGorilla Community Pvt. Ltd.
Publishers Address	: 12/651, First Floor Opp. Arvindo Park, Near Jama Masjid, Indira Nagar, Lucknow, Uttar Pradesh - 226016, India

Copyright

ISBN: 9789355563354

Disclaimer

Compiled and Created by EduGorilla Book Experts

Printed by EduGorilla Community Pvt. Ltd.

SYLLABUS

MATHEMATICS (51)

BIFURCATED SYLLABUS

(As per the Reduced Syllabus for ICSE – Class X Year 2022 Examination)

SEMESTER 2

(Marks: 50)

UNIT NO.	NAME OF THE UNIT
1.	Co – ordinate Geometry
2.	Geometry : Circle
3.	Mensuration
4.	Trigonometry
5.	Statistics
6.	Probability

MATHEMATICS (51)

CLASS X

There will be ***one*** *paper of* ***two and a half*** *hours duration carrying 80 marks and Internal Assessment of 20 marks.*

The paper will be divided into ***two*** *sections, Section I (40 marks), Section II (40 marks).*

Section I: *Will consist of compulsory short answer questions.*

Section II: *Candidates will be required to answer* ***four*** *out of* ***seven*** *questions.*

1. Commercial Mathematics

(i) Goods and Services Tax (GST)

Computation of tax including problems involving discounts, list-price, profit, loss, basic/cost price including inverse cases. Candidates are also expected to find price paid by the consumer after paying State Goods and Service Tax (SGST) and Central Goods and Service Tax (CGST) - the different rates as in vogue on different types of items will be provided. Problems based on corresponding inverse cases are also included.

(ii) Banking

Recurring Deposit Accounts*: computation of interest and maturity value using the formula:*

$$I = P\frac{n(n+1)}{2\times 12}\times\frac{r}{100}$$

$$MV = P\,x\,n + I$$

2. Algebra

(i) Linear Inequations

Linear Inequations in one unknown for $x \in N, W, Z, R$. Solving:

- *Algebraically and writing the solution in set notation form.*
- *Representation of solution on the number line.*

(ii) Quadratic Equations in one variable

(a) Nature of roots

- *Two distinct real roots if $b^2 - 4ac > 0$*
- *Two equal real roots if $b^2 - 4ac = 0$*
- *No real roots if $b^2 - 4ac < 0$*

(b) Solving Quadratic equations by:

- *Factorisation*
- *Using Formula.*

(c) Solving simple quadratic equation problems.

(iii) Ratio and Proportion

(a) Proportion, Continued proportion, mean proportion

(b) Componendo, dividendo, alternendo, invertendo properties and their combinations.

(iv) Factorisation of polynomials:

(a) Factor Theorem.

(b) Remainder Theorem.

(c) Factorising a polynomial completely after obtaining one factor by factor theorem.

Note: f (x) not to exceed degree 3.

(v) Matrices

(a) Order of a matrix. Row and column matrices.

(b) Compatibility for addition and multiplication.

(c) Null and Identity matrices.

(d) Addition and subtraction of 2×2 matrices.

(e) Multiplication of a 2×2 matrix by

- *a non-zero rational number*
- *a matrix.*

(vi) Arithmetic Progression

- *Finding General term.*
- *Finding Sum of first 'n' terms.*

(vii) Co-ordinate Geometry

(a) Reflection

(i) Reflection of a point in a line:

x=0, y =0, x= a, y=a, the origin.

(ii) Reflection of a point in the origin.

(iii) Invariant points.

(b) Co-ordinates expressed as (*x,y*), Section formula, Midpoint formula, Concept of slope, equation of a line, Various forms of straight lines.

(i) Section and Mid-point formula (Internal section only, co-ordinates of the centroid of a triangle included).

(ii) Equation of a line:

- *Slope –intercept form $y = mx + c$*
- *Two- point form $(y-y_1) = m(x-x_1)$*

  Geometric understanding of 'm' as slope/ gradient/ $\tan\theta$ where θ is the angle the line makes with the positive direction of the x axis.

  Geometric understanding of 'c' as the y-intercept/the ordinate of the point where the line intercepts the y axis/ the point on the line where x=0.

- *Conditions for two lines to be parallel or perpendicular.*

Simple applications of all the above.

3. Geometry

(a) Similarity

Similarity, conditions of similar triangles.

(i) Comparison with congruency, keyword being proportionality.

(ii) Three conditions: SSS, SAS, AA. Simple applications (proof not included).

(b) Circles

(i) Angle Properties

- *The angle that an arc of a circle subtends at the centre is double that which it subtends at any point on the remaining part of the circle.*
- *Angles in the same segment of a circle are equal (without proof).*
- *Angle in a semi-circle is a right angle.*

(ii) Cyclic Properties:

- *Opposite angles of a cyclic quadrilateral are supplementary.*
- *The exterior angle of a cyclic quadrilateral is equal to the opposite interior angle (without proof).*

(iii) Tangent and Secant Properties:

- *The tangent at any point of a circle and the radius through the point are perpendicular to each other.*
- *If two circles touch, the point of contact lies on the straight line joining their centres.*
- *From any point outside a circle, two tangents can be drawn, and they are equal in length.*
- *If two chords intersect internally or externally then the product of the lengths of the segments are equal.*
- *If a chord and a tangent intersect externally, then the product of the lengths of segments of the chord is equal to the square of the length of the tangent from the point of contact to the point of intersection.*
- *If a line touches a circle and from the point of contact, a chord is drawn, the angles between the tangent and the chord are respectively equal to the angles in the corresponding alternate segments.*

Note:

- **Proofs of all Theorems EXCLUDED.**
- **Only application of all Circle Theorems in solving numerical problems are included.**

4. Mensuration

Area and volume of solids – Cylinder and Cone.

Three-dimensional solids - right circular cylinder and right circular cone: Area (total surface and curved surface) and Volume. Direct application problems including cost, Inner and Outer volume and melting and recasting method to find the volume or surface area of a new solid. Combination of solids included.

Note: Problems on Frustum are not included.

5. Trigonometry

(a) Using Identities to solve/prove simple algebraic trigonometric expressions

$sin^2 A + cos^2 A = 1$

$1 + tan^2 A = sec^2 A$

$1 + cot^2 A = cosec^2 A;\ 0 \leq A \leq 90°$

(b) *Heights and distances: Solving 2-D problems involving angles of elevation and depression using trigonometric tables.*

Note: Cases involving more than two right angled triangles excluded.

6. Statistics

Statistics – basic concepts, Mean, Median, Mode. Histograms and Ogive.

(a) Computation of:

- *Measures of Central Tendency: Mean*, median class and modal class for continuous grouped data.*
- ** Mean by any method*

Direct : $\frac{\Sigma fx}{\Sigma f}$

Short-cut : $A + \frac{\Sigma fd}{\Sigma f}$ where $d = x - A$

Step-deviation: $A + \frac{\Sigma ft}{\Sigma f} \times i$ where $t = \frac{x - A}{i}$

(b) Graphical Representation. Histograms and Less than Ogive.

- *Finding the mode from the histogram, the upper quartile, lower Quartile and median etc. from the ogive.*
- *Calculation of inter Quartile range.*

7. Probability

Random experiments, Sample space, Events, definition of probability, Simple problems on single events.

SI UNITS, SIGNS, SYMBOLS AND ABBREVIATIONS

(1) Agreed conventions

(a) Units may be written in full or using the agreed symbols, but no other abbreviation may be used.

(b) The letter ‘s’ is never added to symbols to indicate the plural form.

(c) A full stop is not written after symbols for units unless it occurs at the end of a sentence.

(d) When unit symbols are combined as a quotient, *e.g.*, metre per second, it is recommended that it should be written as m/s, or as m s^{-1}.

(e) Three decimal signs are in common international use: the full point, the mid-point and the comma. Since the full point is sometimes used for multiplication and the comma for spacing digits in large numbers, it is recommended that the mid-point be used for decimals.

(2) Names and symbols

In general			
Implies that	⇒	is logically equivalent to	⇔
Identically equal to	≡	is approximately equal to	>>
In set language			
Belongs to	∈	does not belong to	∉
is equivalent to	↔	is not equivalent to	↮
union	∪	intersection	∩
universal set	ξ	is contained in	⊂
natural (counting) numbers	N	the empty set	ø
		whole numbers	W
integers	Z	real numbers	R
In measures			
Kilometre	km	Metre	m
Centimetre	cm	Millimetre	mm
Kilogram	kg	Gram	g
Litre	L	Centilitre	cL
square kilometre	km^2	Square meter	m^2
square centimetre	cm^2	Hectare	ha
cubic metre	m^3	Cubic centimetre	cm^3
kilometres per hour	km/h	Metres per second	m/s

INTERNAL ASSESSMENT

The minimum number of assignments: Two assignments as prescribed by the teacher.

Suggested Assignments

- Comparative newspaper coverage of different items.
- Survey of various types of Bank accounts, rates of interest offered.
- Planning a home budget.
- Conduct a survey in your locality to study the mode of conveyance / Price of various essential commodities / favourite sports. Represent the data using a bar graph / histogram and estimate the mode.
- To use a newspaper to study and report on shares and dividends.
- Set up a dropper with ink in it vertical at a height say 20 cm above a horizontally placed sheet of plain paper. Release one ink drop; observe the pattern, if any, on the paper. Vary the vertical distance and repeat. Discover any pattern of relationship between the vertical height and the ink drop observed.
- You are provided (or you construct a model as shown) - three vertical sticks (size of a pencil) stuck to a horizontal board. You should also have discs of varying sizes with holes (like a doughnut). Start with one disc; place it on (in) stick A. Transfer it to another stick (B or C); this is one move (m). Now try with two discs placed in A such that the large disc is below, and the smaller disc is above (number of discs = n=2 now). Now transfer them one at a time in B or C to obtain similar situation (larger disc below). How many moves? Try with more discs (n = 1, 2, 3, etc.) and generalise.

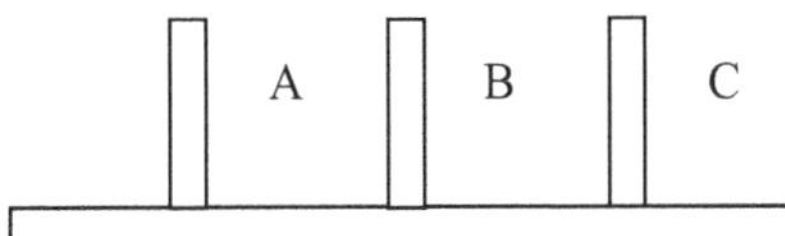

- The board has some holes to hold marbles, red on one side and blue on the other. Start with one pair. Interchange the positions by making one move at a time. A marble can jump over another to fill the hole behind. The move (m) equal 3. Try with 2 (n=2) and more. Find the relationship between n and m.

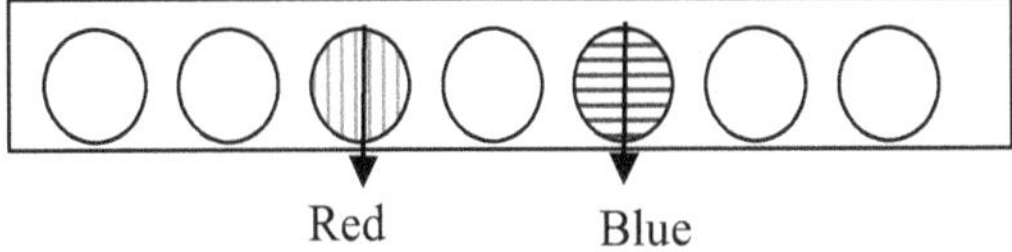

- Take a square sheet of paper of side 10 cm. Four small squares are to be cut from the corners of the square sheet and then the paper folded at the cuts to form an open box. What should be the size of the squares cut so that the volume of the open box is maximum?
- Take an open box, four sets of marbles (ensuring that marbles in each set are of the same size) and some water. By placing the marbles and water in the box, attempt to answer the question: do larger marbles or smaller marbles occupy more volume in a given space?
- An eccentric artist says that the best paintings have the same area as their perimeter (numerically). Let us not argue whether such

sizes increase the viewer's appreciation, but only try and find what sides (in integers only) a rectangle must have if its area and perimeter are to be equal (Note: there are only two such rectangles).

- Find by construction the centre of a circle, using only a 60-30 setsquare and a pencil.
- Various types of "cryptarithm".

EVALUATION

The assignments/project work are to be evaluated by the subject teacher and by an External Examiner. (The External Examiner may be a teacher nominated by the Head of the school, who could be from the faculty, **but not teaching the subject in the section/class**. For example, a teacher of Mathematics of Class VIII may be deputed to be an External Examiner for Class X, Mathematics projects.)

The Internal Examiner and the External Examiner will assess the assignments independently.

Award of Marks	**(20 Marks)**
Subject Teacher (Internal Examiner)	10 marks
External Examiner	10 marks

The total marks obtained out of 20 are to be sent to the Council by the Head of the school.

The Head of the school will be responsible for the online entry of marks on the Council's CAREERS portal by the due date.

INTERNAL ASSESSMENT IN MATHEMATICS - GUIDELINES FOR MARKING WITH GRADES

Criteria	Preparation	Concepts	Computation	Presentation	Understanding	Marks
Grade I	Exhibits and selects a well defined problem. Appropriate use of techniques.	Admirable use of mathematical concepts and methods and exhibits competency in using extensive range of mathematical techniques.	Careful and accurate work with appropriate computation, construction and measurement with correct units.	Presents well stated conclusions; uses effective mathematical language, symbols, conventions, tables, diagrams, graphs, etc.	Shows strong personal contribution; demonstrate knowledge and understanding of assignment and can apply the same in different situations.	4 marks for each criterion
Grade II	Exhibits and selects routine approach. Fairly good techniques.	Appropriate use of mathematical concepts and methods and shows adequate competency in using limited range of techniques.	Commits negligible errors in computation, construction and measurement.	Some statements of conclusions; uses appropriate math language, symbols, conventions, tables, diagrams, graphs, etc.	Neat with average amount of help; assignment shows learning of mathematics with a limited ability to use it.	3 marks for each criterion
Grade III	Exhibits and selects trivial problems. Satisfactory techniques.	Uses appropriate mathematical concepts and shows competency in using limited range of techniques.	Commits a few errors in computation, construction and measurement.	Assignment is presentable though it is disorganized in some places.	Lack of ability to conclude without help; shows some learning of mathematics with a limited ability to use it.	2 marks for each criterion
Grade IV	Exhibits and selects an insignificant problem. Uses some unsuitable techniques.	Uses inappropriate mathematical concepts for the assignment.	Commits many mistakes in computation, construction and measurement.	Presentation made is somewhat disorganized and untidy.	Lack of ability to conclude even with considerable help; assignment contributes to mathematical learning to a certain extent.	1 mark for each criterion
Grade V	Exhibits and selects a completely irrelevant problem. Uses unsuitable techniques.	Not able to use mathematical concepts.	Inaccurate computation, construction and measurement.	Presentation made is completely disorganized, untidy and poor.	Assignment does not contribute to mathematical learning and lacks practical applicability.	0 mark

REVISION TECHNIQUE WHY SHOULD YOU REVISE?

You cannot expect to remember all the mathematics concept that you have studied unless revise. It is important to review all your courses, so that you can answer the examination questions.

WHERE SHOULD YOU REVISE?

In a quiet room, with a table and a clock. The room should be brightly lighted. A reading lamp on the table helps you to concentrate on your work and reduces eyestrain.

WHEN SHOULD YOU REVISE?

Being able to focus and revise whenever you feel like it is a great skill but setting a time and regular schedule prepares your brain activity. Start your revision early morning or early each evening before your brain gets tired.

HOW SHOULD YOU REVISE?

If you sit down to revise without thinking of a definite finishing time, you will find that your learning efficiency falls lower and lower and lower.

If you sit down to revise, saying to yourself that you will stop work after 3 hours, then you're learning efficiency falls at the beginning but rises towards the end as your brain realizes it is coming to the end of the session (see Graph).

We can use this U-shaped curve to help us work more efficiently by splitting a 3-hour session

into 3 shorter sessions, each of about 50 minutes with short, planned breaks between them.

The breaks must be planned so that the graph rises near the end of each short session how much you gain:

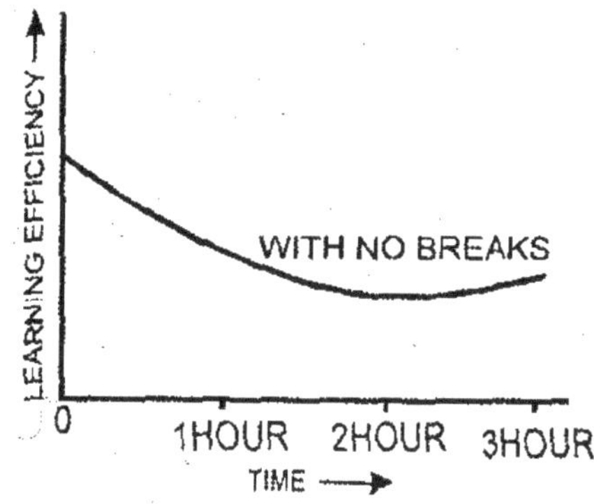

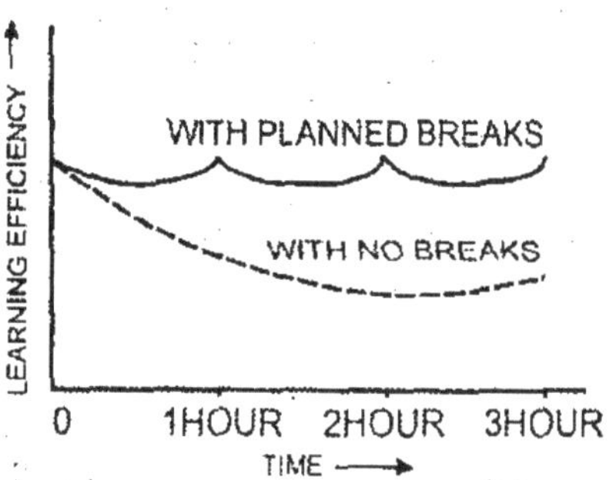

For example, if you start your revision at 6.00 p.m. you should look at your clock or watch and say to yourself. I will work until 7.00 p.m. and then stop — neither earlier and nor later'

At 7.00 p.m. you should leave the table for a relaxation break of 10 minutes (or less), returning by 7.10 p.m. when you should say to yourself, I will work until 8.10 p.m. and then stop neither earlier nor later.'

Continuing in this way is more efficient and causes less strain on you. You get through more work, and you feel less tired.

HOW OFTEN SHOULD YOU REVISE?

The adjoining graphs show the amount of information that your memory can recall at different times after you have finished a revision session the graph rises at the beginning. This is because your brain is still sorting out the information that you have been learning

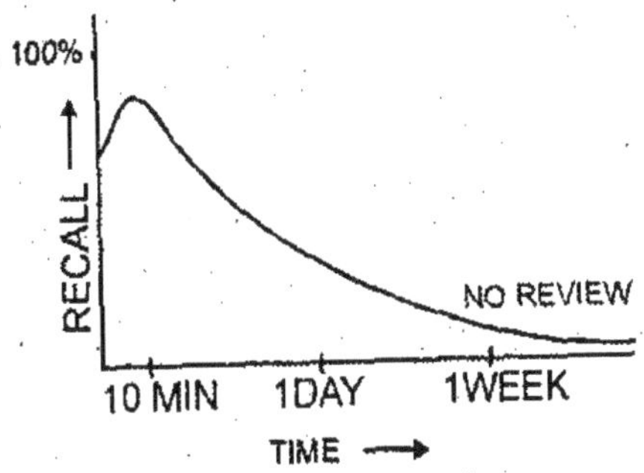

The graph soon falls rapidly so that after 1 day you may remember only about a quarter of what you had learned.

There are two ways of improving your recall process and raising this graph

If you briefly revise the same work again after 10 minutes (at the high point of the graph) then the graph falls much more slowly.

This fits in with your 10-minute break between revision sessions.

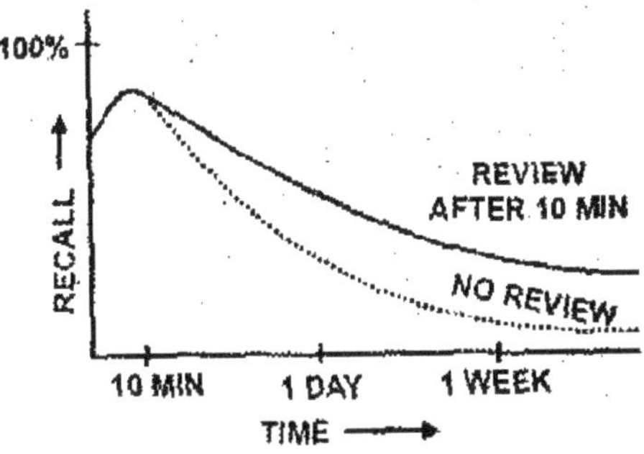

Using the example on the last page, when you return to your table at 7.10 p.m. the first thing you should do is review, the work you learned before 7.00 pm

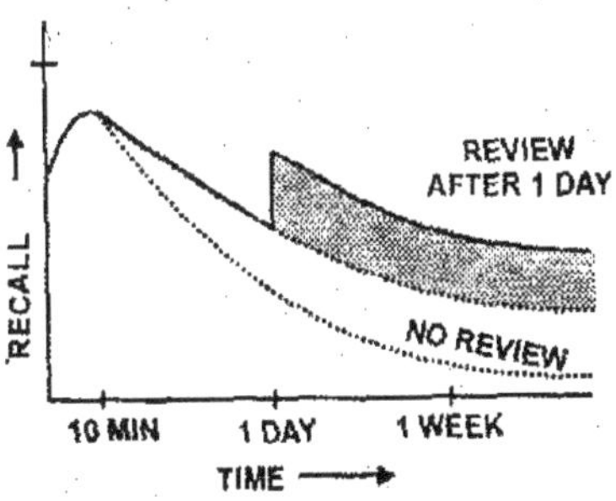

The graph can be lifted again by briefly reviewing the work after 1 day and then again after 1 week. That is, on Tuesday night you should look through the work you learned on Monday night and the work you learned on the previous Tuesday night so that it is fixed equate firmly in your long-term memory.

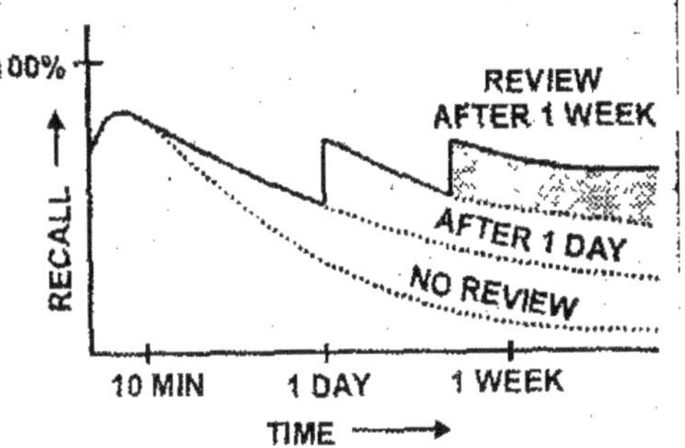

Another method of improving your memory is by taking care to try to understand all parts of your work. This makes all the graphs rise higher.

If you learn your work in a parrot fashion (as you have to do with telephone numbers), all these graphs will be lower. On the occasions when you have to learn facts by heart, try to picture them as exaggerated, colourful images in our mind

REMEMBER

The most important points about revision are that it must occur often and be repeated at the right intervals.

TIPS FOR YOUR BOARD EXAMINATION.

The moment Board Examinations stealthily approach the lives of students, many of them start panicking about the huge syllabus, preparation, revision and the result thereof Students start getting nervous just before the exams and start searching for ways to release their paranoia. To release Then with such stress and tension please follow some steps given below for **10th Board Examination** Preparation.

1. The first step for every student should be to get a thorough knowledge of the latest syllabus by referring to the **ICSE COUNCIL** for **TERM – 2**. After that, they should make a timetable for themselves which would provide them with a schedule, that would help them plan their syllabus and concentrate better.

2. The one thing that students should note before sitting down to study is to make sure that the place in which they are going to study is free from gadgets like computers, TV, radio, mobile, etc. Another thing that equally needs to be avoided is talking with friends while studying; they can do so when they are finished with studying or when they are free.

3. Students are also provided with previous year sample papers by many publications which can be of great help as they can be solved on an everyday basis. They help in analyzing the mistakes that are being committed and that can be worked upon. By having the latest papers students get an idea of the type of questions expected, and the level of difficulty in the Board Exam.

4. In order to score high marks students, tend to revert to the use of malpractices. In many cases, they cram down the syllabus, instead of trying to understand it. They need to understand that both of these methods are wrong in the present and for the future. Cramming without understanding, will take them nowhere, and using wrong means can lead to them being caught and not being able to attempt the paper.

5. In order to feel fresh and energetic the whole day, students should always **eat and sleep well**. They should always have an early dinner and should not study till late night (specially a night before the exam). Fast food and greasy food should be avoided as much as possible and a habit of getting up early to study should be adopted.

6. Making notes and practicing all the problems by **writing them down** rather than verbally learn in them is one of the best tricks to remember and understand the course. Students can also make brief notes of every chapter so that they can refer to them without needing to open their textbook every time.

7. Taking help when in doubt or in any kind of problem should be done by the students well on time. Doubts can be cleared by meeting the concerned teachers, friends, and seniors.

8. The idea of not taking breaks in between and studying continually is a mistake often committed by students.

9. Students should avoid mood swings and personal problems that may prevent them from studying and completing their work. They should always try and remain in a jolly and happy mood and ignore the problems that come in their way. This will help them concentrate better.

10. Students should always learn and practice **time management**. They should work on their writing speed so that they can write fast and neat and not miss any questions while attempting the paper.

11. Don't neglect your health. Just because you're short of time doesn't mean you should live on junk foodie Try to get your **fruits** and **vegetables** every day. Remember to **exercise (breathing yoga)** at least 30 minutes a day. Doing these things will support mental, physical, and emotional function:

12. It's not a good idea to pick up your books and start working until you're finished— because you may not have enough time to accomplish all your tasks. Figure out how much time you have for each assignment, and plot this out in your calendar. Try to give yourself some extra time for each assignment in case one takes longer than you expected. When you plot out your time, be sure to schedule study breaks. Working straight through without a break can make you less efficient and somewhat insane.

13. Set a time limit on how long you study for each class. Don't go overboard on one subject and forget that you have several others to catch up on before going to bed. Also, don't rush through studying; take your time and **concentrate**. You may want to set an alarm clock at a certain hour, so when it rings, go to another subject, and reset the alarm.

14. Get at least **6 hours of sleep**. If you have more or less sleep than you should have, you may start lacking in your coursework and become lazy because of the urge or want to sleep.

Tips for Mathematics (which leads to marks deduction):

Don't forget to write a formula before calculation

Write complete solution (don't skip steps). In some problems like equations with variables, one can check the solution(s) by substituting them back in the equation(s).

In graphs, plot them neatly.

Don't forget to write units (if any).

Show complete working, avoid to solve questions in a rough sheet, and write only answers.

Try to write solutions in an aligned manner. Write formulas/theorems or concepts on paper and stick-on walls so that they make an image in your mind.

May the force be with you.

INDEX

ICSE X MATHEMATICS

SOLVED QUESTION PAPERS

UNSOLVED QUESTION PAPERS

UNIT-1

Co-ordinate Geometry

1.1 Introduction: Co-ordinate geometry is the branch of mathematics where a point is located in a plane with reference to a horizontal line ($x - axis$) and a vertical line ($y - axis$). These two numbers which represent the location of a point are called **co – ordinates** of the point. So, in co – ordinate geometry a point is represented by an **ordered pair** i.e. (x, y) or (a, b), etc.

Remark: The ordered pair (a, b) and (b, a) are different unless $a = b$.

1.2 Cartesian plane or Cartesian co – ordinate system: When two numbered lines mutually perpendicular to each other are placed together the resulting configuration is called a **Cartesian co – ordinate system** or a **Cartesian plane**.

1.3 Co – ordinate axes: In the following figure the horizontal number line XOX' is called x-axis; the vertical number line YOY' is called the $y - axis$. Together both lines are called co – ordinate axes. The point of intersection of co – ordinate axes is called **origin**.

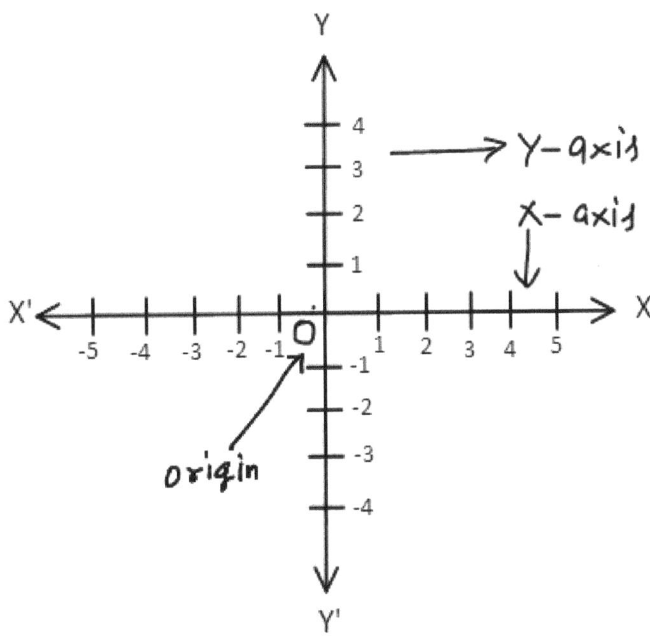

1.4 Co – ordinates of a point: The Co – ordinates of a point indicate its position with reference to co – ordinate axes. Let P be any point in the co – ordinate plane. PQ is the perpendicular from P to XOX' then

(i) OQ is called **x – coordinate** or **abscissa** of P and is usually denoted by x.

(ii) PQ is called **y – coordinate** or **ordinate** of P and is usually denoted by y.

(iii) x *and* y together are called **coordinates** of P and denoted by P (x, y).

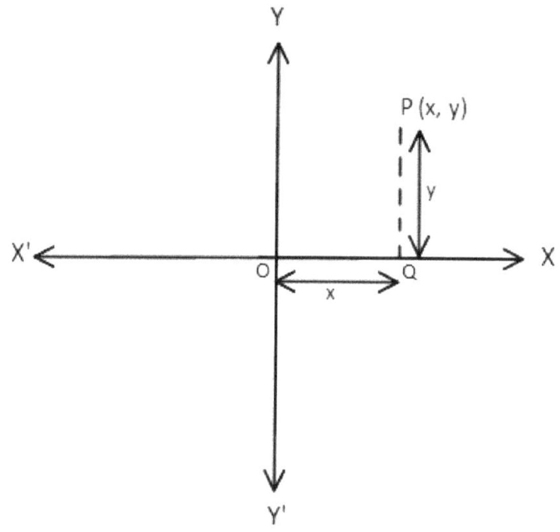

Remark:

(i) When write co – ordinates of a point the abscissa precedes the ordinate i.e. (abscissa, ordinate)
(ii) Co – ordinates of origin O = (0, 0).
(iii) Co – ordinates of a point on $x-\ axis = (x, 0)$ and
(iv) Co – ordinates of a point on $y-\ axis = (0, y)$.

1.5 Convention of signs of co – ordinates: The x-axis and y −axis divide the co – ordinate plane into four parts called **quadrants**, taken in anticlockwise from OX called **1st quadrant**, **2nd quadrant**, **3rd quadrant,** and **4th quadrant**. OX and OY are taken **positive directions** and OX′ and OY′ are taken **negative directions** of x-axis and y-axis respectively.

(i) If a point is in the **1st quadrant**, then the sign of x coordinate and y coordinate will be **(+, +)**, since the 1st quadrant is enclosed by the positive x-axis and the positive y-axis.
(ii) If a point is in the **2nd quadrant**, then the sign of x coordinate and y coordinate will be **(-, +)**, since the 2nd quadrant is enclosed by the negative x-axis and the positive y-axis.

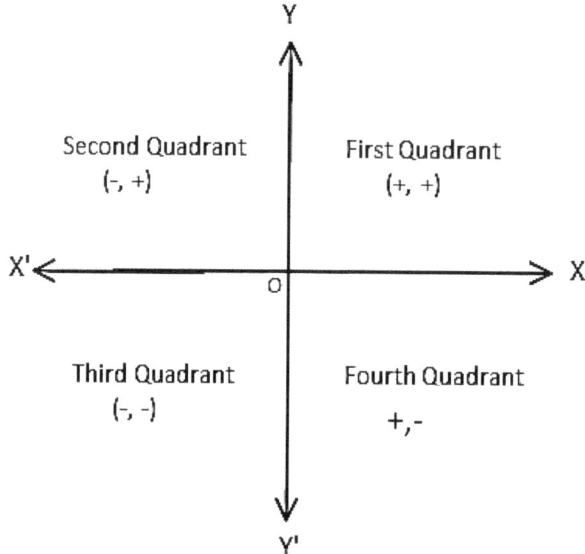

(iii) If a point is in the **3rd quadrant**, then the sign of x coordinate and y coordinate will be **(-, -)** since the 3rd quadrant is enclosed by the negative x-axis and the negative y-axis

(iv) If a point is in the **4th quadrant**, then the sign of x coordinate and y coordinate will be **(+, -)** since the 4th quadrant is enclosed by the positive x-axis and the negative y-axis.

1.6 Plotting a point in co – ordinate plane:

To plot a point in the plane, consider signs of its co – ordinates, then start from the origin first move on the x-axis according to sign of x – coordinate (left or right). From this place move vertically upward or downward on (or parallel) to y-axis according to sign of y – coordinate. Mark a **dot (.)** and name it says P and write its co – ordinates as P (x, y).

For example, to plot the point (-3, 4), follow the instructions:

(i) Start from origin O and move **3 units** along the x-axis to the **left**.

(ii) From this place, move **4 units upwards** (parallel to y-axis) and mark a dot here (in 2nd quadrant). Name this dot P and write its co – ordinates P (-3, 4).

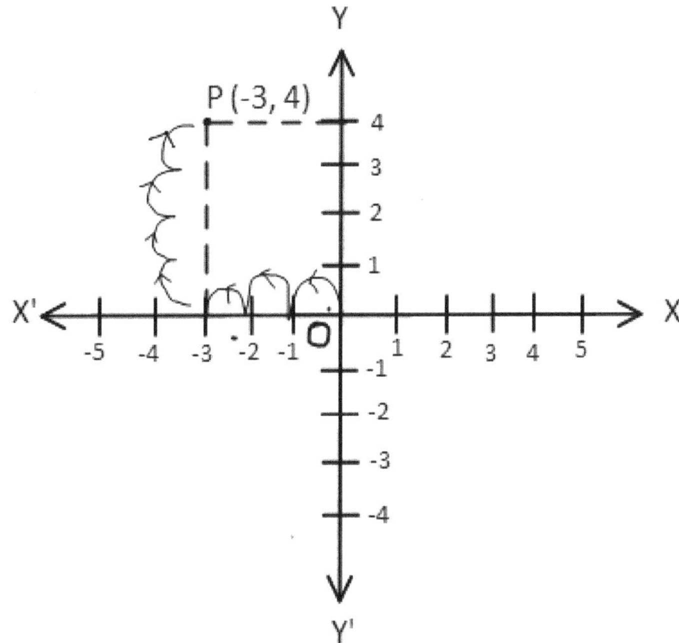

UNIT - 1

CO-ORDINATE GEOMETRY

CHAPTER

Reflection

1.1 Introduction: When you look into a mirror, the image that you see behind the mirror is the image that you see after reflecting in the mirror. **The distance of image from mirror is same as the distance of object from mirror**. Experiments show that if A′ is the image of A upon reflection in **mirror m**, then the line *m* is perpendicular bisector of the line segment AA′.

In the following figure point, **A′** is the image of point **A** in mirror *m*. *m* is the perpendicular bisector of **AA′**, i.e. OA = OA′. Here mirror m is said to be **mediator** or **mirror line** or **reflection line** or **axis of reflection**. So **reflection** of A in line *m* is A′.

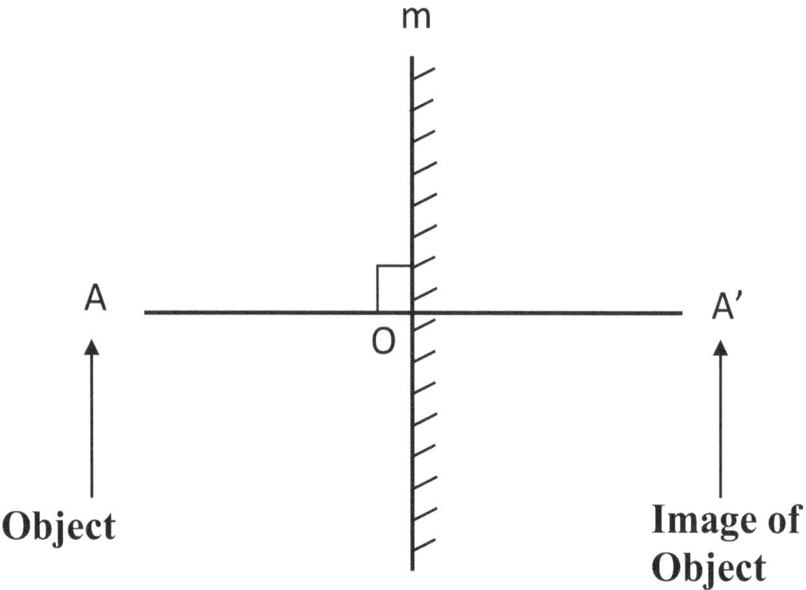

1.2 Notation: Reflection can be denoted in many ways. Ex. We can write as a **reflection of A in *m* is A′**. **Or** Symbolically we can denote reflection as R_m: A = A′.

1.3 Topics to be covered: Following topics are to be covered for examination point of view

- Reflection of a point in the *x*-axis.
- Reflection of a point in the y-axis.
- Reflection of a point in origin.
- Reflection of a point in a line that is parallel to *x*-axis.i.e ($y = a$)
- Reflection of a point in a line that is parallel o y-axis. ($x = a$)
- Reflection of a point in a point.
- Invariant point.

1.4 Reflection of a point in *x*-axis (y = 0): The line $y = 0$ is the equation of $x - axis$.
When a point reflects in *x*-axis (y = 0) the sign of y–coordinate (ordinate) changes. *x* – Axis will act as a mirror. From the figure, it is clear that P' is the image of P under the reflection in *x*-axis.

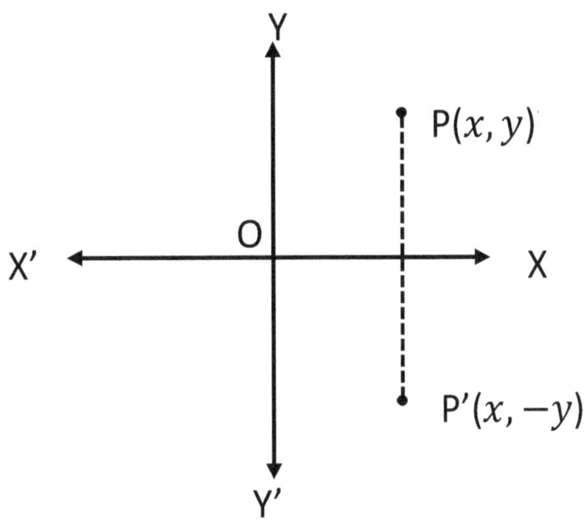

For Example,

Reflection of point (3, 4) in the x – axis = (3, – 4) i.e., R_x (3, 4) = (3, – 4)
Reflection of point (– 3, 4) in the x – axis = (– 3, – 4) i.e., R_x (– 3, 4) = (– 3, – 4)
Reflection of point (4, – 5) in the x – axis = (4, 5) i.e., R_x (4, – 5) = (4, 5)

1.5 Reflection of a point in y – axis (x = 0): The line $x = 0$ is the equation $y - axis$.
When a point reflects in y-axis (x = 0) the sign of x–coordinate (abscissa) changes. y-axis will act as a mirror. From the figure, it is clear that P' is the image of P under the reflection in y-axis.

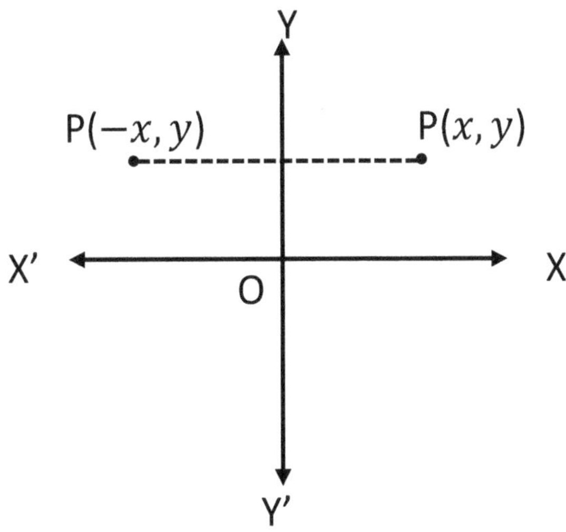

For Example,

Reflection of point $(3, 4)$ in the y – axis = $(-3, 4)$ i.e., R_y $(3, 4) = (-3, 4)$
Reflection of point $(-3, 4)$ in the y – axis = $(3, 4)$ i.e., R_y $(-3, 4) = (3, 4)$
Reflection of point $(4, -5)$ in the y – axis = $(-4, -5)$ i.e., R_y $(4, -5) = (-4, -5)$

1.6 Reflection of a point in the origin:

When a point reflects in origin, the sign of its abscissa and ordinate both change.

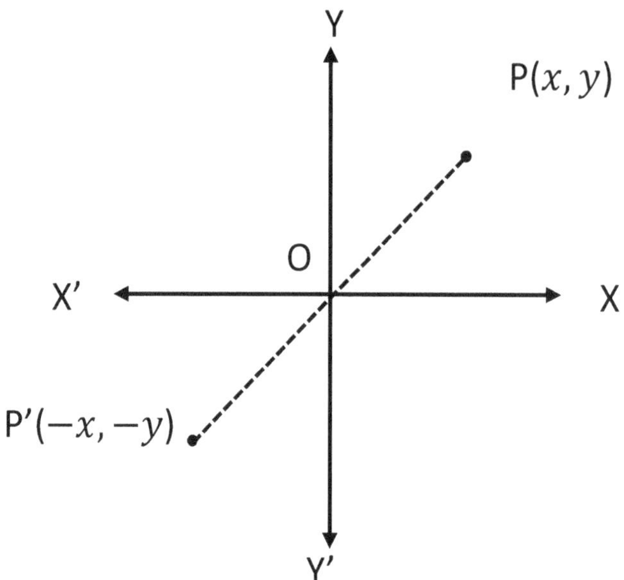

Origin will act as a mirror. From the figure, it is clear that P′ is the image of P under the reflection in the origin.

For Example,

Reflection of point (3, 4) in the origin $= (-3, -4)$ i.e. $R_0\ (3,4) = (-3, -4)$
Reflection of point (− 3, 4) in the origin $= (3, -4)$ i.e. $R_0\ (-3,4) = (3, -4)$
Reflection of point (4, − 5) in the origin $= (-4,5)$ i.e. $R_0(4, -5) = (-4,5)$

1.7 Reflection of a point in a line which is parallel to *x*-axis (y = a): y = a is a line parallel to *x*-axis and at a distance of a unit on either side of *x*-axis depending on the sign of a. If a is positive the line lies on above *x*-axis and if a is negative the line lies below the *x*-axis.

Finding co – ordinates of image using formula: $R_{y=a}: (x, y) = (x, -y + 2a)$

For Example,

(i) Reflection of the point $(4, 5)$in the line y = 2 is the point $(4, -5 + 2.2)$ i.e. $(4, -1)$
(ii) Reflection of the point $(-3, -6)$ in the line y = 2 is the point $(-3, -(-6) + 2.2)$ i.e. $(-3,10)$

Finding co – ordinates of image using Graph: Let P (x, y) be any point in the co – ordinate plane, and AB is a line parallel to *x*-axis.

Equation of the AB is $y = a$, where a is positive. From P drop a perpendicular PM (or count distance of PM on the graph) and produce it to a point P′ such that MP = MP′. Then the point P′ is the **reflection** of the point P in the line AB i.e., y = a.

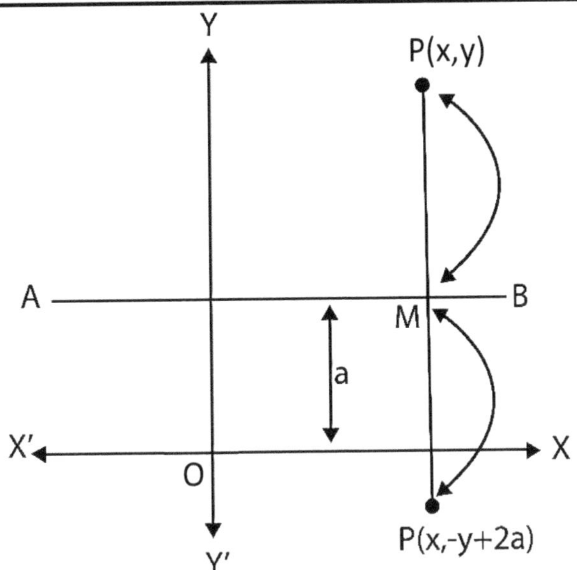

1.8 Reflection of a point in a line that is parallel to y-axis ($x = a$): $x = a$ is a line parallel to y-axis and at a distance of a unit on either side of y - axis depending on the sign of a. If a is positive the line lies on right of y-axis and if a is negative the line lies on left of the y – axis.

Finding co – ordinates of image using formula: $R_{x=a}:(x, y) = (-x + 2a, y)$

For Example,

(i) Reflection of the point (4 ,5) in the line $x = 2$ is the point $(-4 + 2.2,5)$ i.e. $(0,5)$

(ii) Reflection of the point $(-3, -6)$ in the line $x = 2$ is the point $(-(-3) + 2.2, -6)$ i.e. $(7, -6)$.

Finding co – ordinates of image using Graph: Let P (x, y) be any point in the co – ordinate plane,

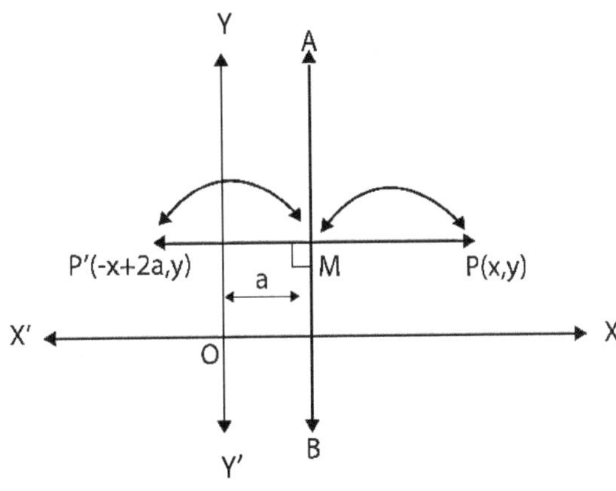

and AB is a line parallel to y - axis.

Equation of the AB is $x = a$, where a is positive. From P drop a perpendicular PM (or count distance of PM on the graph) and produce it to a point P′ such that MP = MP′. Then the point P′ is the **reflection** of the point P in the line AB i.e. x = a.

1.9 Reflection of a point in a point: The reflection of a point P in a given point M is a point P′ so that M is the midpoint of the line segment PP′. Either use midpoint formula (discussed in the next chapter) or use a graph to find the image of P.

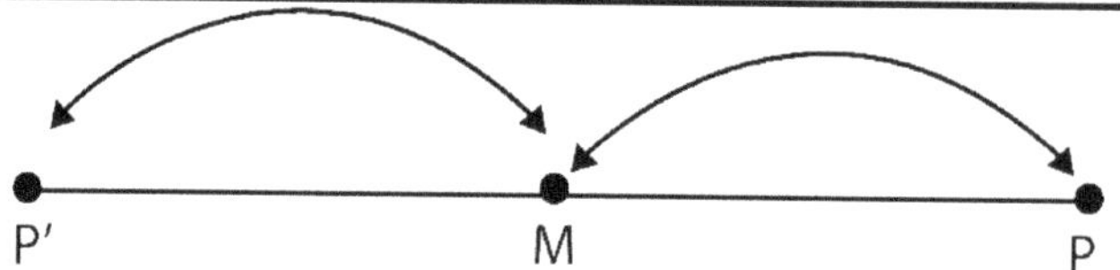

1.10 Invariant Point: If any point remains unaltered (No change in its co–ordinates) after a reflection is called **invariant. For example**, P (5, 0) is a point and is reflected in x-axis. According to the rules of reflection in x-axis, co – ordinates of its image P′ (5, 0). So here P is invariant under reflection in x-axis.

1.11 Single Transformation: If a point reflects in both axis one by one, then this reflection is equivalent to reflection in origin.

For Example: If a point says A (2, −3) 1st reflect in x-axis is and becomes A′ (2, 3). Then A′ (2, 3) reflect in y-axis and becomes A″ (−2,3). So, in a **single transformation,** it is said that the point A reflected in origin as A″.

Practice Questions

1. Write down the co-ordinates of the image of the point (3, –2) when:
   (i) Reflected in the x-axis.
   (ii) Reflected in the y-axis.
   (iii) Reflected in the x-axis followed by a reflection in the y-axis.
   (iv) Reflected in origin.
   (v) State or describe the single transformation of mapping done in part.[iii]

2. A point P is reflected in the x-axis. Co-ordinates of its image are (8, –6).
   (i) Find the Co-ordinates of P.
   (ii) Find the Co-ordinates of the image of P under reflection in the y-axis.

3. A point P is reflected P′ in the x-axis. The co-ordinates of its image are (2, –3) find
   (i) The co-ordinates of P
   (ii) The co-ordinates of the image P under reflection in the y-axis.
   (iii) The co-ordinates of the image Q′ of the point Q (1, 2) in the line PP′.

4. The point (–3, 0) on reflection in a line is mapped as (3,0), and the point (2, –3) on reflection in the same line is mapped as (–2, –3).
   (i) Name the mirror line.
   (ii) Write the co-ordinates of the image of (–3, –4) in the mirror line.

5. A (–2, 4) and B (–4, 2) are reflected in the axis. If A′ and B′ are images of A and B respectively, find:
   (i) The co-ordinates of A′ and B′.
   (ii) Assign a special name to quad. AA′B′B
   (iii) State whether AB′ = BA′

6. Point (3, 0) and (–1, 0) are invariant points under reflection in the line L_1 ; point (0, –3) and (0, 1) are invariant points on reflection on Line L_2.
   (i) Name or write equation for the lines L_1 and L_2
   (ii) Write down the images of points P (3, 4) and Q (– 5, –2) on reflection on L_1. Name the images as P and Q respectively:
   (iii) Write down the images of P and Q on reflection in L_2. Name the images a P″ and Q″ respectively.
   (iv) State or describe a single Transformation that maps P′ into P′.

7. Write down the coordinates of the image of the point (3, –2) when: **(2000)**

(i) Reflected in the x-axis,

(ii) Reflected in the y-axis,

(iii) Reflected in the x-axis followed by a reflection in the y-axis.

(iv) Reflected in the origin.

8. Use graph paper for this question. The point P (5, 3) was reflected in the origin to get the image P′.

(i) Write down the coordinates of P′.

(ii) If M is the foot of the perpendicular from P to the x-axis, find the coordinates of M.

(iii) If N is the foot of the perpendicular from P′ to the x-axis, find the coordinates of N.

(iv) Name the figure PMP′N.

(v) Find the area of the figure PMP′N.

9. Use a graph paper for this question:

(i) The point P (2, –4) is reflected about the line $x = 0$ to get the image Q. Find the co-ordinates of Q.

(ii) Point Q is reflected about the line y = 0 to get the image R. Find the co-ordinates of R.

(iii) Name the figure PQR.

(iv) Find the area of figure PQR.

10. Use graph paper for this question (Take 2 cm = 1 unit along both x and y-axis). ABCD is a quadrilateral whose vertices are A (2,2), B (2, –2), C (0,–1) and D(0,1). **(2018)**

(i) Reflect quadrilateral ABCD on the y-axis and name it as A′B′CD.

(ii) Write down the coordinates of A″ and B′.

(iii) Name two points that are invariant under the above reflection.

(iv) Name the polygon A′B′CD.

11. Use a graph sheet for this question. Take 1 cm = 1 unit along both x and y-axis. **(2019)**

(i) Plot the following points A(0, 5), B(3, 0), C(1, 0) and D(1, –5)

(ii) Reflect the points B, C, and D on the y axis and name them as B′, C′, and D′ respectively.

(iii) Write down the coordinates of B′, C′, and D′.

(iv) Join the points A, B, C, D, D′, C′, B′, A in order and give a name to the closed figure ABCDD′C′B′.

12. Use graph paper for this question. Take 1 cm = 1 unit on both x and y-axis. **(2020)**

(i) Plot the following points on your graph sheets.
A (– 4, 0), B (–3, 2), C (0, 4), D (4, 1) and E (7, 3).

(ii) Reflect the point B, C, D, E on x-axis and name them as B′, C′, D′, and E′ respectively.

(iii) Join the points A, B, C, D, E, E′, D′, C′, B′, and A in order.

(iv) Name the closed figure formed.

13. The triangle OAB is reflected in the origin O to triangle OA′B′. A′ and B′ have co – ordinates (−3, – 4) and (0, −5) respectively.

(i) Find the co – ordinates of A and B.

(ii) Draw a diagram to represent the given information.

(iii) What kind of figure is the quadrilateral ABA′B′?

(iv) Find the co – ordinates of A″, the reflection of A in the origin followed by reflection in the y – axis.

(v) Find the co – ordinates of B″, the reflection of B in the x – axis followed by reflection in the origin.

14. Use a graph paper for this question. (Take 10 small divisions = 1 unit on both axes). P and Q have co-ordinates (0, 5) and (–2, 4).

(i) P is invariant when reflected in an axis. Name the axis.

(ii) Find the image of Q on reflection in the axis found in (i).

(iii) (0, k) on reflection in the origin is invariant. Write the value of k.

(iv) Write the co-ordinates of the image of Q″, obtained by reflecting it in the origin followed by a reflection in x-axis

Answer key

Ans 1.	(i) (3, 2)	(ii) (–3, –2)	(iii) (–3, 2)	(iv) (–3, 2)	(v) Reflection in origin
Ans 2.	(i) (8, 6)	(i) $(-8, 6)$			
Ans 3.	(i) (2, 3)	(ii) (–2, 3)	(iii) (3, 2)		
Ans 4	(i) y – axis	(ii) (3, –4)			
Ans 5.	(i) (2, 4) (4, 2)	(ii) Isosceles trap.	(iii) Yes		
Ans 6.	(i) $L_1 = x$-axis (y = 0), L_2 = y axis (x = 0),	(ii) P′ (3, –4), Q′ (–5, 2)	(iii) P″ (–3, 4) Q″ (5, –2)	(iv) reflection in origin	
Ans 7.	(i) (3, 2)	(ii) (–3, –2)	(iii) (–3, 2)	(iv) (–3, 2)	
Ans 8.	(i) P′ (–5, –3)	(ii) M (5,0)	(iii) N (–5,0)	(iv) || gm	(v) 30 sq. Units
Ans 9.	(i) (–2, –4)	(ii) (–2, 4)	(iii) Right angled triangle	(iv) 16 sq. unit	
Ans 10.	(i) (–2,2), (–2, –2)	(ii) Invariant point (0, –1) (0,1)	(iv) Trapezium		
Ans 11.	(i) $(-3, 0), (-1, 0), (-1, -5)$	(ii) Arrowhead			
Ans 12.	(i) Fish				
Ans 13.	(i) (3, 4), (0, 5)	(iii) Rectangle	(iv) (3, -4)	(v) (0, 5)	
Ans 14.	(i) y-axis	(ii) Q′ (2, 4)	(iii) K = 0	(iv) Q″ (2, 4)	

UNIT - 1

CO-ORDINATE GEOMETRY

CHAPTER

Section and Mid-Point Formula

1.1 Introduction: If P lies between two points A and B somewhere then we say that P divides the join of AB internally in the ratio AP: PB.

To find the co – ordinates of point **P**, which divides internally the line joining A and B, we use **Section formula** or **Mid – Point formula**. There are two cases.

1.2 Case 1: When **P** is **not** the **mid - point** of line segment AB. The formula used to find co – ordinates of **P** is known as **Section or Division Formula.**
Let A (x_1, y_1) and B (x_2, y_2) be the two points and P (x, y) is a point on AB which divides the joining of AB in the ratio m_1: m_2. Then according to **section formula**:

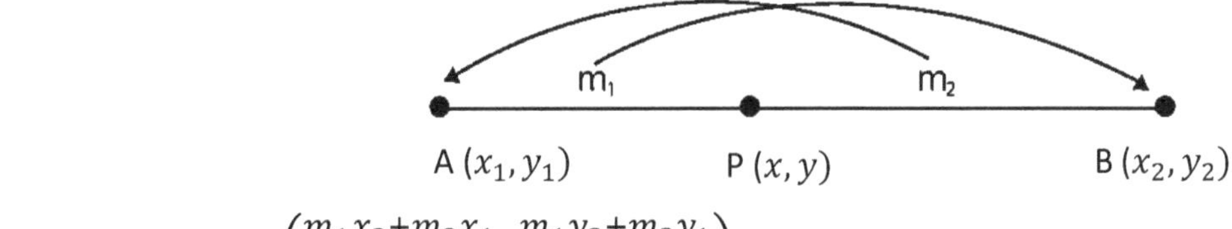

Co – ordinates of P = $\left(\frac{m_1x_2+m_2x_1}{m_1+m_2}, \frac{m_1y_2+m_2y_1}{m_1+m_2}\right)$

Case 2: When **P** is the **mid - point** of line segment AB. The formula used to find co – ordinates of **P** is known as **Mid – point Formula**.
Let A (x_1, y_1) and B (x_2, y_2) be the two points and P (x, y) is a point on AB which divides the joining of AB in the ratio **1:1,** as **P** is the mid – point of AB. Then according to the **Mid – point formula**:

1 P 1

A (x_1, y_1) (x, y) B (x_2, y_2)

Co – ordinates of P = $\left(\frac{x_1+x_2}{2}, \frac{y_1+y_2}{2}\right)$

1.3 Centroid of a triangle: From any vertex of a triangle draw a line segment that bisects its opposite side is called **Median**. Point of intersection of Medians is called the **Centroid**. Since centroid G lies on all three medians, so the medians are **concurrent**.

- A very important **property of centroid** is that it divides the medians in **2: 1**.

Let A (x_1, y_1), B (x_2, y_2), and C (x_3, y_3) be the vertices of the triangle ABC. Let **AD** be the median bisecting its base then **G (*x*, y)** on AD is the centroid which divides AD internally in the ratio **AG: GD = 2: 1**. Hence co – ordinates of **centroid G** are given by:

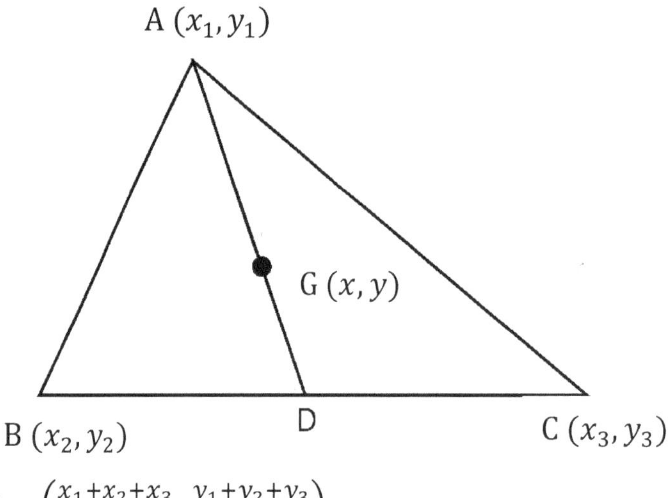

Co – ordinates of G = $\left(\frac{x_1+x_2+x_3}{3}, \frac{y_1+y_2+y_3}{3}\right)$

1.4 Points of Trisection: Let A and B are two points. P and Q are two points between A and B such that **AP = PQ = QB**; then P and Q are called **points of trisection** of AB. In this case P divides the join of AB in the ratio 1:2 and Q divides the join of AB in the ratio 2:1.

1.5 Steps to find the ratio in which the line segment joining of two points (say A and B) divided by *x*-axis or y-axis or a point (say P):

- If co – ordinates of both points (say A and B) are given, and it is internally divided by *x* – axis then use section formula for **y** co – ordinate because on *x*-axis y – coordinate becomes 0.
- If co – ordinates of both point (say A and B) are given, and it is internally divided by y – axis then use section formula for ***x*** co – ordinate because on y-axis *x* – coordinate becomes 0.
- If co – ordinates of both point (say A and B) are given and co – ordinates of P are also given then either use section formula for *x* or for y.

Remember:

- Co – ordinates of a point lies on *x*-axis = (*x*, 0).
- Co – ordinates of a point lies on y-axis = (0, y).
- If a line *x* = a divides the join of two points (say A and B) in m_1: m_2. Then co – ordinates of the point which divide the join of A and B = (a, y).
- If a line $y = a$ divides the join of two points (say A and B) in m_1: m_2. Then co – ordinates of the point which divide the join of A and B = (*x*, a).

Practice Sheet

1. P divides the line segment joining A (– 2, 1) and B (1, 4) in the ratio 2:1. Find the co-ordinate of P.

2. Find the points of trisection of the line segment joining the points (–4, 2) and (3, 7).

3. The co-ordinates of A and B are (–3, a) and (1, $a + 4$). The mid-point of AB is (–1, 1). Find the value of a.

4. The line segment joining the point A (2, –3) and B (3, 4) cuts the *x*-axis at P. Find the ratio in which P divides the line segment AB.

5. Calculate the ratio in which the line segment joining A (6, 5) and B (4, –3) is divided by the line y = 2. [**Hint**: The line y = 2 divide the join of A and B in the ratio $m_1 : m_2$ at the point $(x, 2)$]

6. Three consecutive vertices of a parallelogram ABCD are A (10, –6), B (2, –6), and C (–4, –2). Find the fourth vertex D.

7. The line joining the points A (4,–5) and B (4,5) is divided by the point P such that $\frac{AP}{AB} = \frac{4}{5}$, find the co-ordinates of P.

8. Find the ratio in which the point (2, a) divides the join of (– 4, 3) and (6, 3). Hence find a.

9. Two vertices of a triangle are (3, 2) and (1, 2). Find the third vertex given that the centroid is (0, 3).

10. Given a line segment AB joining the points A(– 4, 6) and B(8, –3). Find:
(i) The ratio in which AB is divided by the y-axis.
(ii) Find the coordinates of the point of intersection.

11. Calculate the ratio in which the line joining A(– 4, 2) and B(3, 6) is divided by point P(x, 3). Also, find x:

12. The slope of a line joining P(6, k) and Q (1–3k, 3) is $\frac{1}{2}$. Find.
(i) k
(ii) Midpoint of PQ, using the value of 'k' found in (i).

13. In what ratio is the line joining P (5, 3) and Q (-5, 3) divided by the y – axis? Also, find the co – ordinates of point of intersection.

14. M and N are two points on the X-axis and Y-axis respectively. P (3, 2) divides the line segment MN in the ratio 2:3. Find:
(i) The coordinates of M and N.
(ii) Slope of the line MN.

15. M is the mid – point of the line segment joining the points A (0, 4) and B (6, 0). M also divides the line segment OP in the ratio 1:3. Find:
(i) Co – ordinates of M.
(ii) Co – ordinates of P.

Answer key

Ans 1.	(0, 3)
Ans 2.	$\left(\frac{-5}{3}, \frac{11}{3}\right)$ and $\left(\frac{2}{3}, \frac{16}{3}\right)$
Ans 3.	-1
Ans 4.	3:4
Ans 5.	3:5
Ans 6.	(4, –2)
Ans 7.	$(4, -1)$
Ans 8.	3:4, 3
Ans 9.	$(-4,5)$
Ans 10.	1:2, (0,3)
Ans 11.	1:3, $\frac{-9}{4}$
Ans 12.	$-11, (20, -4)$
Ans 13.	1:1 ,(0,3)
Ans 14.	M (5, 0), N (0, 5), slope = -1
Ans 15.	M (3, 2), P (12, 8)

UNIT - 1

CO-ORDINATE GEOMETRY

CHAPTER

Equation of a Line

1.1 Introduction: We all familiar with straight lines. In earlier classes we have studied about linear (first degree) equations in two variables or one variable, like $2x + 3y = 8$, $x = 4$, $y = -3$ etc. Each such type of equation represents a straight line or conversely. Every straight line can be represented by a linear equation. In a plane, a line could be **horizontal** (parallel to x – axis), **vertical** (parallel to y – axis) or **oblique** (neither parallel to x – axis nor parallel to y-axis).

Remember:

(i) A straight line passes through many points. Co – ordinates of each point will satisfy the equation of the straight line.

For Example:

To check, whether a line $4x - 3y = 2$ passes through (5, 6).

Substitute $x = 5$ and $y = 6$ in the given equation, we get:

$4 \times 5 - 3 \times 6 = 2 \Rightarrow 20 - 18 = 2$, which is true. It means point (5, 6), **satisfies** the given equation so the given line passes through the point or point lies on the given line. Graphically:

(ii) Any point, through which a line passes, will always satisfy the equation of the line.

$4x - 3y = 2$ (5,6)

For Example:

The line given by the equation $4x + 3y + 6 = 0$ passes through the point (k, 2), calculate the value of k.

Solution:

Since it is given that the line passes through the point (k, 2). So, this co – ordinates will satisfy the equation. On substituting $x = k$ and $y = 2$ in the given equation, we get:

$4 \times k + 3 \times 2 + 6 = 0 \Rightarrow 4k + 12 = 0 \Rightarrow 4k = -12 \Rightarrow k = -3$ **Ans.**

1.2 Terms related to the equation of a straight line:

Inclination of a line: When a line passes in a plane and intersect with x – **axis**, it makes two angles with x - axis. One angle in **positive** direction of x**-axis** and other in **negative** direction of x**-axis**.

The **angle (θ)** which a straight line makes with the positive direction of x-axis (from positive x-axis, in anticlockwise direction towards the line) is called **inclination** of a line.

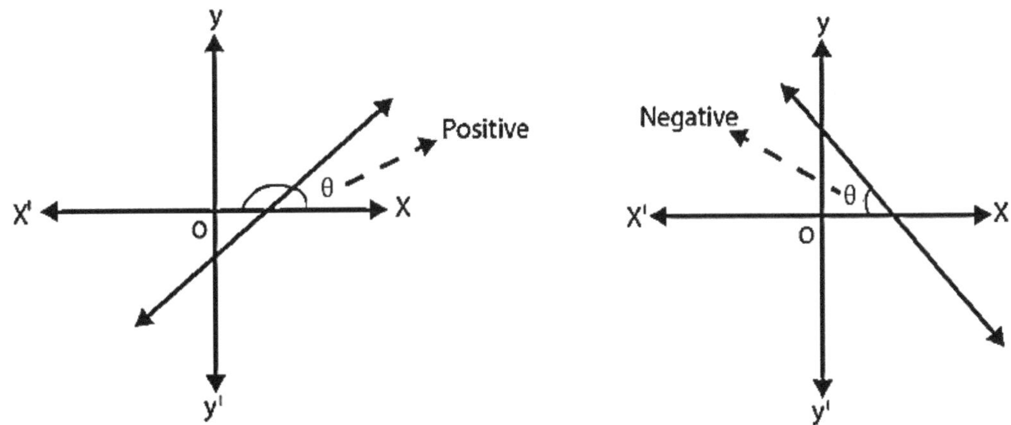

Remark:

1. In our syllabus $0° \leq \theta \leq 90°$
2. If a line does not intersect with x – axis then (inclination) $\theta = 0°$

Slope or gradient of a straight line: Slope is basically the ratio of vertical rise and horizontal distance of a line. **Slope is the most important element in the equation of a straight line**. Usually, it is denoted by **m**. There are 5 ways to find slope of a line.

(i) If inclination (θ) is given then **slope (m) = tan θ**

(ii) If a straight line passing through two given fixed points (or co – ordinates of two points lies on the line are given).

Let A (x_1, y_1) and B (x_2, y_2) be any to fixed points. Then **slope (m)** of the line through AB is given by the formula:

$$m = \frac{y_2 - y_1}{x_2 - x_1} \text{ or } m = \frac{y_1 - y_2}{x_1 - x_2}$$

(iii) Relation of slopes between two parallel lines:

Let AB and PQ are two parallel lines so that their angles of inclination are θ and α respectively. Since lines are parallel so θ and α will be corresponding and equal. So, **slope of line AB (let m_1) = slope of line PQ (let m_2).**

Therefore, **if two lines are parallel their slopes are equal.**

$$\boldsymbol{m_1 = m_2}.$$

Conversely, **if the slopes of two lines are equal, the lines are parallel to each other**.

(iv) Relation of slopes between two lines which are perpendicular to each other:

Let AB and PQ are two lines which are **perpendicular** to each other than product of their slope = -1.

Therefore, **if two lines are perpendicular to each other then:**

$$\boldsymbol{m_1 . m_2} = -1.$$

Conversely, **if the product of the slopes of two lines = −1, the lines are mutually perpendicular**.

(v) Finding slope (m) of a line whose equation is given in standard form (ax + by + c = 0):

(a) Convert the given equation in **slope intercept from** i.e. $\boldsymbol{y = mx + c}$.

(b) Here coefficient of x is slope (**m**) and the constant term (**c**) is y – intercept (Proper sign for slope and y – intercept is important).

For Example,

Find the slope m and y – intercept of the line $3x - 4y - 5 = 0$.

Solution:

Given equation is $3x - 4y - 5 = 0$

Make **y** as subject $\Rightarrow -4y = -3x + 5 \Rightarrow y = \frac{3}{4}x - \frac{5}{4}$

Therefore Slope (m) of the given line = $\frac{3}{4}$ and its y – intercept (c) = $-\frac{5}{4}$

1.3 Intercepts made by a line on the axes: If a straight line meets the x – axis at A and y – axis at point B (as shown in the given figure), then:

(i) The distance from origin O to point A (OA) is called **x – intercept**. Equivalent to a point on x – axis. So if x – intercept = 6; the corresponding point on x – axis = (6, 0). If x – intercept = -7; the corresponding point on x – axis = $(-7, 0)$ and so on.

(ii) The distance from origin O to point B (OB) is called **y – intercept**. Equivalent to a point on y – axis.

So if y – intercept = 6; the corresponding point on y – axis = (0, 6). If y – intercept = −7; the corresponding point on y – axis = (0, −7) and so on.

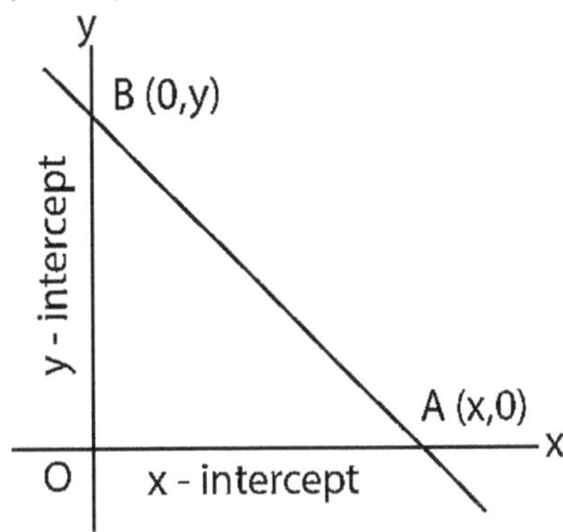

1.4 Condition for colinearity of three points: If three points A, B and C lies on the same straight line, they are said to be colinear. Then **slope of AB = slope of BC**.

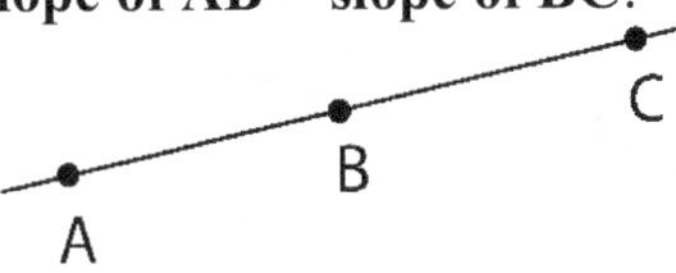

Practice Sheet – 1 (Based on slope of a line)

1. Find, which of the following points lie on the line $x - 2y + 5 = 0$
(i) (1, 3) (ii) (0, 5) (iii) (–5, 0)
(iv) (5, 5) (v) (2, –1.5) (vi) (–2, –1.5).

2. Does the line $2x - 3y + 7 = 0$ pass through the point (2, 3)?

3. The line given by the equation $\frac{y}{2} = x - p$ passes through the point (– 4, 4). Find p.

4. For what value of k will the point (3, – k) lie on line $9x + 4y = 3$?

5. The line $y = 3x–2$ bisects the join of (a, 3) and (2, –5), find the value of a.
[**Hint**: First find the mid points of (a, 3) and (2, -5) in terms of a. Then substitute the co – ordinates of mid-point $\frac{1}{\sqrt{3}}$ in the given equation]

6. Find the slope of a line whose inclination is:
(i) 0° (ii) 30° (iii) 45° (iv) 60°

7. Find the slope of a line passing through:
(i) A (4, 6) and B (2, 3) (ii) P (–2, –1) and Q (6, 4) (iii) D (a, –b) and E (b, – a)

8. Find k, if the slope of the line joining (k, 2) and (8, –11) is $\frac{-3}{4}$.

9. Find the slope of a line parallel to AB if:
(i) A = $(-2, 4)$ and B = $(0, 5)$ (ii) A = $(0, -4)$ and B = $(-7, 3)$

10. If $2x - 3y + 5 = 0$ and $px + 6y + 7 = 0$ are parallel lines, find the value of p.

11. Given that the line $\frac{y}{2} = x - p$ and the line $ax + 5 = 3y$ are parallel, find the value of a.

12. Find the slope of a line perpendicular to the line AB if:
(i) A $(0,8)$ and B $(-5,2)$
(ii) A $(1, -11)$ and B (5, 2)

13. Find the value of 'p' for which the line $5x - 3y + 2 = 0$ and $6x - py + 7 = 0$ are perpendicular to each other. **(2020)**

14. The line passing through $(-4, -2)$ and $(2, -3)$ is perpendicular to the line passing through $(a, 5)$ and $(2, -1)$, find a.

15. The slope of a line joining P (6, k) and Q ($1–3k$, 3) is $\frac{1}{2}$. Find.
(i) k
(ii) Midpoint of PQ, using the value of 'k' found in (i). **(2016)**

16. Find the slope and y-intercept of the following lines:

(i) $3x + 5y + 7 = 0$ (ii) $\frac{x}{3} + \frac{y}{4} = 1$ (iii) $y - 3 = 0$

17. The point (k, 3), (2, −4) and (−k + 1, −2) are collinear. Find k.

18. A (5, 4), B (−3, −2) and C (1, −8) are the vertices of a triangle ABC. Find:

(i) The slope of AB

(ii) The slope of the altitude of AB

(iii) The slope of the median AD

Answer key

Ans 1.	(i), (iii) and (iv)			
Ans 2.	No			
Ans 3.	-6			
Ans 4.	6			
Ans 5.	$\frac{-4}{3}$			
Ans 6.	(i) 0	(ii) $\frac{1}{\sqrt{3}}$	(iii) 1	(iv) $\sqrt{3}$
Ans 7.	(i) $\frac{3}{2}$	(ii) $\frac{5}{8}$	(iii) 1	
Ans 8.	$\frac{-28}{3}$			
Ans 9.	(i) $\frac{1}{2}$	(ii) -1		
Ans 10.	$p = -4$			
Ans 11.	$a = 6$			
Ans 12.	(i) $-\frac{5}{6}$	(ii) $-\frac{4}{13}$		
Ans 13.	$p = -10$			
Ans 14.	$a = 3$			
Ans 15.	−11, (20,−4)			
Ans 16.	(i) $\frac{-3}{5}, \frac{-7}{5}$	(ii) $\frac{-4}{3}$, 4	(iii) 0, 3	
Ans 17.	$-\frac{1}{3}$			
Ans 18.	(i) $\frac{3}{4}$	(ii) $-\frac{4}{3}$	(iii) $\frac{3}{2}$	

Equation of a straight line in different forms:

1.5 Equation of a straight line parallel to x - axis: Let AB be a straight line parallel to x – axis. Equation of the line will be **y = b**, where **b** is the perpendicular distance of line from x - axis. It may passes from above or below the x-axis.

If the line passes from above the x-axis, then its equation will be y = b.

If the line passes from below the x-axis, then its equation will be y = −b.

For Example

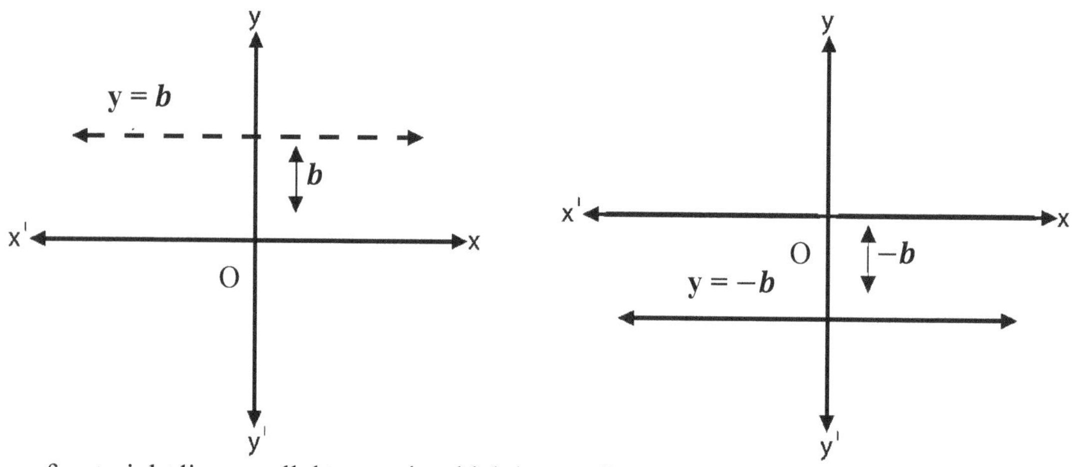

Equation of a straight line parallel to x-axis which is at a distance:

(i) 2 units above it ⇒ y = 2

(ii) 3 units below it ⇒ y = −3.

Remark: The equation of x axis is y = 0. Means when b = 0 then the line AB coincides with x-axis.

1.6 Equation of a straight line parallel to y - axis: Let AB be a straight line parallel to y – axis. Equation of the line will be **x = a**, where **a** is the perpendicular distance of line from y – axis. It may passes to the right or left or the y – axis.

If the line passes to the right of the y – axis, then its equation will be x = a.

If the line passes to the left of the y – axis, then its equation will be x = −a.

For Example:

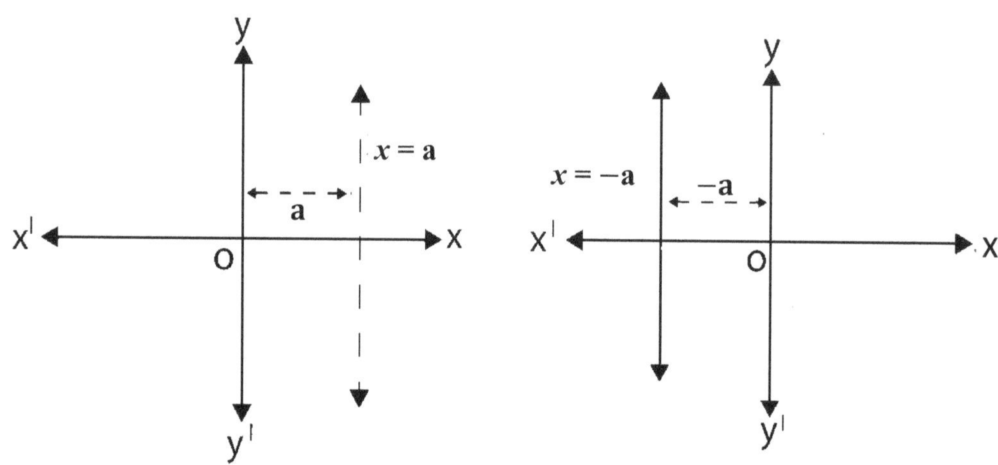

Find the equation of a straight line parallel to y-axis which is at a distance:

(i) 3 units to the right of it ⇒ $x = 3$

(ii) 2 units to the left of it ⇒ $x = -2$.

Remark: The equation of y axis is x = 0. Means when a = 0 then the line AB coincides with y-axis.

1.7 Slope intercept from of a line: Slope intercept form of the equation of a straight line is **y = mx + c**. Where **m** is the slope and **c** is the **y – intercept**. In the figure of **section 1.3,** B (0, y) is the y-intercept. Since y-intercept is the distance from the origin to the point, where given/required line intersects the y – axis, so we can write **B (0, c)** too. When slope and y – intercept of a line are given then find the equation of line using **y = mx + c**.

For Example:

Find the equation of a line whose inclination = 60°, y-intercept = 2.

Solution:

Since inclination $\theta = 60°$, so slope m = tan 60° ⇒ m = $\sqrt{3}$ and y intercept c = 2 So, substituting the values of m and c in the equation y = mx + c, we get: y = $\sqrt{3}\,x + 2$; which is the required equation.

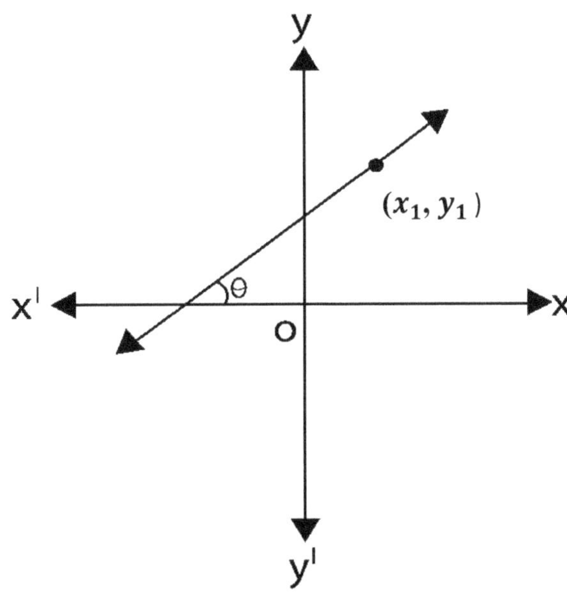

1.8 Point slope form of a line: Point slope form of the equation of a straight line is **$y - y_1 = m(x - x_1)$**. Where **m** is the slope of the line and **(x_1, y_1)** is the co – ordinates of a point on the given/required line.

For Example:

Find the equation of a line that passes through (5, 4) and makes an angle of 60° with the positive direction of the x-axis.

Solution: Given that inclination $\theta = 60°$,so slope m = tan 60° ⇒ m = $\sqrt{3}$ and required line passes through (5, 4), so $(x_1, y_1) = (5, 4)$. Substituting in $y - y_1 = m(x - x_1)$, we get:

$$y - 4 = \sqrt{3}(x - 5)$$

$y = \sqrt{3}x - 5\sqrt{3} + 4$, which is the required equation. **Ans.**

1.9 Two point's form of a line: When co – ordinates of two points lie on the line are given, then equa tion of the line can be find using following steps:

(i) Find slope of the line using the formula $m = \frac{y_2 - y_1}{x_2 - x_1}$

(ii) Now from two given point's co – ordinates take any one point's co – ordinate as (x_1, y_1) and substitute values in $y - y_1 = m(x - x_1)$.

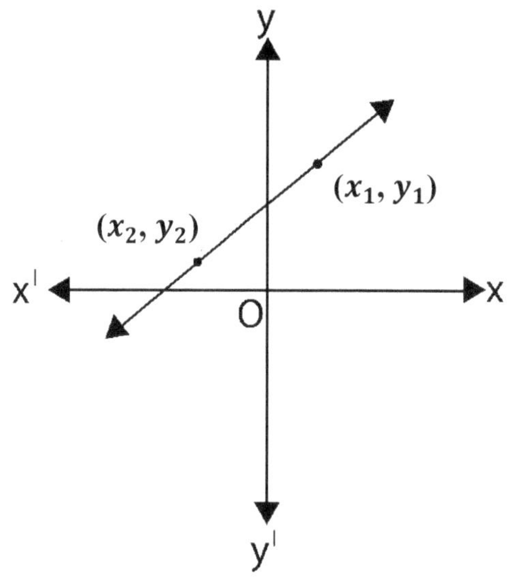

For Example:

Find the equation of line passing through A (4, –2) and B (5, 2)

Solution:

Let $(4, -2) = (x_1, y_1)$ and $(5, 2) = (x_2, y_2)$

Therefore, slope of the line is $= m = \frac{y_2 - y_1}{x_2 - x_1} = \frac{2+2}{5-4} = 4$

Now equation of the line: $y - y_1 = m\,(x - x_1)$

$y - (-2) = 4\,(x - 4) \Rightarrow y + 2 = 4x - 16 \Rightarrow y = 4x - 18$ **Ans.**

1.10 Equally inclined line to the co – ordinate axes: When a line makes equal angles with both the co – ordinate axes, it is called equally inclined line.

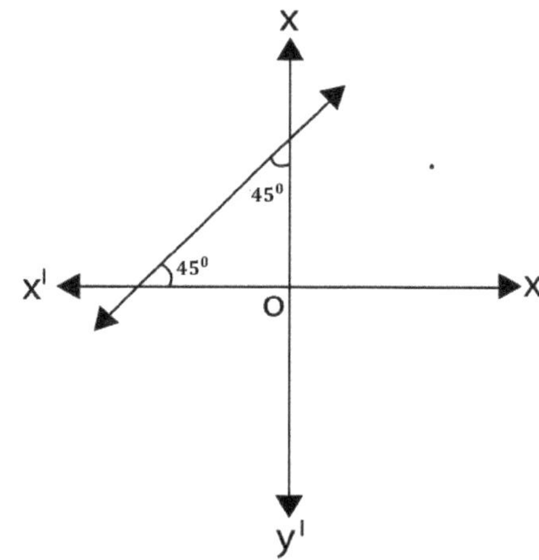

Tips to find equation of a line:

(i) First find slope **(m)** of that line for which equation is to be found (by any one of the 5 methods mentioned above).

(ii) Then find co–ordinates of a point on that line as (x_1, y_1).

(iii) Use $y - y_1 = m\,(x - x_1)$ to find the equation of the given line.

Practice Sheet – 2 (Based on Equation of straight line)

1. Find the equation of a line whose:
(i) Slope = 3, y-intercept = – 5 units
(ii) Inclination = 30°, y-intercept = 2

2. A-line through (5, 3) whose inclination is 45°, intersects y-axis at Q.
(i) Write the slope of the line.
(ii) Write the equation of the line.
(iii) Find the co – ordinates of Q.

3. Find the equation of a straight line that cuts an intercept –2 units from y-axis and is equally inclined with positive x-axis and negative y-axis.

4. Write down the equation of a line parallel to the line $3x + 2y = 8$ and passing through the point (0, 1).

5. If the image of the point (2, 1) with respect to a line l be (5, 2). Find:
(i) The slope of the line l.
(ii) The equation of the line l.

6. A line AB meets x – axis at A and y – axis at B. P (4, –1) divides AB in the ratio 1: 2. Find:
(i) The co – ordinates of A and B.
(ii) The equation of the line through P and perpendicular to AB.

7. The graph of the equation $y = mx + c$ passes through the points (1, 4) and (–2, –5). Determine the values of m and c.

8. Write down the equation of the line whose gradient is $\frac{3}{2}$ and which passes through P, where P divides the line segment joining A (–2, 6) and B (3, –4) in the ratio 2: 3.

9. A (1, –5), B (2, 2) and C (–2, 4) are the vertices of triangle ABC. Find the equation of:
(i) The altitude of the triangle through B
(ii) The line through C and parallel to AB.

10. A straight line passes through the points P (2, –5) and Q (4, 3). Find:
(i) The slope of the line PQ
(ii) The equation of the line PQ
(iii) The value of p if PQ passes through the point $(p - 1, p + 4)$.

11. Find the equation of a line passing through the point (2, −5) and making an intercept of –3 on the y-axis.

12. Find the equation of the perpendicular from the point P (–1, –2) on the line $3x + 4y - 12 = 0$. Also find the co-ordinates of the foot of the perpendicular.

13. Find the equation of the line passing through the point of intersection of $7x + 6y = 71$ and $5x - 8y = -23$; and perpendicular to the line $4x - 2y = 1$.

14. ABCD is a rhombus. The coordinates of A and C are (3, 6) and (–1, 2) respectively. Write down the equation of the diagonal BD.

15. A (1, 4), B (3, 2), and C (7, 5) are the vertices of an ABC. Find:

(i). The coordinates of the centroid G of ABC.

(ii). The equation of a line, through G and parallel to AB.

16. Find the equation of a line passing through the point (– 2, 3) and having the x-intercept of 4 units.

17. Find the value of 'p' for which the line $5x - 3y + 2 = 0$ and $6x - py + 7 = 0$ are perpendicular to each other. Hence find the equation of line passing through $(-2, -1)$ and parallel to $6x - py + 7 = 0$. **(2020)**

18. A (2, 5), B $(-1, 2)$, and C (5, 8) are the vertices of a triangle ABC, 'M' is a point on AB so that AM: MB = 1: 2. Find the co – ordinates of 'M'. Hence find the equation of the line passing through the points C and M.

19. A $(1, -5)$, B (2, 2) and C (-2, 4) are the vertices of triangle ABC. Find the equation of:

(i) The median of the triangle through A.

(ii) The altitude of the triangle through B.

(iii) The line through C and parallel to AB.

20. Points A and B have coordinates (7, –3) and (1, 9) respectively. Find:

(i) The slope of AB.

(ii) The equation of the perpendicular bisector of the line segment AB.

(iii) The value of 'p' if $(-2, p)$ lies on it.

Answer key

Ans 1.	(i) $y = 3x - 5$	(ii) $x - \sqrt{3}y + 2\sqrt{3} = 0$	
Ans 2.	(i) 1	(ii) $x - y - 2 = 0$	(iii) Q $(0, -2)$
Ans 3.	$x - y - 2 = 0$		
Ans 4	$3x + 2y - 2 = 0$		
Ans 5.	(i) $m = -3$	(ii) $3x + y - 12 = 0$	
Ans 6.	(i) A $(6, 0)$, B $(0, -3)$	(ii) $2x + y - 7 = 0$	
Ans 7.	$m = 3, c = 1$		
Ans 8.	$3x - 2y + 4 = 0$		
Ans 9.	(i) $3y = x + 4$	(ii) $y = 7x + 18$	
Ans 10.	(i) 4	(ii) $4x - y - 13 = 0$	(iii) $p = 7$
Ans 11.	$x + y + 3 = 0$		
Ans 12.	$4x - 3y - 2 = 0, (\frac{44}{25}, \frac{42}{25})$		
Ans 13.	$x + 2y = 17$		
Ans 14.	$x + y = 5$		
Ans 15.	(i) $\frac{11}{3}, \frac{11}{3}$	(ii) $3x + 3y - 22 = 0$	
Ans 16.	$x + 2y = 4$		
Ans 17.	$p = -10$,	$3x + 5y + 11 = 0$	
Ans 18.	M $(1, 4)$, $x - y + 3 = 0$		
Ans 19.	(i) $8x + y = 3$	(ii) $x - 3y + 4 = 0$	(iii) $y = 7x + 18$
Ans 20.	(i) -2,	(ii) $x - 2y + 2 = 0$,	(iii) 0

1.1 Introduction: Set of all points in a plane that are at a constant distance from a fixed point. Or the locus (path) traced out by a moving point, at a fixed distance from a fixed point in the same plane.

- The fixed point is called the **centre** of the circle and the constant distance is called **radius** of the circle.
- The outer boundary or perimeter of the circle is called **circumference**.
- A line which intersects the circle at two distinct point is called **secant**.
- A line segment, which touches the circle at two distinct points is called **chord**.
- A chord which passes through centre is called **diameter**. It is the **longest** chord of the circle. Its length is double of the **radius**. Diameter = 2 × radius.

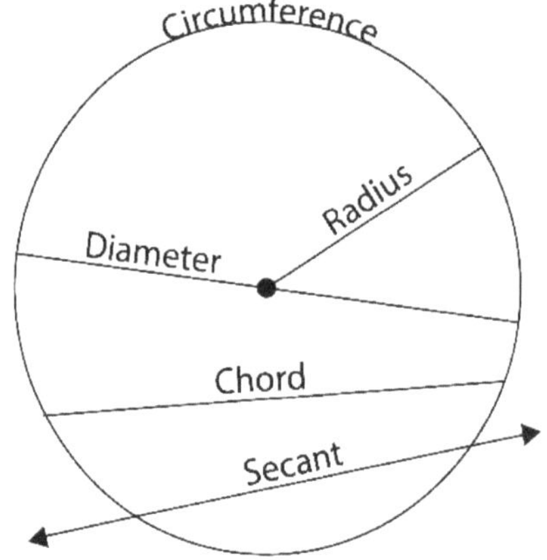

1.2 Equal or congruent circles: Circles having equal radius are called **equal** or **congruent** circles.

1.3 Concentric circles: Circles having common centre and different radii (plural of radius) are called **concentric** circles.

1.4 Circumscribed circle: If a circle contains a polygon inside itself so that all vertices of the polygon touches boundary of the circle, called **circumscribed** circle. The centre of circumscribed circle is called **circumcenter** and the polygon is called **inscribed** polygon. The following figures are examples of circumscribed circle.

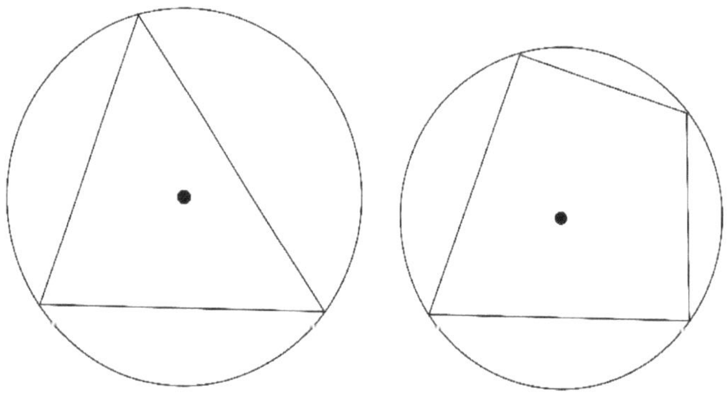

1.5 Inscribed circle: A circle, inside a polygon so that the circle touches all the sides of the polygon, is called **inscribed circle**. The centre of the circle is called **in centre** and the polygon is called **circumscribed polygon**.

The following figures are examples of **inscribed circle**.

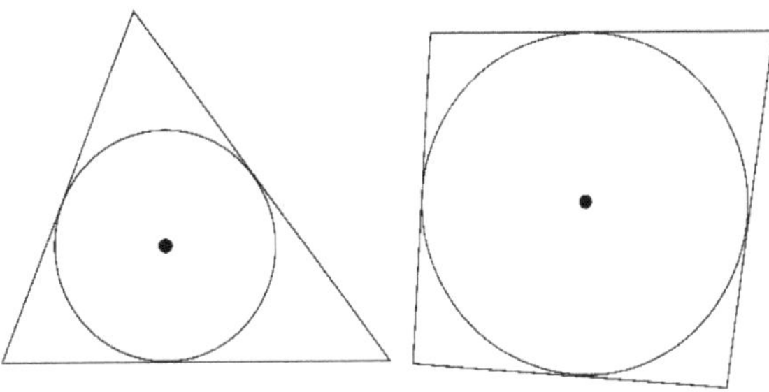

1.6 Parts of circle:

(i) Arcs: Part of the circumference of a circle is called an **arc**. If the figure, the whole circumference is divided into two parts arc APB and arc AQB. The arc APB, which is smaller is called the **minor arc** and the arc AQB, which is greater is called the **major arc**. circumference is the longest arc of a circle.

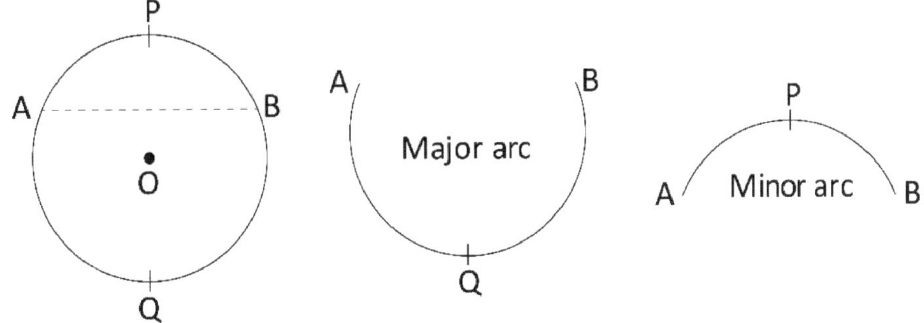

(ii) Segment: Plane region bounded between an arc and a chord is called **segment**. Larger part is called **major segment** and lesser part is called **minor segment**.

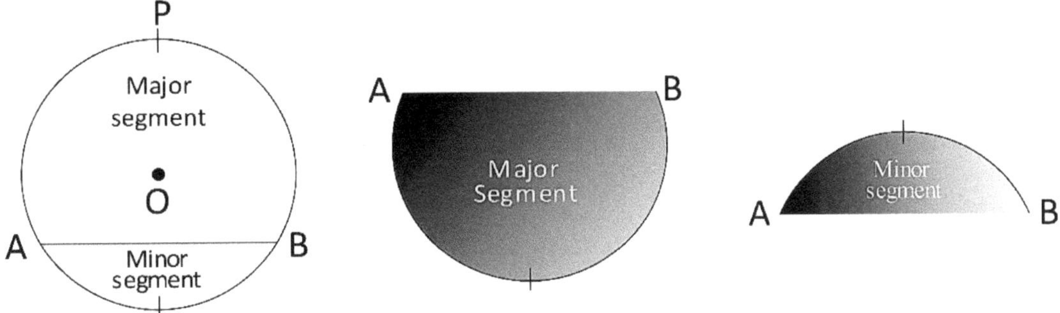

(iii) Sector: The plane region enclosed between an arc and its corresponding radii are called sector of a circle. Larger area containing part is called **major sector** and smaller area containing part is called **minor sector.**

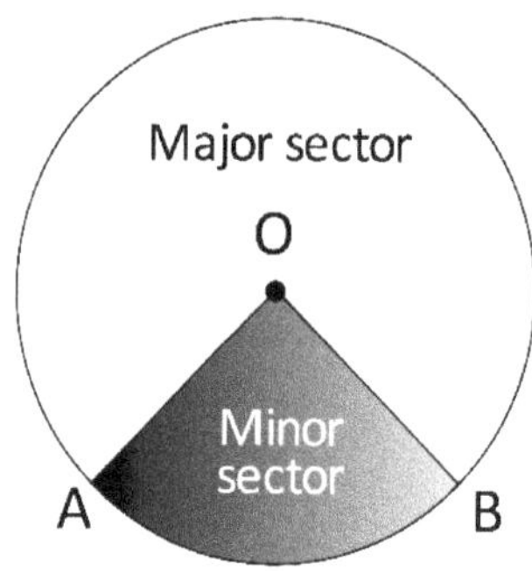

1.7 Cyclic quadrilateral: If all the four vertices of a quadrilateral lie on the circumference of a circle, then it is called cyclic quadrilateral. If ABCD is a cyclic quadrilateral then A, B, C and D are called concyclic points.

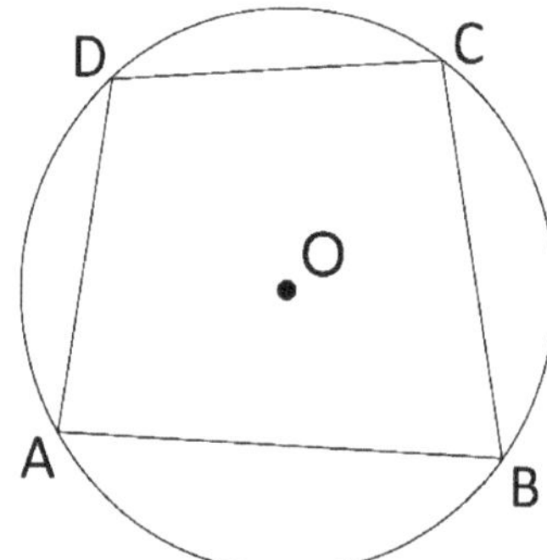

1.8 Chord properties of a circle: Recall theorems you have studied in your IXth class. They may be helpful in few questions.

(i) Perpendicular dropped from centre to a chord bisects the chord.

(ii) If a straight line drawn from centre to chord bisects the chord, makes 90° with the chord.

(iii) Perpendiculars dropped from centre to equal chords are equal also (Equal chords are equidistant from the centre).

(iv) If perpendiculars from centre to chords are equal, then chords will be equal too.

(v) Equal arcs/chords suntend equal angles at the centre.

1.9 Properties of angle made by chord in circles:

Theorem 1: Angles in the same segment of a circle are equal.

$$\angle ARB = \angle APB = \angle AQB$$

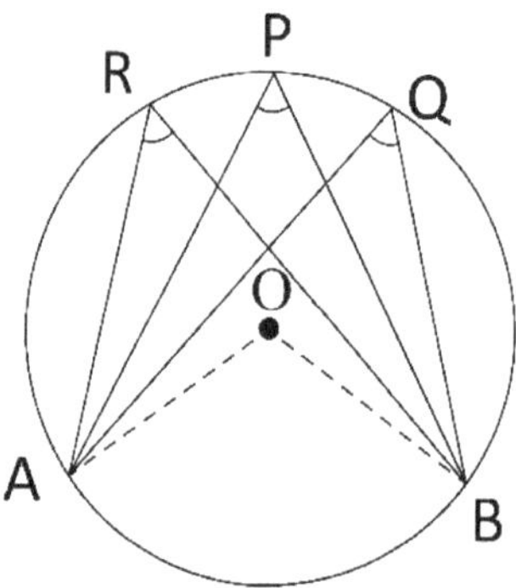

Theorem 2: The angle subtended by a chord at the centre is double the angle subtended by the same arc at the remaining part of the circumference.

$$\angle AOB = 2\angle APB$$

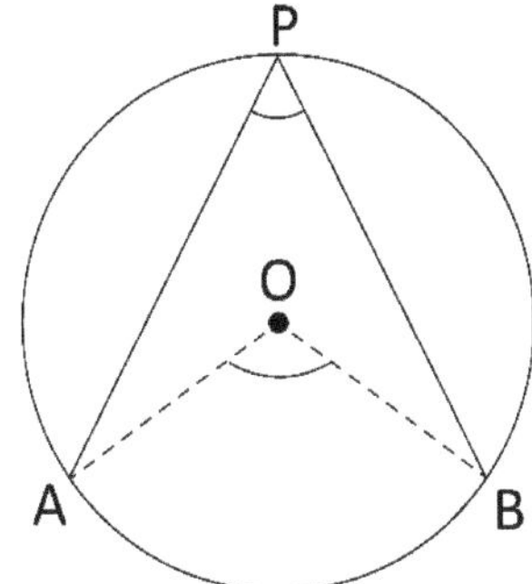

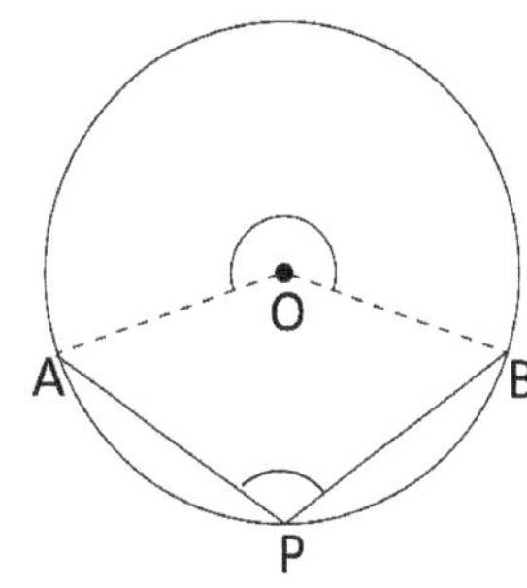

Theorem 3: Angle in a semi-circle is a right angle. AB is the diameter so ∠APB = 90°

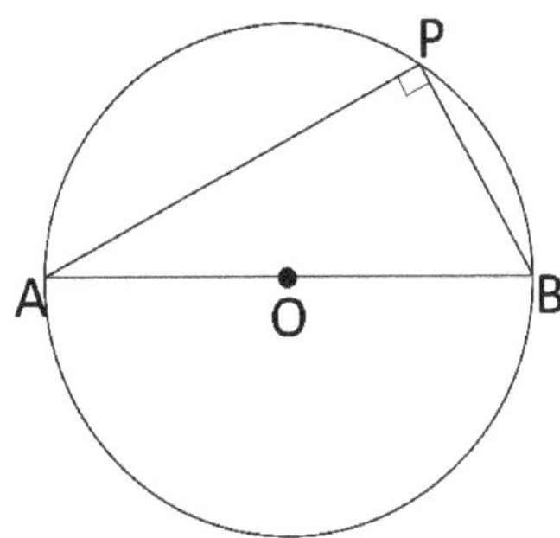

Converse of theorem 3, If a chord subtends 90°at the circumference of a circle, the chord will be **diameter**.

1.10 Cyclic properties: See section **1.7** for cyclic quadrilateral.

Theorem 4: The opposite angles of a cyclic quadrilateral are supplementary. If ABCD is a cyclic quadrilateral, then ∠A + ∠C = 180° and ∠B + ∠D = 180°

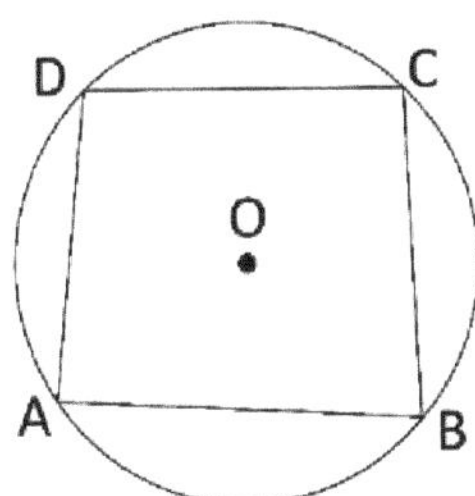

Converse of theorem 4: If a pair of opposite angles of a quadrilateral are supplementary, then it is a cyclic quadrilateral.

Theorem 5: The exterior angle of a cyclic quadrilateral is equal to the opposite interior angle.In cyclic quadrilateral ABCD. ∠ADC=∠CBE

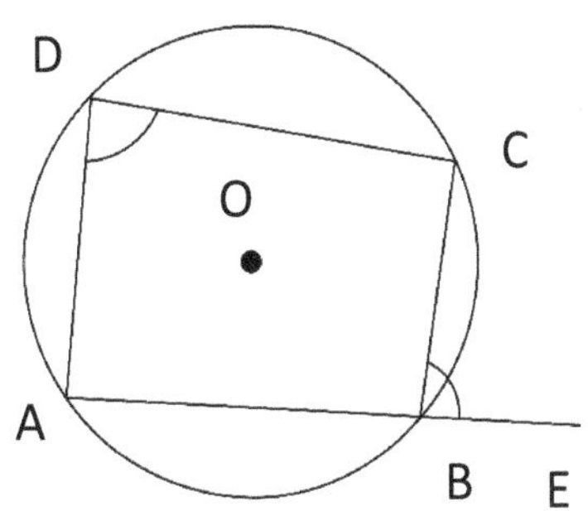

Practice Sheet – 1

1. In the fig. – 1 given below AOC = 110° calculate: (i) ∠ADC (ii) ∠ABC (iii) ∠OAC
2. In the fig. – 2 given below, BAD = 65°, ∠ABD = 70° and ∠BDC = 45°.Find: (i) ∠BCD (ii) ∠ADB, Hence show that AC is a diameter.

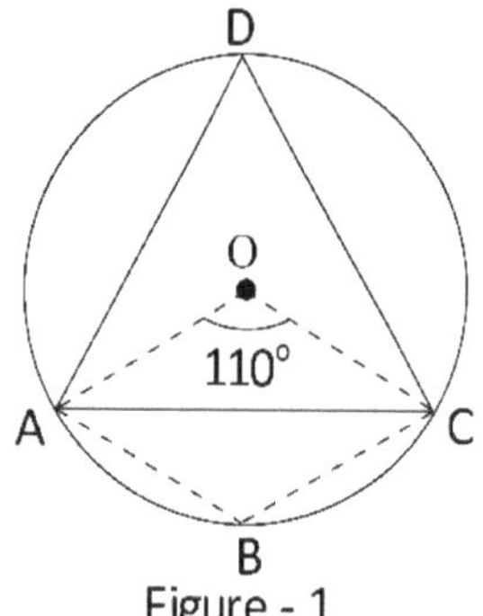

Figure - 1

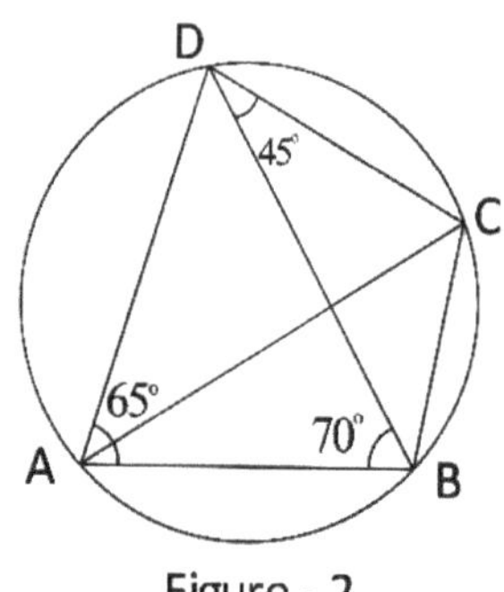

Figure - 2

3. In the adjoining figure AB is a diameter of the circle with centre O. BOC = 120°, find the measure of ∠ADC.

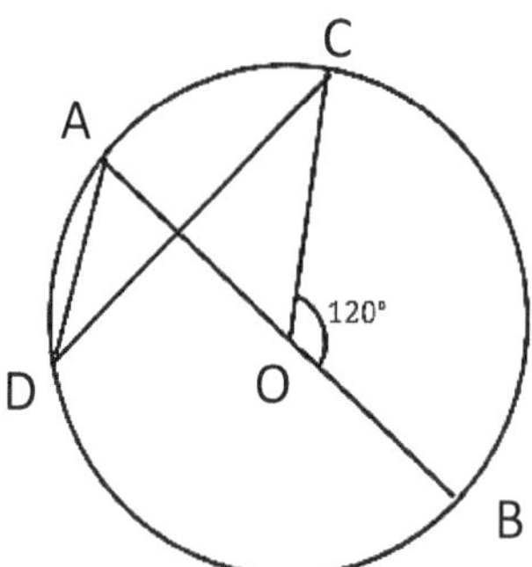

4. In the adjoining figure AC and BD are two chords of a circle. If ∠ACB = 65° and ∠BDC = 40°, find ∠ABC.

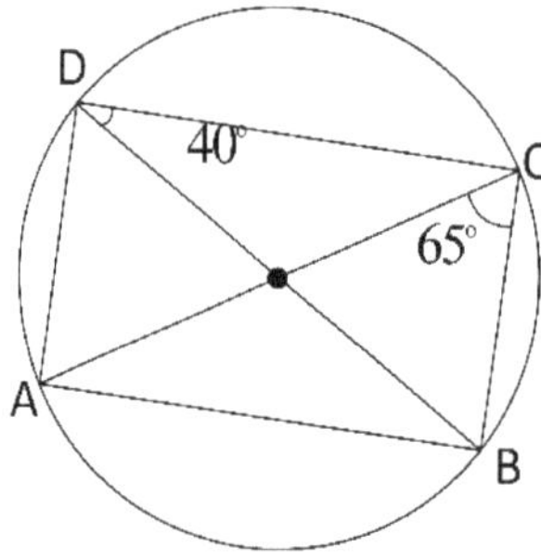

5. In the given figure AB is a diameter of the circle with centre O. If BCD =120°, find (i) ∠BAD (ii) ∠DBA

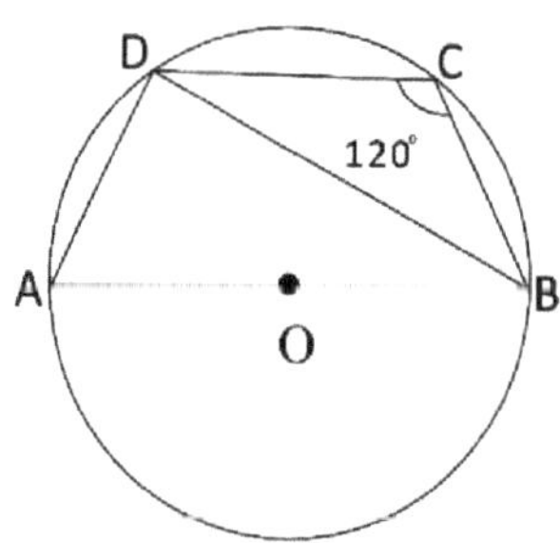

6. In the following figures find the values of x:

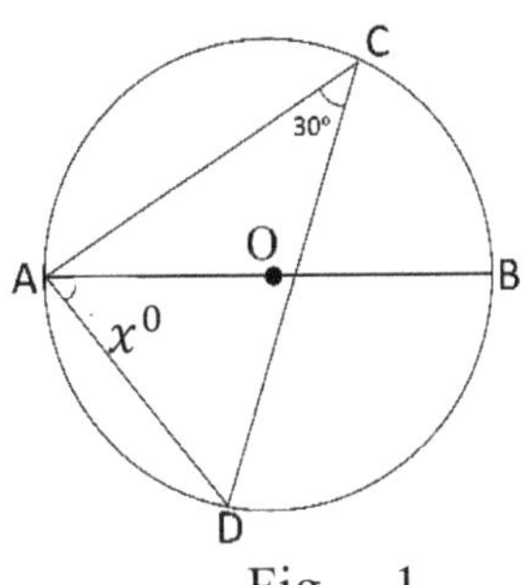

Fig. – 1

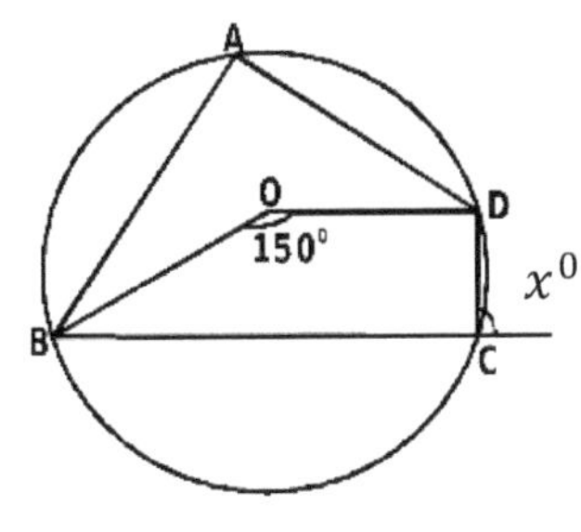

Fig. – 2

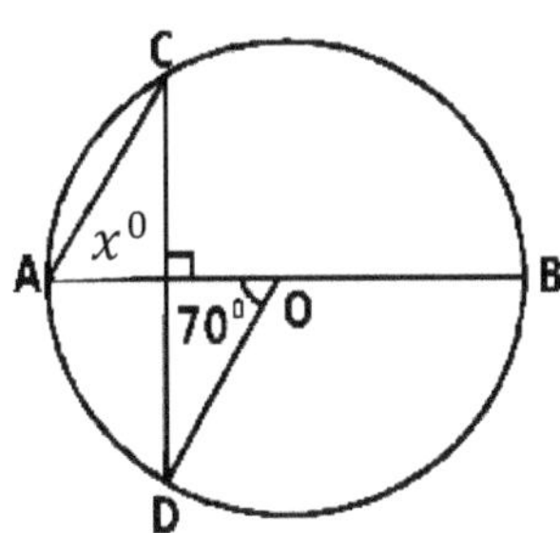

Fig. – 3

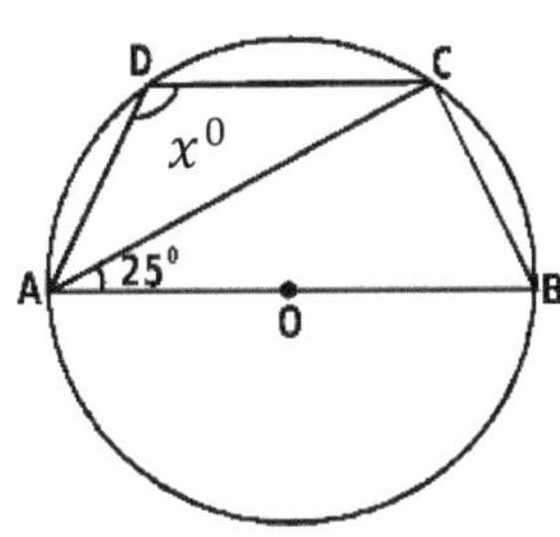

Fig. – 4

7. Find the value of x.

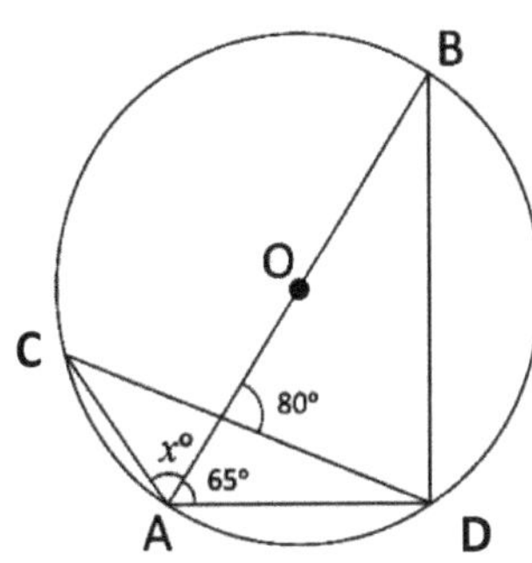

8. In figure P and Q are the centers of the two circles intersecting at B and C Find .

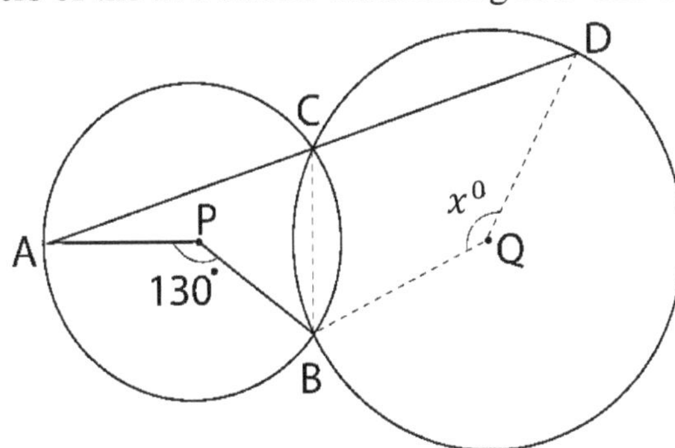

9. In the diagram given alongside, AC is the diameter of the circle, with centre O. CD and BE are parallel.
Angle $\angle AOB = 80°$ and angle $\angle ACE = 10°$.
Calculate: (i) $\angle BEC$ (ii) $\angle BCD$ (iii) $\angle CED$

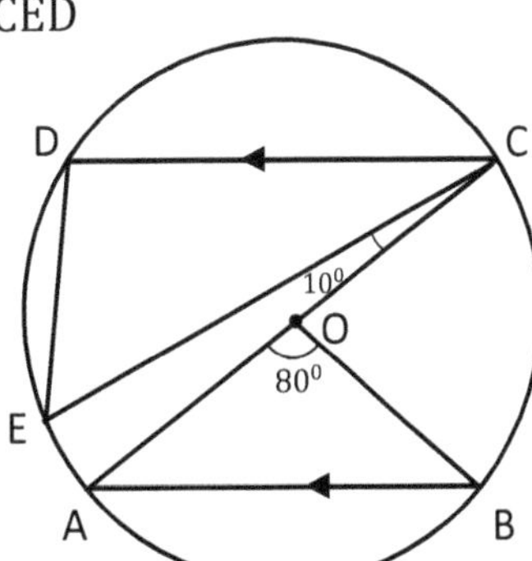

10. In the figure given alongside, AD is the diameter of the circle. If $\angle BCD = 130°$ calculate:
(i) $\angle DAB$ (ii) $\angle ADB$.

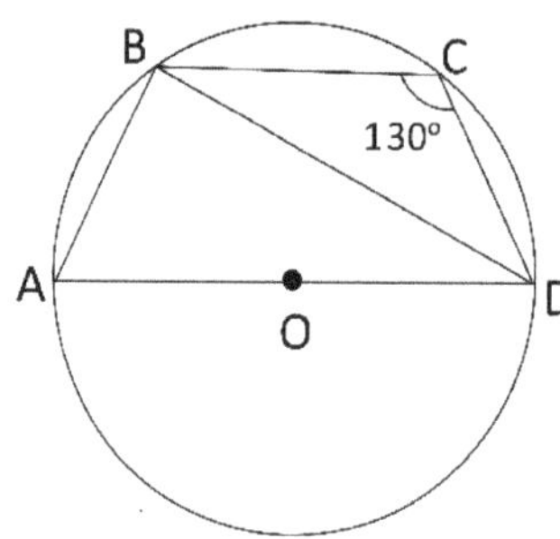

11. In the given figure, AB is the diameter of a circle with centre O and BCD is 120°.
Find: (i) ∠DBA and (ii) ∠BAD

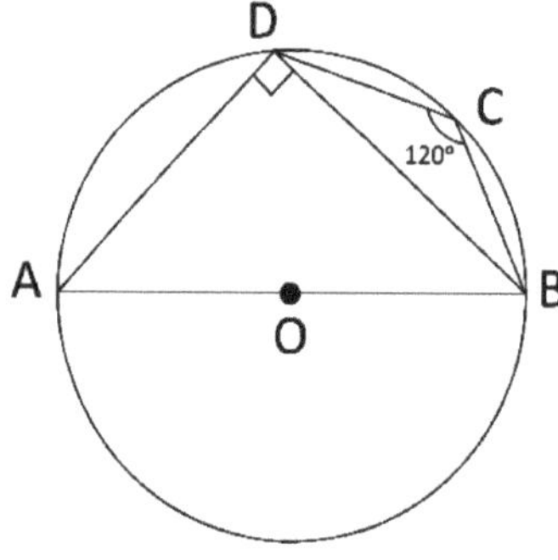

12. In the figure, ∠DBC = 58° BD is a diameter of the circle.
Calculate: (i) ∠BDC (ii) ∠BEC (iii) ∠BAC **(2014)**

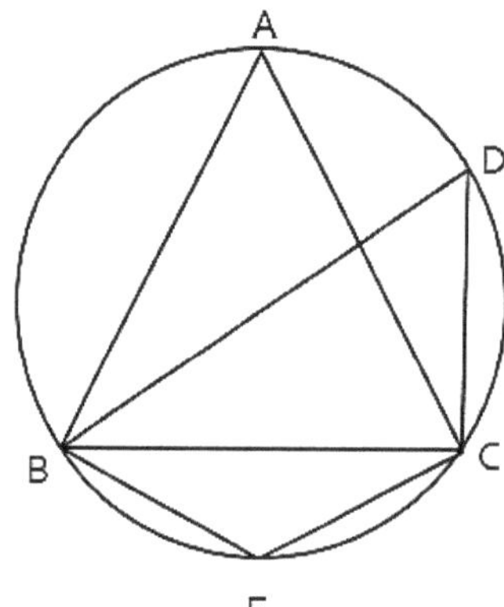

13. In the figure given below, AD is a diameter. O is the centre of the circle. AD is parallel to BC and ∠CBD = 32°. Find. (i) ∠OBD (ii)∠AOB (iii) ∠BED **(2016)**

14. In the given figure, ABCDE is a pentagon inscribed in a circle such that AC is a diameter and side BC || AE. If angle BAC = 50°, find giving reasons: **(2019)**
(i) ∠ACB (ii) ∠EDC (iii) ∠BEC Hence prove that BE is also a diameter.

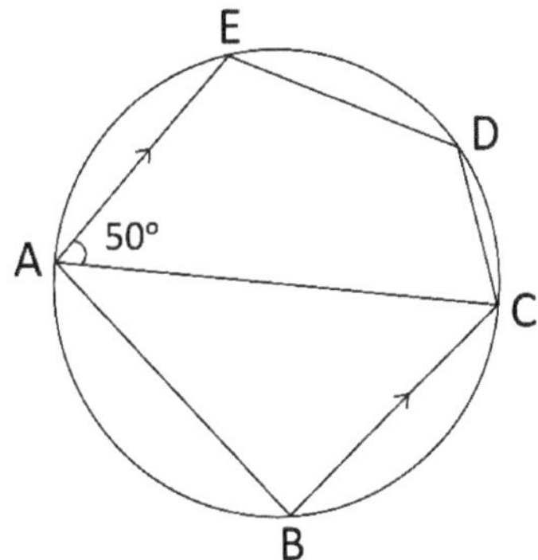

15. In the given figure, O is the centre of the circle and AB is a diameter. If AC = BD and ∠AOC = 72°, find: (i) ∠ABC (ii)∠BAD (iii)∠ABD

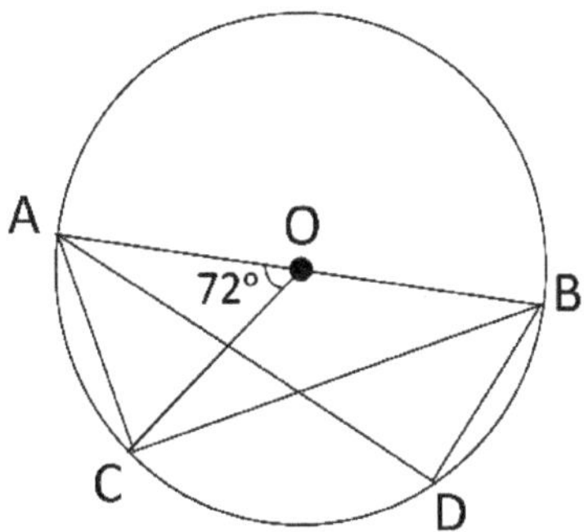

16. In the figure, ABF is a straight line and BE || DC. If ∠DAB = 92°, find (i) $\angle BCD$ (ii) $\angle ADC$

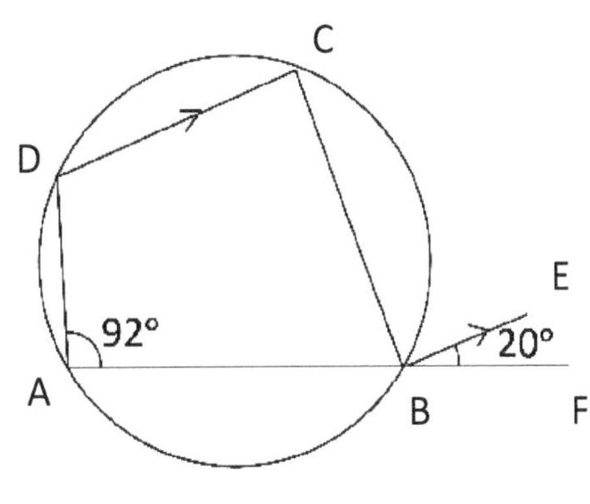

Answer key

Ans 1.	(i) 55°	(ii) 125°	(iii) 35°	
Ans 2.	(i) 115°	(ii) 45°		
Ans 3.	(i) 30°			
Ans 4.	(i) 75°			
Ans 5.	(i) 60°	(ii) 30°		
Ans 6.	(i) 60°	(ii) 75°	(iii) 55°	(iv) 115°
Ans 7.	(i) 75°			
Ans 8.	(i) 130°			
Ans 9.	(i) 50°	(ii) 100°	(iii) 30°	
Ans 10.	(i) 50°	(ii) 40°		

Ans 11.	(i) 30°	(ii) 60°		
Ans 12.	(i) 32°	(ii) 148°	(iii) 32°	
Ans 13.	(i) 32°	(ii) 64°	(iii) 58°	
Ans 14.	(i) 40°	(ii)130°	(iii) 40°	
Ans 15.	(i) 36°	(ii) 36°	(iii) 54°	
Ans 16.	(i) 88°	(ii) 108°.		

1.11 Tangent and secant properties: If a circle and a straight line lie in a plane, then with respect to each other one of the following three situations may exist:

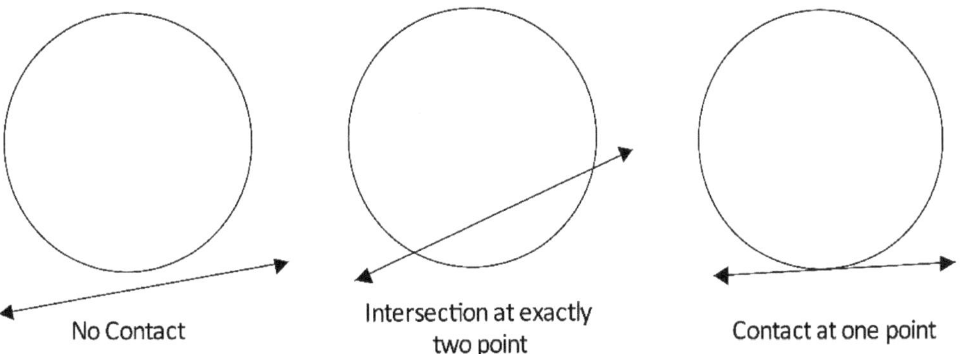

The line is called **secant** if it intersects circle at two points

The line which touches circle at one point is called the **tangent of the circle**. The point on the circumference, where the line touches is called the **point of contact**.

Theorem 6: The tangent at any point of a circle and the radius through the point are perpendicular to each other.

If we draw a number of line segment from the centre to the line, the perpendicular (OP here) is the shortest.

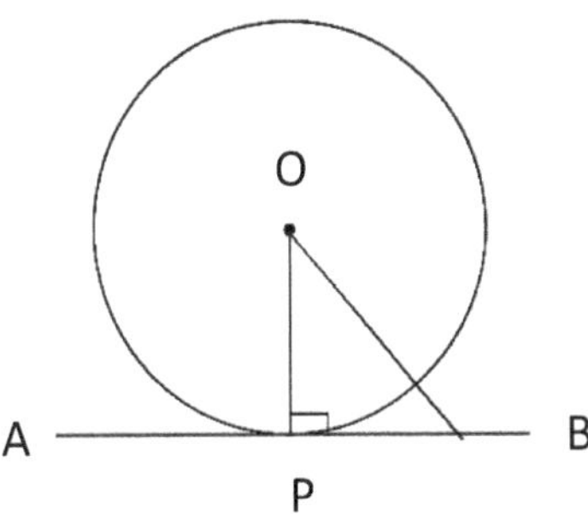

Theorem 7: From any point outside a circle, **only** two tangents can be drawn, then

(i) The lengths of tangents are equal. PA = PB

(ii) The tangents subtend equal angles at the centre of the circle. ∠AOP = ∠BOP

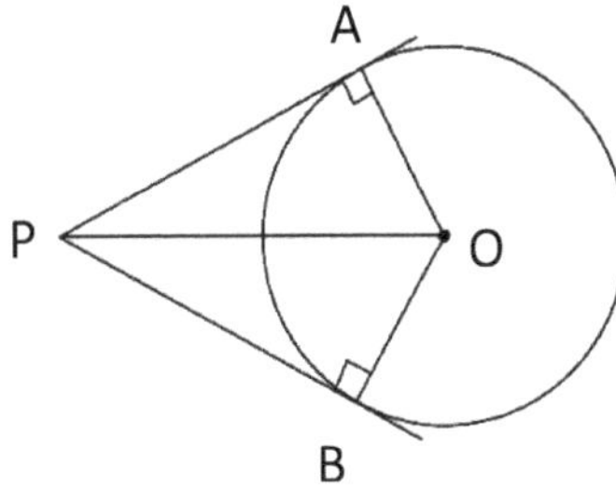

(iii) The tangents are equally inclined to the line joining the point and the centre of the circle. ∠APO = ∠BPO

Theorem 8: If two circles touch internally or externally, the point of contact lies on the straight line joining their centers.

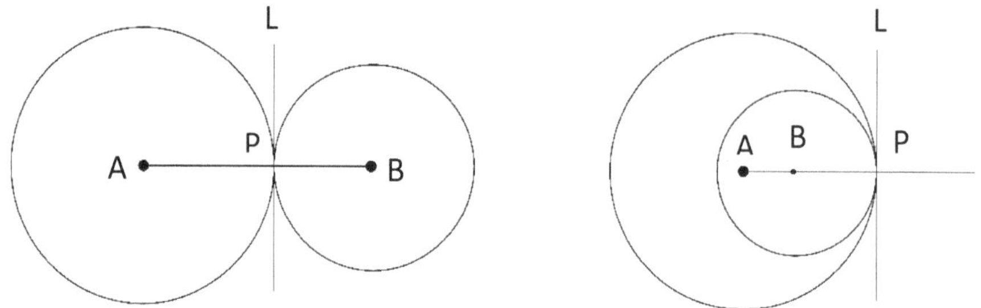

1.12 Segments of a chord: If P is a point lies on a chord internally or externally, then it divides chord

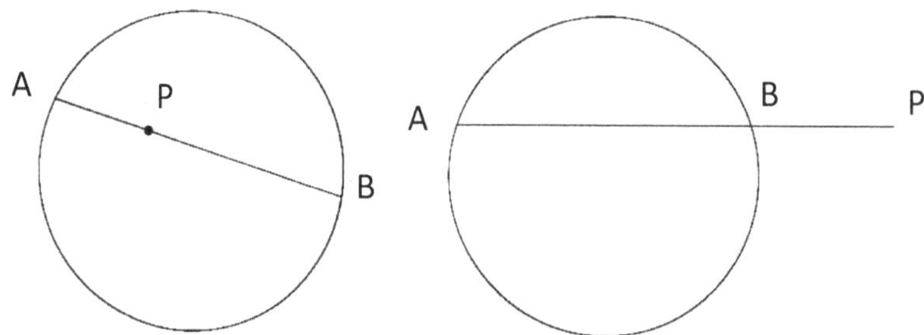

into two segments PA and PB. In first figure P divides AB internally and in second figure P divides externally.

Theorem 9: If two chords intersect internally or externally then the product of the lengths of the segments are equal $PA \times PB = PC \times PD$

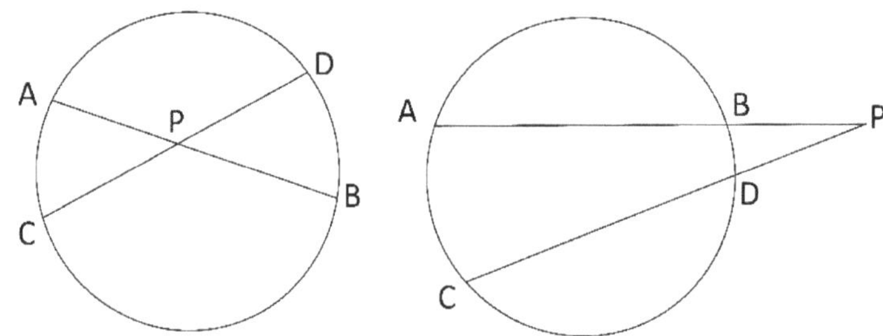

Theorem 10: If a chord and a tangent intersect externally, then the product of the lengths of segments of the chord is equal to the square of the length of the tangent from the point of contact to the point of intersection. $PA \times PB = PT^2$

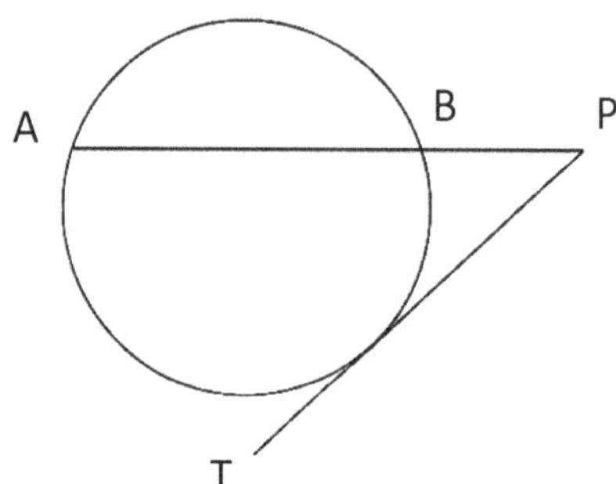

1.13 Angles in the alternate segments see theorem – 11: Recall two theorems "radius makes 90° at point of contact with tangent" and "angle in a semicircle is a right angle", and see in the figure given:

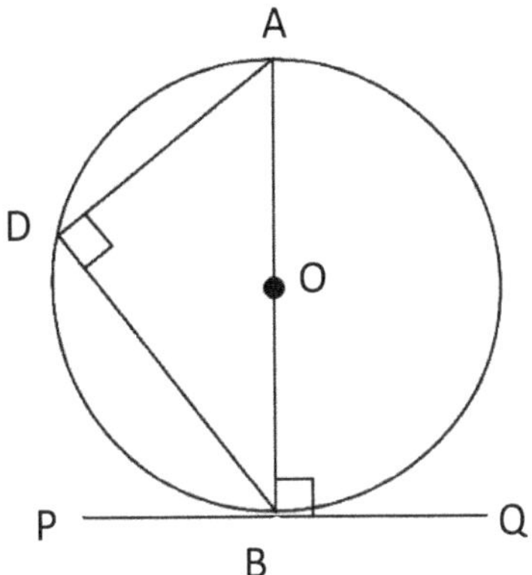

In the figure, $\angle ADB = 90°$(angle in a semi-circle)
$\angle ABQ = 90°$(radius makes 90° at point of contact with tangent)
So $\angle ADB = \angle ABQ$
These angles remain equal if we move point A and D on circumference, and result in a theorem called angles in the alternate segment.

Theorem 11: If a line touches a circle and from the point of contact, a chord is drawn, the angles between the tangent and the chord are respectively equal to the angles in the corresponding alternate segments.

Or

Angles in the alternate segments are equal, so from the figure, $\angle ADB = \angle ABQ$

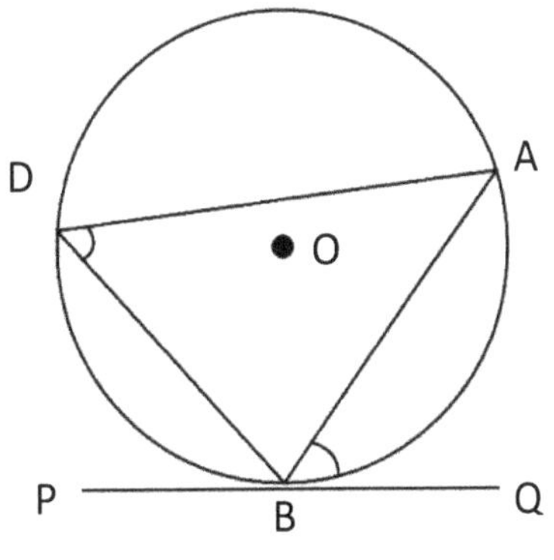

Practice Sheet – 2

1. In the figure given: from an external point P, tangents PA and PB are drawn to a circle. CE is a tangent to the circle at D. If AP = 15 cm, find the perimeter of the triangle PEC.

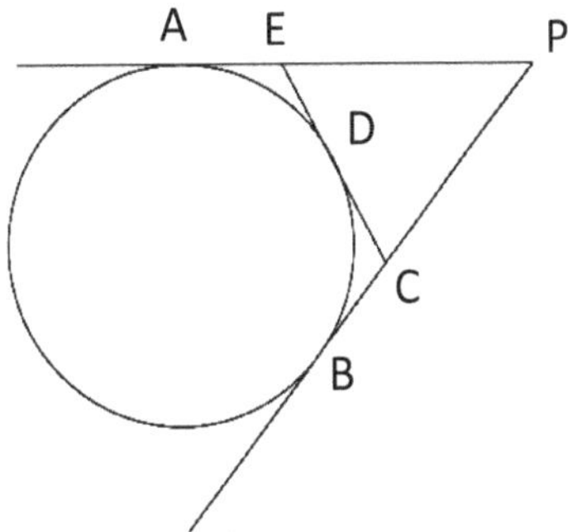

2. In the adjoining figure, a circle is inscribed in the quadrilateral ABCD. Given that BC = 38 cm, QB = 27 cm, and DC = 25 cm, and that AD is perpendicular to DC, find the radius of the circle.

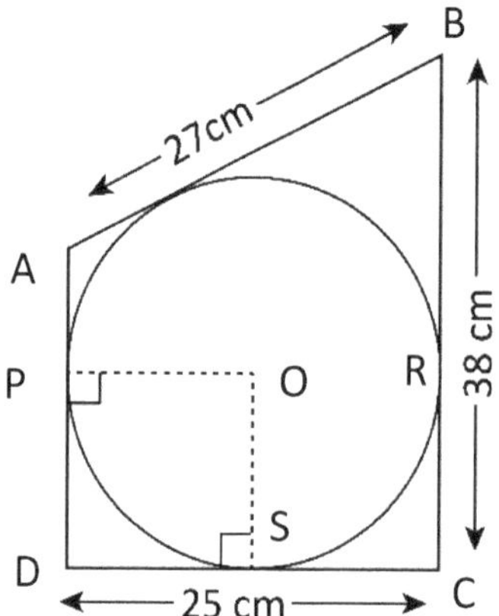

3. In the adjoining figure, AT is a tangent to a circle at A. If ∠CAB = 60° and ∠TAB = 55°, find ∠ABC.

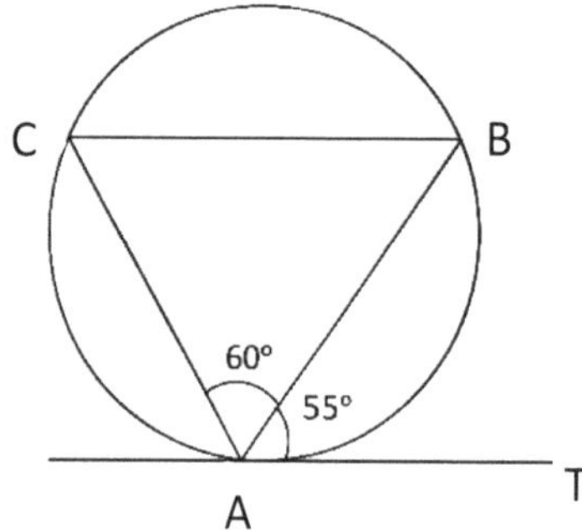

4. In the figure given, PQ is a tangent to the circle at A, DB is a diameter, ∠ADB = 30° & ∠CBD = 60° calculate : (i)∠QAB (ii)∠PAD (iii)∠CDB.

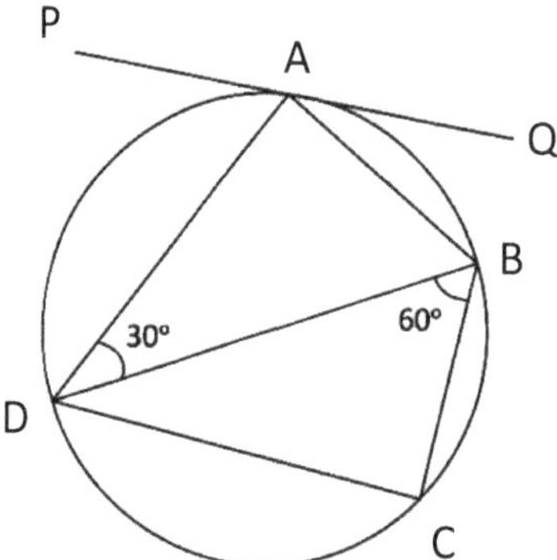

5. Find the unknown length x in each of the following figures:

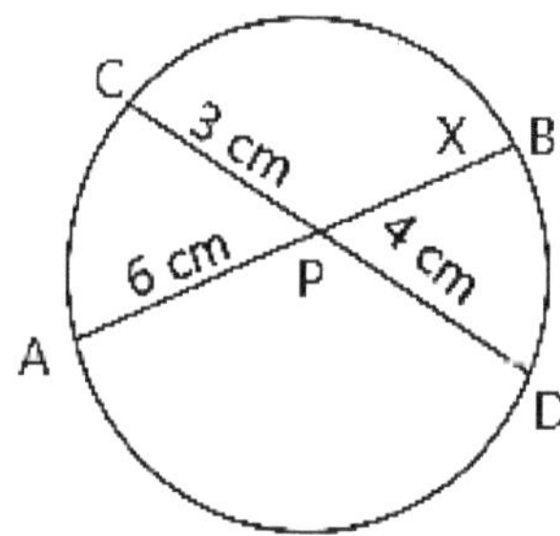

6. In the figure, if PA = 16 cm, PC = 10 cm, and PD = 8 cm, find AB.

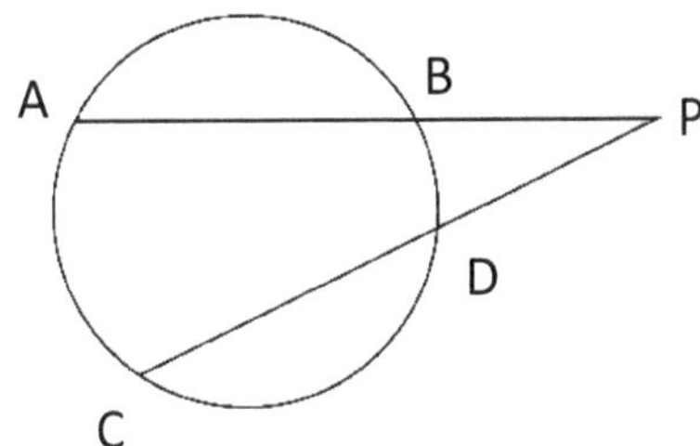

7. In the given figure, the angle A of the triangle ABC is a right angle. The circle on AC as diameter cuts BC at D. If BD = 9 cm, and DC = 7 cm, calculate the length of AB.

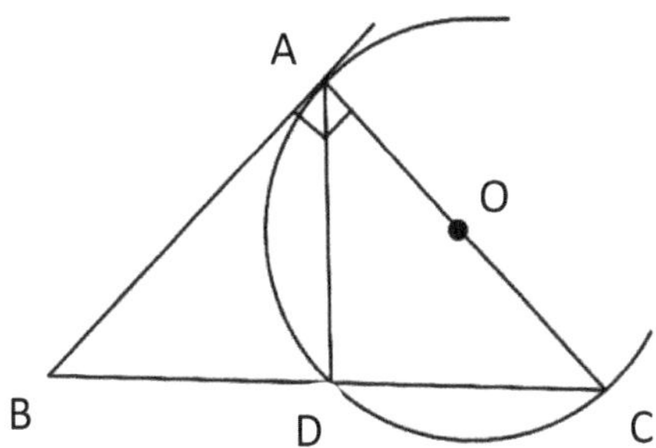

8. In the figure given below, diameter AB and chord CD of a circle meet at P. PT is a tangent to the circle at T. CD = 7.8 cm, PD = 5 cm, PB = 4 cm. Find: **(2014)**

(i) AB

(ii) the length of tangent PT.

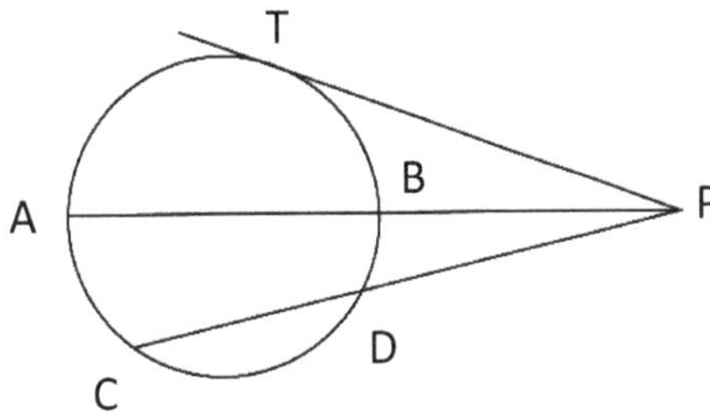

9. In the following figure O is the centre of the circle and AB is a tangent to it at point B. BDC = 65 °. Find ∠BAO.

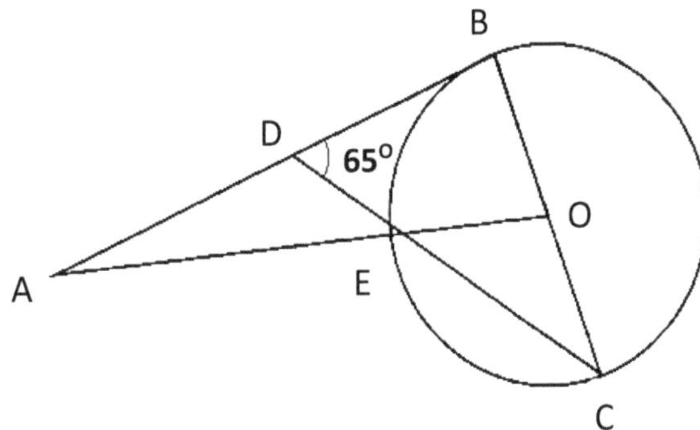

10. In the figure given below, O is the centre of the circle and SP is a tangent. If ∠SRT = 65°, find the value of x, y and z. **(2015)**

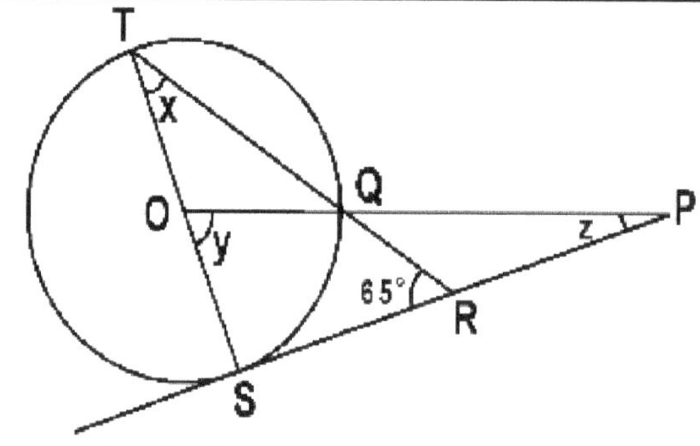

11. In the figure given, O is the centre of the circle.∠DAE = 70°. Find giving suitable reasons, the measure of: (i)∠BCD (ii)∠BOD (iii)∠OBD **(2017)**

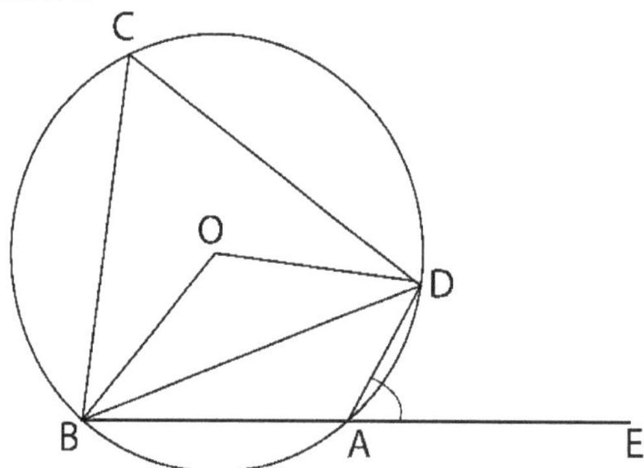

12. In the given figure AC is a tangent to the circle with centre O. If ∠ADB = 55°, find x and y. Give reason for your answer.

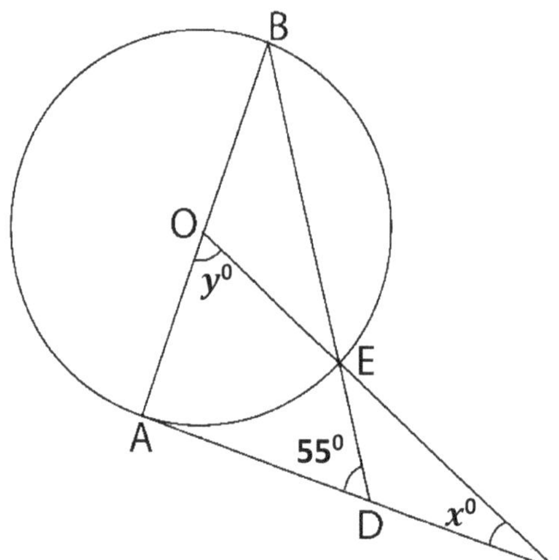

13. In the given figure TP and TQ are two tangents to the circle with centre O, touching at A and C respectively. If ∠BCQ = 45° and ∠BAP = 60°. Find: **(2020)**

(i) ∠OBA and ∠OBC
(ii) ∠AOC
(iii) ∠ATC

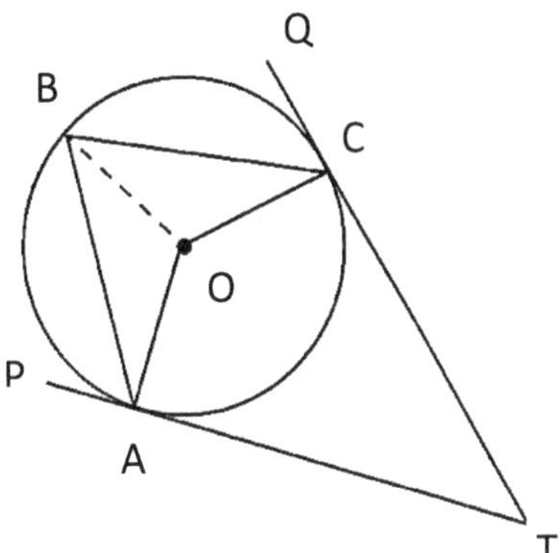

14. In the given circle with centre O, ∠ABC = 100°, ∠ACD = 40°, and CT is a tangent to the circle at C. Find ∠ADC and ∠DCT

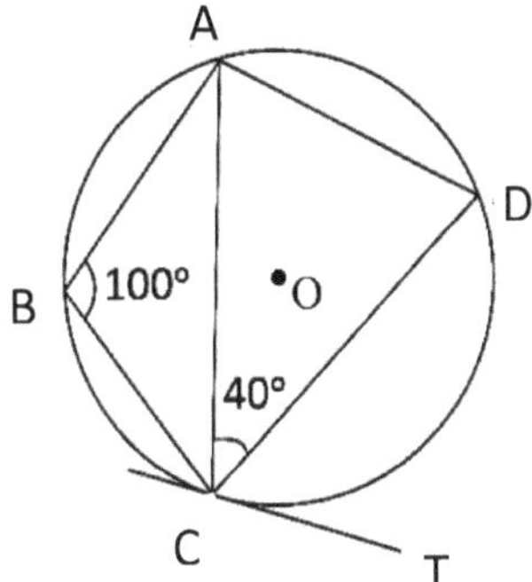

15. In the given figure. XY is the diameter of the circle and PQ is a tangent to the circle at Y. If ∠AXB = 50° and ∠ABX = 70°, find ∠BAY and ∠APY

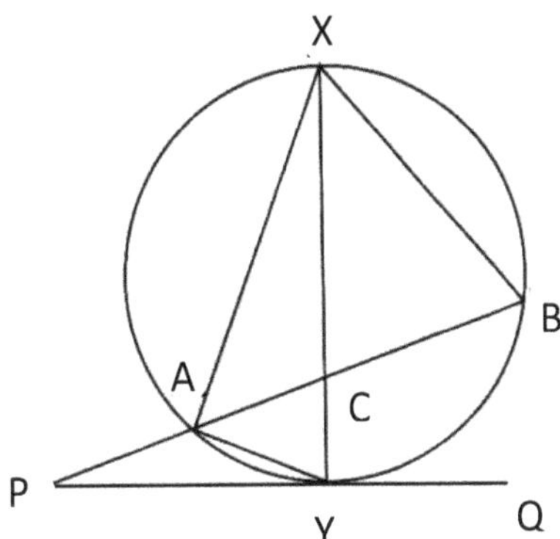

16. In the given figure, QAP is the tangent at point A and PBD is a straight line. If ∠ACB = 36° and ∠APB = 42°, find: (i) ∠BAP (ii) ∠ABD (iii) ∠QAD (iv) ∠BCD

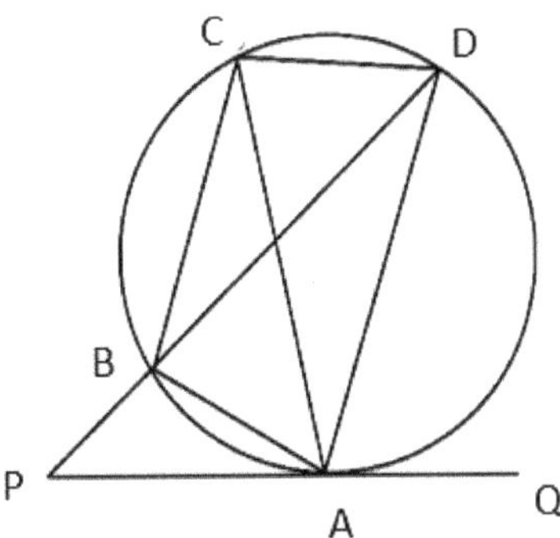

17. In the given figure, O is the centre of the circle. The tangents at B and D intersect each other at point P. If AB is parallel to CD and $\angle ABC = 55°$, find:

(i). $\angle BOD$ (ii). $\angle BPD$

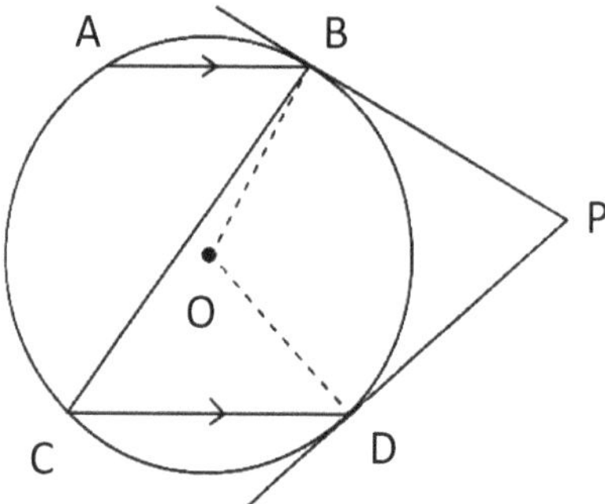

18. Two circles intersect each other at point A and B. Their common tangent touches the circles at point P and Q as shown in the figure. Show that the angles PAQ and PBQ are supplementary.

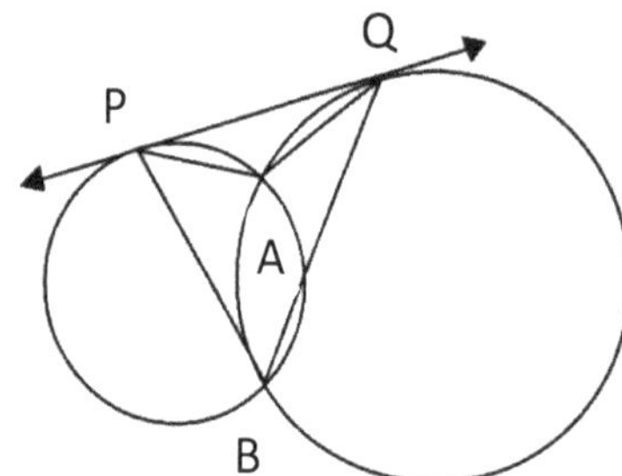

19. In the given figure, O is the centre of the circle, $OM \perp AB$. If $\angle ABC = 42°$, calculate:

(i). $\angle AOC$ (ii). $\angle ODC$

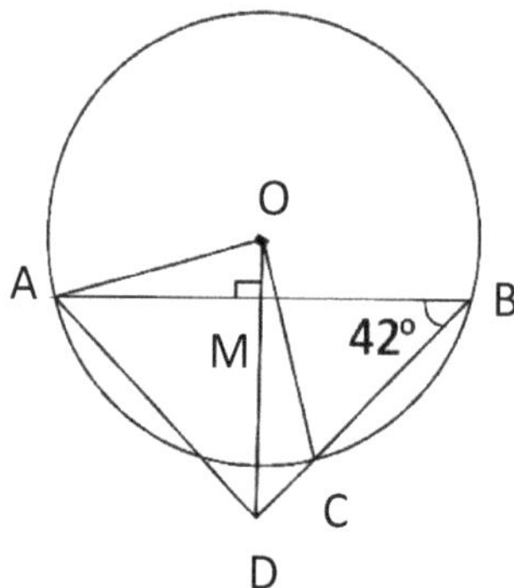

20. In the given figure, the side of the quadrilateral touches the circle. Prove that AB + CD = BC + DA.

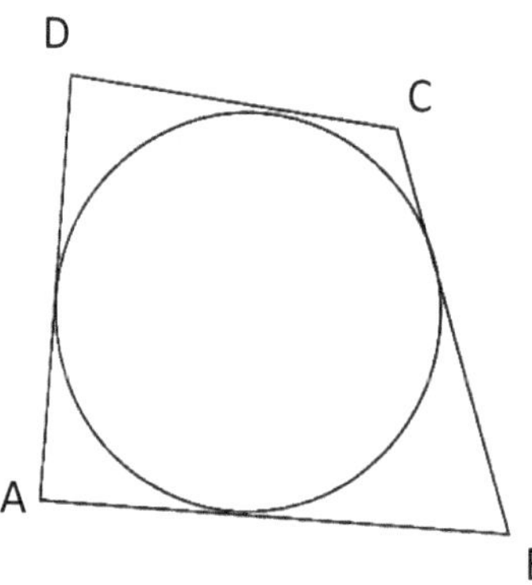

21. AB and CD are two chords of a circle intersecting at P. Prove that PA × PB = PC × PD.

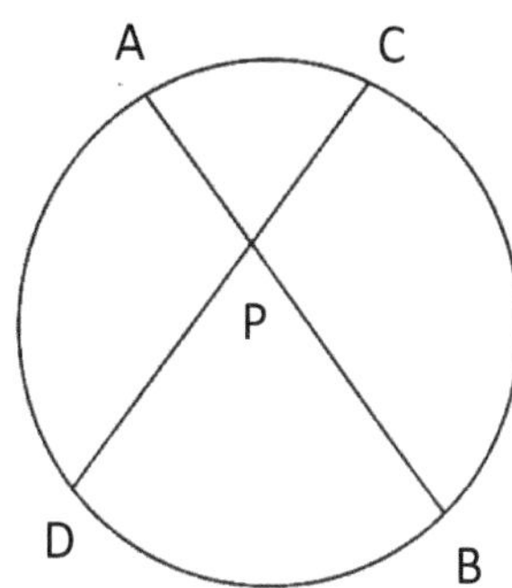

22. In the given figure, PM is a tangent to the circle and PA = AM. Prove that:

(i) ΔPMB is an isosceles triangle.

(ii) PA. PB $= MB^2$

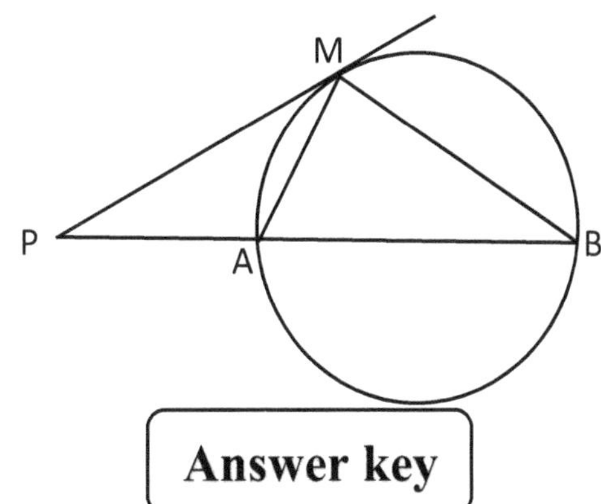

Answer key

Ans 1.	30 cm			
Ans 2.	14 cm			
Ans 3.	65°			
Ans 4.	(i) 30°	(ii) 60°	(iii)30°	
Ans 5	2 cm			
Ans 6.	11 cm			
Ans 7.	12 cm			
Ans 8.	(i) 12 cm	(ii) 8 cm		
Ans 9.	40°			
Ans 10.	$x = 25°, y = 40°, z = 40°$			
Ans 11.	(i) 70°	(ii) 140°	(iii) 20°	
Ans 12.	$x = 20°$, y = 70°			
Ans 13.	(i) 30° and 45°	(ii) 150°	(iii) 30°	
Ans 14.	80°, 60°			
Ans 15.	30°, 10°			
Ans 16.	(i) 36°	(ii) 78°	(iii) 78°	(iv) 114°
Ans 17.	(i) 110°	(ii) 70°		
Ans 19.	(i) 84°	(ii) 48°		

Cylinder, Cone and Sphere

1.1 Introduction: We see many objects/articles around us. These objects can be categorized into two categories:

(i) Two dimensional or 2D: These are also called **plane figure** that has no thickness. They lie entirely in **one plane**. These objects can be composed of line segments, curves, or a combination of the two. They occupy space in one plane only, so we can calculate their **area** and **perimeter**. **For example** circle triangle, quadrilateral, etc.

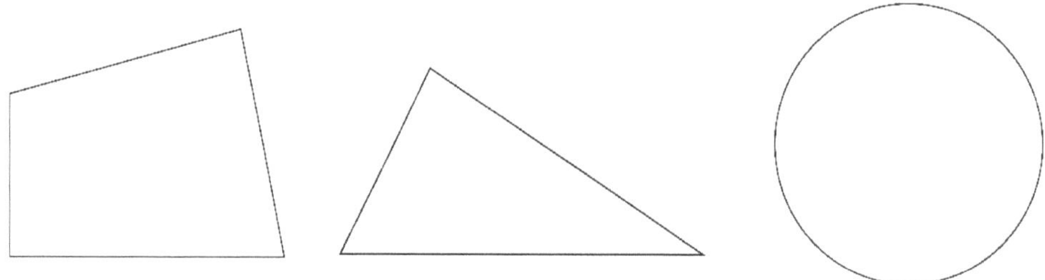

(ii) Three dimensional or 3D: These are also called **solids**, or we can say **2D figure with thickness/height**. They occupy space in two planes so we can determine their **surface area** and **volume**. **For example** cylinder, cone, sphere, prism, etc.

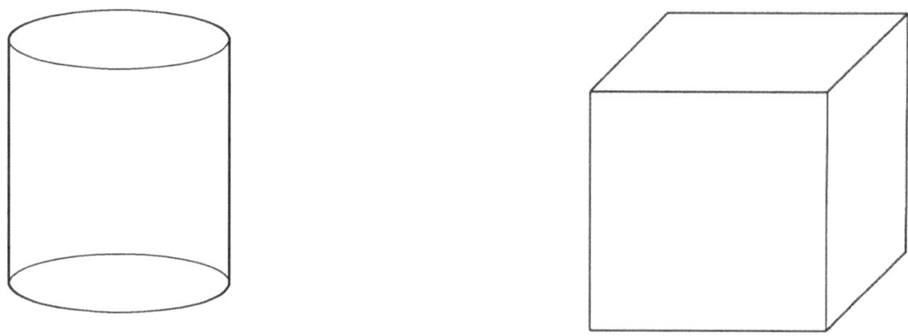

1.2 Cross Section of a solid: Every solid has a plane figure in its base, which is called **cross section**. **For example,** cylinders and cones have a circular cross section, cubes and cuboids have a quadrilateral cross section etc.

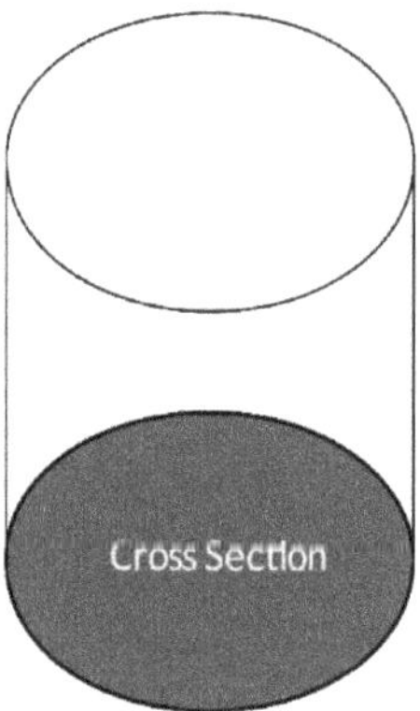

1.3 Surfaces in solids: When we look at the faces of these solids, we find that some are **flat,** and some are **curved**. These faces are not only seen but can also be touched. Like in a **closed cylinder** we have **2 flat surfaces** and **1 curved surface**, in a **closed cylinder** we have **1 flat** and **1 curved surface**.

Cylinder

A solid obtained by revolving a rectangular paper about one of its sides is called a right circular rectangle. Or in other words a solid of height h whose ends are circles (which are congruent to each other) is called a right circular cylinder. Radius (r) and height (h) are its basic elements.
We will study about right circular cylinder (or simply cylinder) of the following two types:

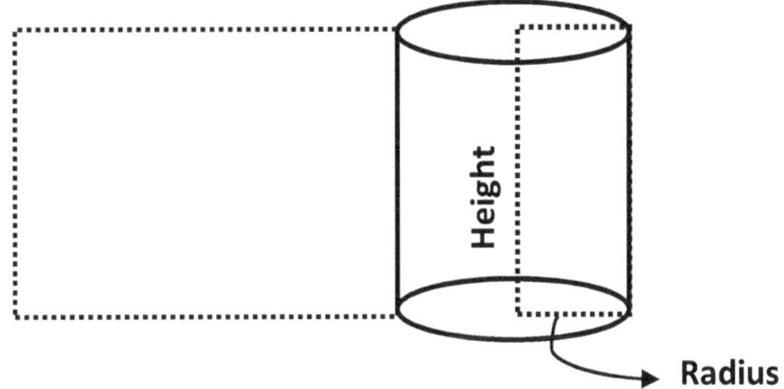

1.4 Solid cylinder: Let r be the radius and h be the height of a solid right circular cylinder, then:

(i) Curved (lateral) surface area or area of walls

= perimeter of cross-section × height= $2\pi rh$ (unit^2)

(ii) Total surface area = curved surface area + area of both circular ends

= $2\pi rh + 2\pi r^2$

=$2\pi r(h + r)$ (unit^2)

(iii) Volume = area of cross section × height

= $\pi r^2 h$(unit^3)

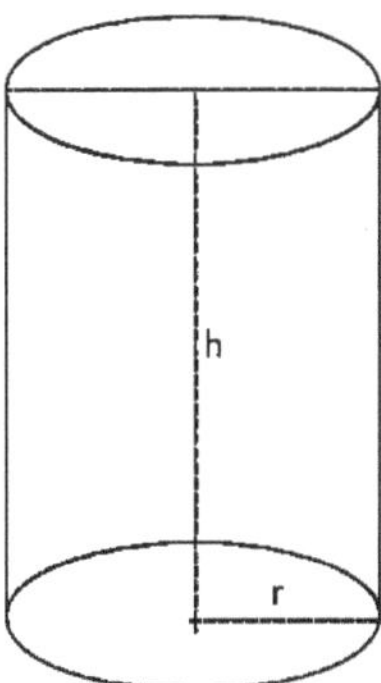

1.5 Hollow Cylinder (Pipe): There are two cylinders whose height is same and radius of outer (R) > radius of inner (r). There are total 4 surfaces. 1 inner curved surface, 1 outer curved surface, two rings.

(i) Thickness of cylinder = R – r

(ii) Area of cross-section (Ring) = $\pi(\mathrm{R}^2 - \mathrm{r}^2)$

(iii) External curved surface area = $2\pi Rh$

(iv) Internal curved surface area = $2\pi rh$

(v) Total surface area = External CSA + Internal CSA + area of both rings.

$= 2\pi Rh + 2\pi rh + 2\pi(R^2 - r^2)$

(vi) Volume of material = Volume of external cylinder (material + air) – volume of internal cylinder (air)

$= \pi R^2 h - \pi r^2 h$

$= \pi(R^2 - r^2)h$

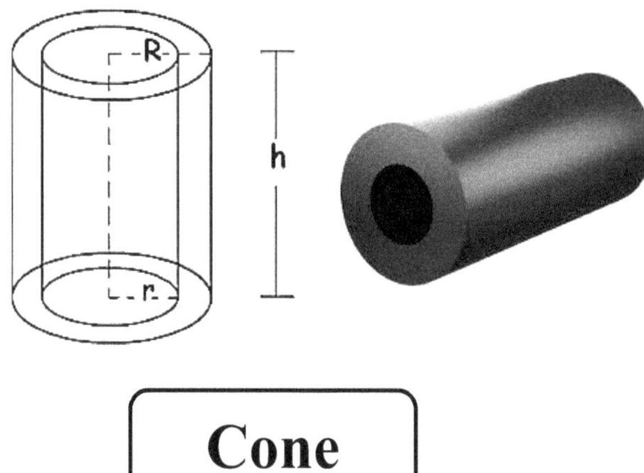

Cone

A solid obtained by revolving a right angled triangle about its perpendicular or base, is called a right circular cone (or simply cone). Its basic elements are radius (r), height (h) and slant height (l), which are connected with the formula $l^2 = h^2 + r^2$.

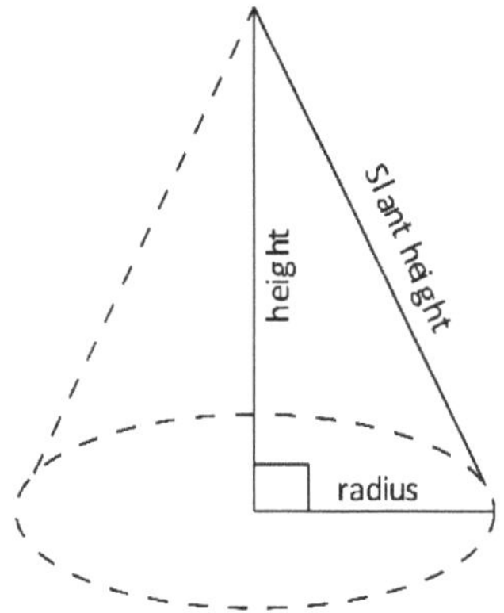

1.6 Surface area and volume of a cone:

(i) Slant height $l = \sqrt{h^2 + r^2}$

(ii) Curved surface area (CSA) $= \pi rl$

(iii) Total surface area (TSA) = CSA + area of base

$= \pi rl + \pi r^2$

$= \pi r(l + r)$

(iv) Volume $= \frac{1}{3}\pi r^2 h$

1. 7 Combinations of two or more solids: In our daily life we come across a number of solids made of combinations of two or more solids.

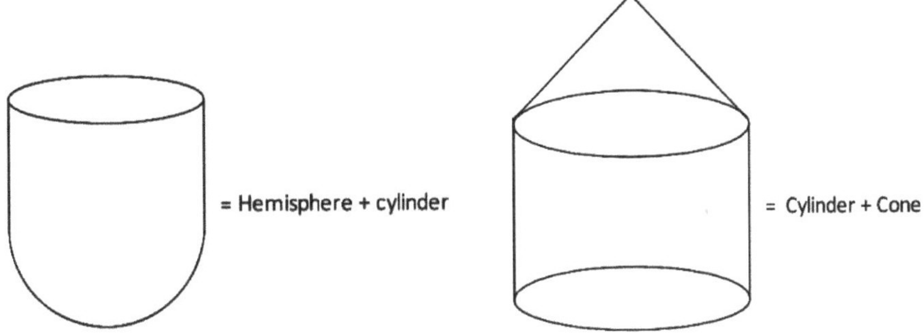

Remark: To find surface area and volume of such combinations we have formulas. But be careful while applying them. Because while calculating volume it is easy to say that volume of whole solid = volume of solid 1 $\pm$ volume of solid 2, but **while calculating surface area, it is not that straight**. Because when two or more solids combined their surfaces overlap each other and may be vanished. As in the following combinations a closed cone has 2 surfaces (1 flat and 1 curved) and a closed cylinder has two surfaces (2 flat and 1 curved) so there are total 5 surfaces. But when we combined them there are only 3 surfaces: 1 flat surface of cylinder,1 curved surface of cylinder and 1 curved surface of cone. So now to calculate the surface area of this solid, we will consider only curved surface of cone + curved surface of cylinder + flat surface of cylinder.

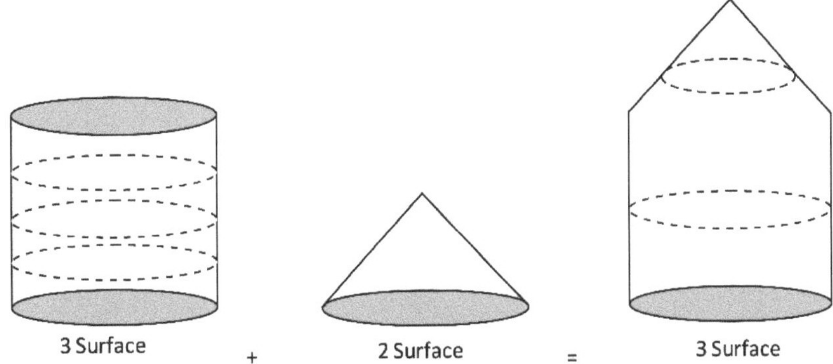

1.8 Recast after melting and number of solids:

(i) When a solid melts and recast into another solid, its volume remain change.

(ii) When a big solid melts and recast into number of small solids then:

$$\text{Number of small solid} = \frac{\text{Volume of big solid}}{\text{Volume of small solid}}$$

Practice Sheet

1. The height of a right circular cylinder is 21 cm, and its radius is 14 cm. Find:
(i) Volume (ii) Curved surface area (iii) Total surface area

2. The area of curved surface of a right circular cylinder is 4400 cm^2 and the circumference of its base is 110 cm. Find the height of the cylinder.

3. Find the volume of a circular cone whose height is 3 cm and slant length is 5 cm.

4. A solid right circular copper cone of height 15 cm and radius 6 cm is melted, and smaller copper cones of height 3 cm and radius 2 cm are made. How many smaller cones can be made?

5. A solid metallic right cone is melted, and a number of solid right cylinders are made with the material. Find the number of cylinders if the radius of the base of each cylinder is half the radius of the cone and the height of each cylinder is one-third the height of the cone.

6. The height of a right circular cone is 3.6 cm. and the radius of its base is 1.6 cm. It is melted and recast into a right circular cone with radius of its base as 1.2 cm., find its height.

7. A circus tent is in the shape of a cylinder surmounted by a right cone. The height of the cylindrical part is 11 decimeters. The base of the tent has a diameter of 24 decimeters and the total height of the tent is 16 decimeters. Find the area of the canvas required to make the tent.

8. A conical hole is drilled in a circular cylinder of height 12 cm. and base radius 5 cm. The height and base radius of the cone is also the same. Find the whole surface and volume of the remaining portion of cylinder. Leave you answer in terms of π.

9. If the diameter of the cross-section of a wire is decreased by 5%, how much percent will the length be increased so that the volume remains the same.

10. A solid metallic cylinder has radius 3 cm and height 5 cm. It is made of metal A. To reduce its weight, a conical hole is drilled in the cylinder from one of its ends and is completely filled with a lighter metal B. The conical hole has radius of 3/2 cm and its depth is 8/9 cm. Calculate the ratio of the volume of the metal A to the volume of the metal B in the solid.

11. An exhibition tent is in the form of a cylinder surmounted by a cone. The height of the tent above the ground is 85 m and the height of the cylindrical part is 50 m. If the diameter of the base is 168 m, find the quantity of canvas required to make the tent. Allow 20% extra for folds and for stitching. Give your answer to the nearest m^2.

12. A girl fills a cylindrical bucket 32 cm in height and 18 cm in radius with sand. She empties the bucket on the ground and makes a conical heap of the sand. If the height of the conical heap is 24 cm. find: (i) its radius and (ii) its slant height. **(2004)**

13. A vessel in the form of an inverted cone is filled with water to the brim. Its height is 20 cm and diameter is 16.8 cm. Two equal solid cones are dropped in it so that they are fully submerged. As a result, one third of the water in the original cone overflows. What is the volume of each of the solid cones submerged? **(2006)**

14. The volume of a conical tent is 1232 m^3 and the area of the bare floor is 154 m^2.
    Calculate the:
    (i) radius of the floor.
    (ii) height of the tent.
    (iii) length of the canvas required to cover this conical tent if its width is 2 m. **(2008)**

15. A conical hole is drilled in a circular cylinder of height 12 cm and base radius 5 cm. The height and base radius of the cone is also the same. Find the total surface area and volume of the remaining solid.

16. From a solid wooden cylinder of height 28 cm and diameter 6 cm, two conical cavities are hollowed out. The diameter of the cones are also of 6 cm and height 10.5 cm. Taking $\pi = \frac{22}{7}$, find the volume of remaining solid. **[Boards 2020]**

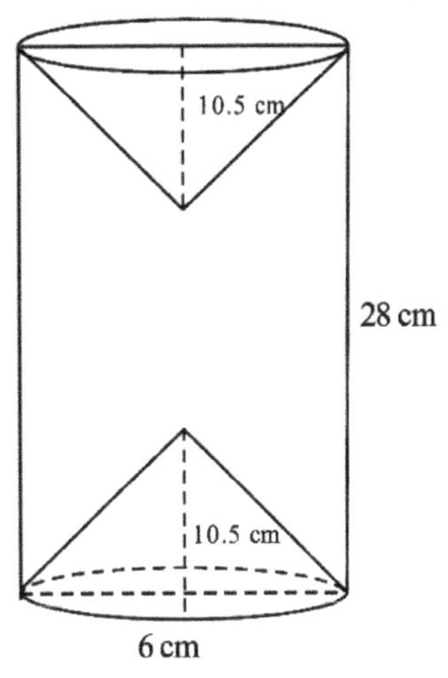

Answer key

Ans 1.	(i) 3234 cm^3	(ii)1848 cm^2	iii) 3080 cm^2.
Ans 2.	40 cm		
Ans 3.	50.3 cm^3		
Ans 4.	45		
Ans 5.	4		
Ans 6.	6.4 cm		
Ans 7.	1320 dm^2		
Ans 8.	210 π cm^2, 200 π cm^3		
Ans 9.	10.8% approx.		
Ans 10.	133:2		
Ans 11.	60509 m^2		
Ans 12.	36 cm, 43.27 cm		
Ans 13.	246.4 cm^3		
Ans 14.	(i) 7m	(ii) 24m	(iii) 275m
Ans 15.	210 πcm^2 and 200 πcm^2		
Ans 16.	594 cm^3.		

UNIT - 4

TRIGONOMETRY

CHAPTER

Trigonometrical Identities

1.1 Introduction: We studied relationships between angles of triangle. Sum of all angles of a triangle equals 180°. If two angles are given, then we can find third angle using **Angle sum property of Triangle**. Missing side of a triangle can be find using **Pythagoras formula**. So we have studied the relationship either between angles or sides of triangles. **Trigonometry** is the branch of mathematics that study the **relationship between sides and angles** of triangle. It is based on a right angle triangle but its applications are beyond a right angle triangle.

1.2 Trigonometrical ratios: We have studied **Trigonometrical ratios (T. Ratio)**, which establishes a relationship between sides and angles of triangles. Let's have a brief description of T. Ratio.

(i) $\sin\theta = \dfrac{\text{Perpendicular}}{\text{Hypotenuse}}$ (ii) $\text{cosec}\,\theta = \dfrac{\text{Hypotenus}}{\text{Perpendicular}}$

(iii) $\cos\theta = \dfrac{\text{Base}}{\text{Hypotenus}}$ (iv) $\sec\theta = \dfrac{\text{Hypotenuse}}{\text{Base}}$

(v) $\tan\theta = \dfrac{\text{Perpendicular}}{\text{Base}}$ (vi) $\cot\theta = \dfrac{\text{Base}}{\text{perpendicular}}$

Chapter: Trigonometrical Identities

In mathematics **Identity** means an equation which is always true, no matter what values are substituted in the variable. $3x + 4x = 7x$, is an identity because it is always true for all values of x.

1.3 Trigonometric identities are equations that involve trigonometrical ratios of an angle and are true for every value of the angle for which both sides of the equality are defined. In latest syllabus of ICSE – X questions only regarding to Trigonometrical identities will be asked. These are the three Trigonometrical identities or square relations:

(i) $\sin^2\theta + \cos^2\theta = 1$
(ii) $1 + \tan^2\theta = \sec^2\theta$
(iii) $1 + \cot^2\theta = \text{cosec}^2\theta$

Remark: The square relation given above are the main relations. But by changing the subject we can create more relations from them.

(i) $\sin^2\theta + \cos^2\theta = 1$ $\Rightarrow \cos^2\theta = 1 - \sin^2\theta$ $\Rightarrow \sin^2\theta = 1 - \cos^2\theta$
(ii) $1 + \tan^2\theta = \sec^2\theta$ $\Rightarrow \sec^2\theta - \tan^2\theta = 1$ $\Rightarrow \sec^2\theta - 1 = \tan^2\theta$
(iii) $1 + \cot^2\theta = \text{cosec}^2\theta$ $\Rightarrow \text{cosec}^2\theta - \cot^2\theta = 1$ $\Rightarrow \text{cosec}^2\theta - 1 = \cot^2\theta$

and many more.........

1.4 Few more relations which are helpful in solving questions:

(i) Reciprocal Relations:

(i) $\sin\theta = \dfrac{1}{\text{cosec}\,\theta}$ and $\text{cosec}\,\theta = \dfrac{1}{\sin\theta}$ (sin θ and cosec θ are reciprocal of each other)

(ii) $\cos\theta = \dfrac{1}{\sec\theta}$ and $\sec\theta = \dfrac{1}{\cos\theta}$ (cos θ and sec θ are reciprocal of each other)

(iii) $\tan\theta = \dfrac{1}{\cot\theta}$ and $\cot\theta = \dfrac{1}{\tan\theta}$ (tan θ and cot θ are reciprocal of each other)

(ii) Quotient Relations:

$$\tan\theta = \frac{\sin\theta}{\cos\theta} \text{ and } \cot\theta = \frac{\cos\theta}{\sin\theta}$$

Tips: Tips couldn't help unless practice well. But few lines and examples related to them are given below:

(i) Try to break up left hand identity in $\sin\theta$ and $\cos\theta$.

(ii) Multiplication by conjugate in numerator and denominator of a fraction. (Conjugate of $a - b$ is $a + b$ and vice versa)

Example 1: Prove that: $\dfrac{\sin A}{1+\cos A} = \text{cosec } A - \cot A$

Solution:

L.H.S.

$$= \frac{\text{Sin A}}{1+\cos A} \times \frac{1-\cos A}{1-\cos A} \quad \text{(Multiply and divide by } 1 - \cos A\text{)}$$

$$= \frac{\sin A(1-\cos A)}{1-\cos^2 A}$$

$$= \frac{\sin A(1-\cos A)}{\sin^2 A}$$

$$= \frac{(1-\cos A)}{\sin A}$$

$$= \frac{1}{\sin A} - \frac{\cos A}{\sin A}$$

$$= \text{cosec A} - \cot A = \text{R.H.S}$$

Example 2: Prove that: tan A + cot A = sec A. cosec A

Solution:

L.H.S.

$$= \tan A + \cot A$$

$$= \frac{\sin A}{\cos A} + \frac{\cos A}{\sin A}$$

$$= \frac{\sin^2 A + \cos^2 A}{\cos A \cdot \cos A}$$

$$= \frac{1}{\cos A \cdot \sin A}$$

$$= \frac{1}{\cos A} \cdot \frac{1}{\sin A} \quad \because (\sin^2 A + \cos^2 A = 1)$$

$$= \sec A \cdot \text{cosec A} = \text{R.H.S} \quad (\because \sec A = \frac{1}{\cos A} \text{ and cosec } A = \frac{1}{\sin A})$$

Practice Sheet

Prove the following Identities:

1. $\frac{\sec A-1}{\sec A+1}=\frac{1-\cos A}{1+\cos A}$

2. $\tan^2 A-\frac{1}{\cos^2 A}+1=0$

3. $\tan^2 A-\frac{1}{\cos^2 A}+1=0$

4. $(\cot A-\operatorname{cosec} A)^2=\frac{1-\cos A}{1+\cos A}$

5. $(\operatorname{cosec}^2 A-1)(\sec A+1)(\sec A-1)=1$

6. $\frac{\sin^3 A-\cos^3 A}{\sin A-\cos A}-\sin A\cdot\cos A=1$

7. $\frac{\cos A}{1-\tan A}+\frac{\sin^2 A}{\sin A-\cos A}=\sin A+\cos A$

8. $\frac{1+\cos A}{1-\cos A}=\frac{\tan^2 A}{(\sec A-1)^2}$ **(2012)**

9. $\frac{1+\sec A-\tan A}{1+\sec A+\tan A}=\frac{1-\sin A}{\cos A}$

10. $\frac{\cot A+\operatorname{cosec} A-1}{\cot A-\operatorname{cosec} A+1}=\frac{1+\cos A}{\sin A}$

11. $\frac{1+\cos A+\sin A}{1+\cos A-\sin A}=\frac{1+\sin A}{\cos A}$

12. $\sqrt{\frac{1-\cos A}{1+\cos A}}=\operatorname{cosec} A-\cot A$ **(2000)**

13. $\sqrt{\frac{1-\cos A}{1+\cos A}}=\frac{\sin A}{1+\cos A}$ **(2000, 2013)**

14. $\frac{\cos A}{1-\tan A}+\frac{\sin A}{1-\cot A}=\cos A+\sin A$ **(2015)**

15. $\tan^4 A+\tan^2 A=\sec^4 A-\sec^2 A$

16. $1+\frac{\cot^2 A}{1+\operatorname{cosec} A}=\operatorname{cosec} A$

17. $\sin^6 A+\cos^6 A=1-3\sin^2 A\cdot\cos^2 A$

18. $\sqrt{\sec^2 A+\operatorname{cosec}^2 A}=\tan A+\cot A$ **(2018)**

19. $\sin A(1+\tan A)+\cos A(1+\cot A)=\sec A+\operatorname{cosec} A$

20. $\frac{\sin A}{1+\cot A}-\frac{\cos A}{1+\tan A}=\sin A-\cos A$ **(2020)**

21. If $x = a \cos A + b \sin A$ and $y = a \sin A - b \cos A$, prove that: $x^2 + y^2 = a^2 + b^2$

Heights and Distances

1.1 Introduction: Using Trigonometrical ratios we can find the missing sides of a triangle. Using the same concept, we can find the heights or distances of some real-life objects, like height of a building, a hill etc. **Heights and Distances** is one of the most important applications of Trigonometry.

Line of sight: To understand the line of sight consider two situations given below:

(i) A person standing at A (at some distance from the foot of a tower) and is looking at the top of the tower (Figure – 1)

(ii) A Person standing at the top of the tower and looking at an object at point A (Figure – 2).

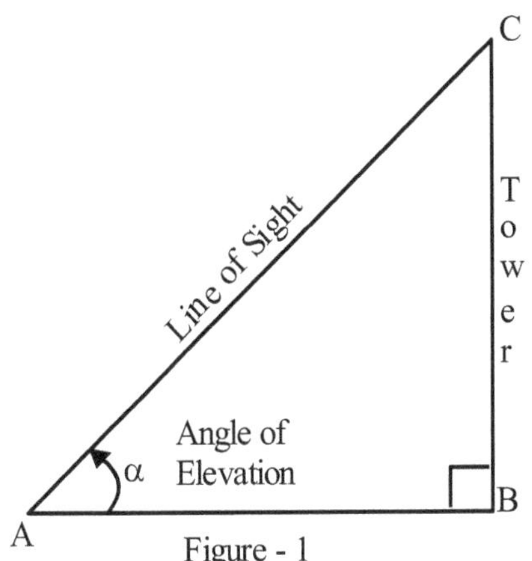

Figure - 1

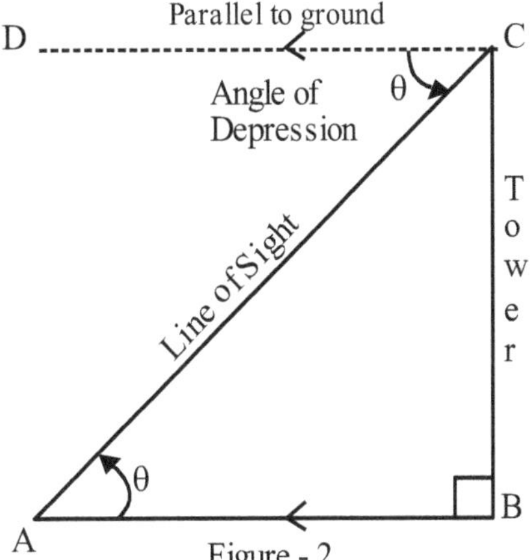

Figure - 2

1.2 Angle of Elevation: The angle made by the line of sight with the horizontal when a person raise his head to see the top of a tower **C** is called **angle of elevation**. In the figure – 1 given above $\angle BAC$ is the angle of elevation.

1.3 Angle of Depression: The angle made by the line of sight with the horizontal when a person down his head to see the point at A (at some distance from the foot of the tower) is called **angle of depression**. In the figure – 2 given above $\angle DCA$ is the angle of depression, which in turn equals to the angle of elevation. So $\angle DCA = \angle BAC$ (alternate).

Angle of elevation = Angle of depression

Remark:

1. Use required trigonometrical ratio with angle of elevation or depression to find the unknown quantity.
2. Heights and distances is completely based on **diagram**. Focus on making diagram according to question. Calculation is secondary.

Practice Sheet

1. A tower is 100 m high. Find the angle of elevation of its top from a point 100 m away from its foot.

2. A kite flying at a height of 75 m from the level ground is attached to a straight string inclined at 60° to the horizontal ground. Find the length of the string to the nearest meter.

3. From the top of a tower, a man finds that the angle of depression of a car on the ground is 30°. If the car is at a distance 40 m away from the tower, find the height of the tower in nearest meter.

4. From a point P on level ground, the angle of elevation of the top of a tower is 30°. If the tower is 100 m high, how far is P from the foot of the tower?

5. A pole being broken by the wind,the top struck the ground at an angle of 30° and at a distance of 8 m from the foot of the pole. Find the whole height of the pole?

6. A ladder rests against a vertical wall such that the top of the ladder reahes the top of the wall. The ladder is inclined at 60° with the ground, and the bottom of the ladder is 1.5 m away from the foot of the wall. Find:
(i) The length of the ladder
(ii) The height of the wall

7. A tower is 64 m tall. A man standing erect at a distance of 36 m from the tower observes the angle of elevation of the top of the tower to be 60°. Find the height of the man.

8. From the top of a cliff 150 m high, the angles of depression of two boats are 60° and 30°. Find the distance between the boats, if the boats are:
(i) On the same sides of the cliff.
(ii) On the opposite sides of the cliff.

9. From a point on the ground 40 m away from the foot of a tower, the angle of elevation of the top of the tower is 30°. The angle of elevation to the top of a water tank (on the top of the tower) is 45°. Find the:
(i) Height of the tower
(ii) The depth of the tank

10. A person standing on the bank of a river observes that the angle of elevation of the top of a tree standing on the opposite bank is 60°. When he retreats 40 m away from the bank, he finds that the angle of elevation to be 30°. Find:
(i) The height of the tree
(ii) The width of the river, correct to two decimal places

11. From the top of a cliff 90 m high, the angles of depression of the top and bottom of a tower are observed to be 30° and 60° respectively. Find the height of tower.

12. The angle of elevation of a jet plane from a point A on the ground is 60°. After flight of 15 seconds, the angle of elevation changes to 30°. If the jet plane is flying at a constant height of $1500\sqrt{3}$ m, find the speed of the jet plane.

13. The angle of elevation of the top Q of a vertical tower PQ from a point X on the ground is 60°. At a point Y, 40 m vertically above X, the angle of elevation is 45°. Find the height of the tower PQ and the distance XQ.

14. The angle of elevation of a cloud from a point *h* meter above a lake is 30° and the angle of depression of the reflection of cloud in the lake is 45°. If the height of the cloud be 200 m. Find h.

15. The angle of elevation from a point P of the top of a tower QR, 50m high is 60° and that of the tower PT from a point Q is 30°. Find the height of the tower PT, correct to the nearest meter. **(2018)**

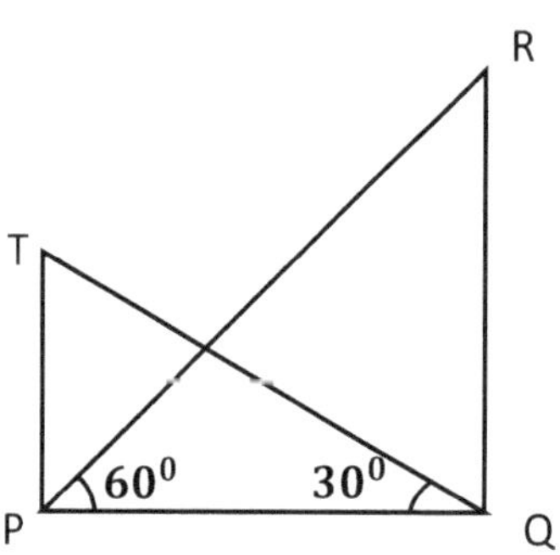

16. A man observes the angle of elevation of the top of the tower to be 45°. He walks towards it in a horizontal line through its base. On covering 20 m the angle of elevation changes to 60°. Find the height of the tower correct to two significant figures. **(2019)**

17. From the top of a cliff, the angle of depression of the top and bottom of a tower are observed to be 45° and 60° respectively. If the height of the tower is 20 m. Find: **(2020)**
(i) The height of the cliff.
(ii) The distance between the cliff and the tower.

18. The angle of elevation of the top of a tower from two points P and Q at distances a and b respectively, from the base and in the same straight line with it, are complementary. Prove that the height of the tower is $\sqrt{ab}$.

19. From the top of the tower the angle of depression of an object on the horizontal ground is found to be 60°. On descending 20 m vertically downwards from the top of the tower, the angle of depression of the object is found to be 30°. Find the height of the tower.

20. A vertical tower stands on a horizontal plane and is surmounted by a vertical flagstaff of height h meter. At a point on the plane, the angle of elevation of the bottom of the flagstaff is α and that of the top of flagstaff is β. Prove that the height of the tower is: $\frac{h \tan \alpha}{\tan \beta - \tan \alpha}$.

21. The angle of elevation of the top of a building from the foot of the tower is 30° and the angle of elevation of the top of the tower from the foot of the building is 60°. If the tower is 60 m high, find the height of the building.

Answer key

Answer 1.	60°
Answer 2.	87 m
Answer 3.	23 m
Answer 4.	173.2 m
Answer 5.	13.86 m
Answer 6.	(i) 3m (ii) 2.6 m
Answer 7.	1.65 m
Answer 8.	(i) 173.2 m (ii) 346.4 m
Answer 9.	(i) 23.1 m (approx.) (ii) 16.9 m (approx.)
Answer 10.	(i) 34.64 m (ii) 20 m
Answer 11.	60 m
Answer 12.	720 km/hr
Answer 13.	94.64 m, 109.3 m
Answer 14.	53.6 m
Answer 15.	16.67m
Answer 16.	47 m
Answer 17.	27.32 m
Answer 19.	30 m
Answer 21.	20 m

1.1 Introduction: The basic idea of statistics is the extraction of meaningful information from raw data. Statistics deals with collection, organization, analysis and interpretation of data. To represent and find meaningful information from the data we use two approaches:

1. Graphical Approach: In this approach statistical data represented by diagrams. We shall be studying only the following diagrams:

(i) Histogram
(ii) Frequency Polygon
(iii) Ogive (Cumulative frequency curve)

2. Calculative Approach: In this approach statistical data represented by some numerical expressions, called **Measures of Central Tendency** or **averages.** Out of many types of statistical averages, only three averages will be studied here:

(i) Arithmetic Mean (or simply Mean)
(ii) Median
(iii) Mode

Remark: For calculation of any Measures of Central Tendency **class intervals** should be **continuous**. If they are not continuous, make them continuous first using **adjustment factor**. Here is an example for this:

$$\text{Adjustment Factor} = \frac{\text{Lower limit of a class} - \text{Upper limit of previous class}}{2}$$

Now rewrite class intervals by (lower limit – adjustment factor) and (upper limit + adjustment factor).

For example:

Marks	11-20	21-30	31-40	41-50	51-60	61-70	71-80
No. of students	2	6	10	12	9	7	4

Solution:

Here class intervals are discontinuous, so adjustment factor = $\frac{21-20}{2} = 0.5$

Marks (before adjustment)	Marks (after adjustment)
11 – 20	10.5 – 20.5
21 – 30	20.5 – 30.5
31 – 40	30.5 – 40.5
41 – 50	40.5 – 50.5
51 – 60	50.5 – 60.5
61 – 70	60.5 – 70.5
71 – 80	70.5 – 80.5

Mean

Arithmetic mean is the sum of a collection of data divided by the sum of the data.

For example:

The mean of n numbers $x_1, x_2, x_3, \ldots\ldots\ldots\ldots, x_n$ is $= \frac{x_1+x_2+x_3+\cdots\ldots\ldots\ldots\ldots+x_n}{n} = \frac{\Sigma x}{n}$

The Greek later Σ (Sigma) means sum of number. This method is used when data is ungrouped (Non tabular).

1.2 Arithmetic mean of Tabulated (grouped data): The arithmetic mean can be obtained by using any one of the following three methods:

(i) Direct method
(ii) Short cut Method (assumed mean method)
(iii) Step–deviation method

1.3 Direct Method: Mean using direct method: Mean = $\frac{\Sigma fx}{\Sigma f}$

Steps:

1. Find the class mark (x) of each class (if not given already).

$$\text{Class Mark} = \frac{\text{Lower limit} + \text{Upper limit}}{2}$$

2. Calculate fx for each x.
3. Find Σfx and Σf.
4. Use the formula to calculate the mean.

Example: Find mean of the following data using direct method. **(2006)**

Class interval	20 - 30	30 – 40	40 – 50	50 – 60	60 - 70	70 - 80
Frequency	10	6	8	12	5	9

Solution:

Class interval	**class mark (x)**	**Frequency (f)**	***fx***
20 – 30	25	10	250
30 – 40	35	6	210
40 – 50	45	8	360
50 – 60	55	12	660
60 – 70	65	5	325
70 – 80	75	9	675
	$\Sigma f = 50$		$\Sigma fx = 2480$

$$\text{Mean} = \frac{\Sigma fx}{\Sigma f}$$

$$= \frac{2480}{50}$$

$$= 49.6$$ **Ans**

1.4 Short – cut Method (Assumed mean method): Mean using shortcut method:

$$\text{Mean} = A + \frac{\Sigma fd}{\Sigma f}$$

Steps:

1. Find the class mark (x) of each class (if not given already).

$$\text{Class Mark} = \frac{\text{Lower limit} + \text{Upper limit}}{2}$$

2. Choose a suitable number from the middle of class mark (x) column, known as assumed mean (A)
3. Calculate the deviation (d) of each x from assumed mean i.e. d = x – A
4. Calculate fd for each x.
5. Find Σfd and Σf.
6. Use the formula to calculate the mean.

Example: Find mean of the table given in **section 1.3** using short cut method.

Solution:

Class interval	class mark (x)	Frequency (f)	Deviation (d) $d = x - A$	fd
20 – 30	25	10	-30	-300
30 – 40	35	6	-20	-120
40 – 50	45	8	-10	-80
50 – 60	55 = A	12	0	0
60 – 70	65	5	10	50
70 – 80	75	9	20	180
	$\Sigma f = 50$			$\Sigma fd = -270$

$$\text{Mean} = A + \frac{\Sigma fd}{\Sigma f}$$

$$= 55 + \left(\frac{-270}{50}\right)$$

$$= 49.6 \qquad \textbf{Ans.}$$

1.5 Step – deviation method: Step – deviation method is used when the values of f and x are large. For large numbers the calculation of direct method and step deviation method becomes tedious.

Mean using step – deviation method: $\text{Mean} = A + \frac{\Sigma fu}{\Sigma f} \times h$

Steps:

1. Find the class mark (x) of each class (if not given already).

$$\text{Class Mark} = \frac{\text{Lower limit+Upper limit}}{2}$$

2. Choose a suitable number from the middle of class mark (x) column, known as assumed mean (A)
3. Calculate the deviation (d) of each x from assumed mean i.e. $d = x - A$
4. Calculate u $= \frac{x-A}{h}$ for each d = x – A, where h is the class size. (h = upper limit – lower limit).
5. Calculate fu for each x.
6. Find Σfu and Σf.
7. Use the formula to calculate the mean.

Example: Find mean of the table given in **section 1.3** using step deviation method.

Solution:

Class interval	class mark (x)	Frequency (f)	Deviation (d) $d = x - A$	$u = \frac{d}{h}$	fu
20 – 30	25	10	-30	-3	-30
30 – 40	35	6	-20	-2	-12
40 – 50	45	8	-10	-1	-8
50 – 60	55 = A	12	0	0	0
60 – 70	65	5	10	1	5
70 – 80	75	9	20	2	18
	Σf = 50				Σfd = – 27

$$\text{Mean} = A + \frac{\Sigma fu}{\Sigma f} \times h$$
$$= 55 + \left(\frac{-27}{50}\right) \times 10$$
$$= 49.6 \quad \textbf{Ans.}$$

Practice Sheet -1 (Based on Mean)

1. Calculate the arithmetic mean of first five prime numbers.

2. The mean of marks scored by 100 students was found to be 40. Later on it was discovered that a score of 53 was misread as 83. Find the correct mean.

3. Find the mean of the following distribution.

x	4	6	9	10	15
f	5	10	10	7	8

4. Find the value of p, if the mean of the following distribution is 7.5.

x	3	5	7	9	11	13
f	6	8	15	p	8	4

5. Find the mean of the following distribution using (i) Direct method (ii) Short – cut method

Class	0 – 10	10 - 20	20 – 30	30 – 40	40 - 50
Frequency	12	16	6	7	9

6. The following are the marks obtained by 100 students in a class test.

Marks	0 – 10	10 - 20	20 – 30	30 – 40	40 – 50	50 – 60
No. of students	12	18	27	20	17	6

Calculate the mean marks by:

(i) Short cut method

(ii) Strep – deviation Method

7. Calculate the mean of the distribution, given below, using the short cut method: **(2014)**

Marks	11-20	21-30	31-40	41-50	51-60	61-70	71-80
No. of students	2	6	10	12	9	7	4

8. The arithmetic mean of the following distribution is 25. Determine the value of p

Class	0 – 10	10 - 20	20 – 30	30 - 40	40 - 50
Frequency	5	18	15	p	6

9. The marks obtained by 120 students in mathematics test is given in the following distribution.

Marks	0 – 20	20 - 40	40 – 60	60 – 80	80 – 100	Total
No. of students	17	f_1	32	f_2	19	120

The mean of the following distribution is 50 and the sum of the frequencies is 120. Find the missing frequencies f_1 and f_2.

10. Find the value of p, if the mean of the following distribution is 20.

x	15	17	19	20 + p	23
f	2	3	4	5p	6

11. The mean of the following data is 16. Calculate the value of f. **(2020)**

Marks	5	10	15	20	25
No. of Students	3	7	F	9	6

12. The data on the number of patients attending a hospital in the morning are given below. Find the average (mean) number of patients attending the hospital in a month by using the shortcut method.
Take the assumed mean as 45. Give your answer correct to 2 decimal places.

No. of patients	10 – 20	20 – 30	30 – 40	40 – 50	50 – 60	60 – 70
No. of days	5	2	7	9	2	5

Answer key

Ans 1.	5.6
Ans 2.	39.7
Ans 3.	9
Ans 4.	P = 3
Ans 5.	22
Ans 6.	28
Ans 7.	46.9
Ans 8.	p = 16
Ans 9.	$f_1 = 28$, $f_2 = 24$
Ans 10.	p = 1
Ans 11.	f = 15
Ans 12.	40.33

Median

Median is the value of **middle** most observation of the **arranged** data either in ascending or descending order.

1.6 Median for raw data:

Steps:

1. First arrange the data in ascending or descending order.

2. Find n (number of observations).

3. If n is odd then median = $\left(\frac{n+1}{2}\right)^{\text{th}}$ term.

4. If n is even, then median = $\dfrac{\left(\frac{n}{2}\right)^{\text{th}} \text{term} + \left(\frac{n}{2}+1\right)^{\text{th}} \text{term}}{2}$

1.7 Median for tabulated data (When class intervals are not given):

Steps:

1. First construct a cumulating frequency distribution table.

2. Find n (sum of all frequencies). If $\boldsymbol{n}$ is **odd,** then from the cumulative frequencies find the value just greater than or equal to $\left(\frac{n+1}{2}\right)$ and take the corresponding value from **class mark ($\boldsymbol{x}$)**. This is the required **median**.

3. If **n** is **even** then from the cumulating frequencies find the value just greater than or equal to $\frac{n}{2}$ and $\frac{n}{2}+1$, and take the corresponding values from **class marks ($\boldsymbol{x}$)**. The mean of these observations is the required median.

1.8 Median for tabulated data (When class intervals are given): The **Ogive** can be used to find the median of frequency distribution when the class intervals are given. First, make the class intervals **continuous** (if not) with the help of adjustment factor (**see example in remark in section 1.1**).

Ogive: The curve obtained by graphically representing cumulative frequency distribution is called a **cumulative frequency curve** or **Ogive**. Ogives are of two types:

(i) Less than ogives.

(ii) More than ogives (Not in syllabus)

Steps to draw less than ogive:

1. Represent class intervals (continuous) on x – axis and cumulative frequencies on y – axis with a suitable scale.

2. Plot points (upper limit, cumulative frequency) on the graph and join them smoothly to get the curve (ogive). **Less than ogives:** Now plot **cumulative frequencies against upper limits** of their respective class intervals.

3. Find n (sum of frequencies). Find $\left(\frac{n}{2}\right)^{\text{th}}$ if n is even and $\left(\frac{n+1}{2}\right)^{\text{th}}$ if n is odd, and find the number on y – axis.

4. Draw a horizontal line which meets the curve at a point, from this point draw a vertical line which meets x – axis at a point. Take this value of x – axis, which is the required **median**.

Remark: The class interval, to which the median for the given data belongs, is called **Median class**.

Example: Draw the ogive for the following distribution and find median.

Class intervals	0 – 10	10 - 20	20 – 30	30 - 40	40 - 50
Frequency	5	7	10	8	5

Solution:

Step 1. Draw a cumulative frequency distribution table from the following data.

Class interval	Frequency (f)	Cumulative Frequency
0 – 10	5	5
10 – 20	7	5 + 7 = 12
20 – 30	10	12 + 10 = 22
30 – 40	8	22 + 8 = 30
40 – 50	5	30 + 5 = 35
	$n = 35$	

Step 2. On a graph paper, mark class intervals on x – axis and cumulative frequencies on y – axis with a suitable scale.

Step 3. On this graph mark point (10, 5), (20, 12), (30, 22), (40, 30) and (50, 35). Join them so that smoothly so that curve start from lower limit of first class and ends up upper limit of last class.

Since = 35 (odd)

Median = $\left(\frac{n+1}{2}\right)^{\text{th}}$ term

$= \left(\frac{35+1}{2}\right)^{\text{th}}$ term

$= 18^{th}$ term

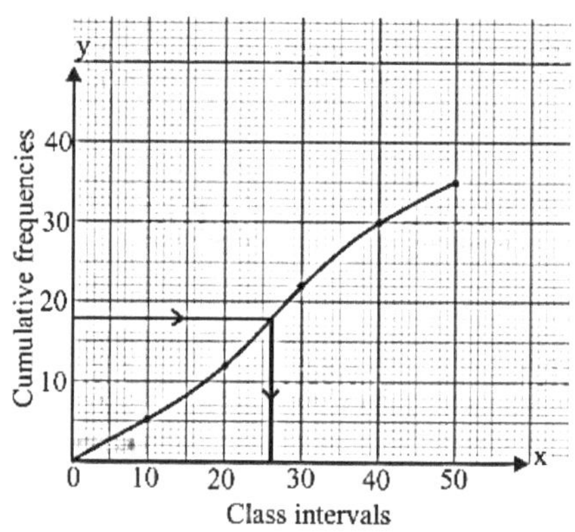

Step 4. Through 18th mark on y – axis, draw a horizontal line which meets the curve at a point, through this point draw a vertical line which meets x – axis at a point. This value on x – axis is required median. According to the ogive drawn median = 26.5 which belong to 20 – 30, so median class is 20 –30.

1.9. Quartile:

Quartile is the values of statistical data which divide the whole set of observations (x) into four equal parts. For finding quartile, the given data are always arranged in ascending order.

To understand quartile, let's take an example. Let say some data arranged along a line from A to B. Q_1, Q_2 and Q_3 are marks on this line segment so that the line segment is divided into four equal parts ($AQ_1 = Q_1Q_2 = Q_2Q_3 = Q_3B$). Then **$Q_1$** (1/4 th part) is called **Lower quartile, Q_2** is called the **middle quartile** (median) and **Q_3** (3/4 th) is called **upper quartile** for same set of data.

A ——— **$\frac{1}{4}$ Q_1** ——— **Median Q_2** ——— **$\frac{3}{4}$ Q_3** ——— **B**

Value of n	Lower Quartile (Q_1)	Middle Quartile (Median)	Upper Quartile (Q_3)
If n is odd	$\left(\frac{n+1}{4}\right)^{\text{th}}$ term	$\left(\frac{n+1}{2}\right)^{\text{th}}$ term	$\left(\frac{3(n+1)}{4}\right)^{\text{th}}$ term
If n is even	$\left(\frac{n}{4}\right)^{\text{th}}$ term	$\left(\frac{n}{2}\right)^{\text{th}}$ term	$\left(\frac{3n}{4}\right)^{\text{th}}$ term

Remark: Process of calculation of lower quartile (Q_1) and upper quartile (Q_3) from the ogive is same as median.

1.10. Inter quartile range: For a given set of data the difference between the upper quartile and lower quartile is called inter quartile range.

Inter quartile range = $Q_3 - Q_1$ and semi inter quartile range = $\frac{Q_3 - Q_1}{2}$

Practice Sheet -2 (Based on Median)

1. In a class test, the marks obtained by 11 students are 13,17, 20, 5, 3, 19, 7, 6, 11, 15, 17. Find:
(i) median
(ii) lower quartile
(iii) upper quartile
(iv) inter quartile

2. The marks obtained (out of 50) by 100 students in a test are given below. Find the median marks.

Marks	20	29	28	33	42	38	43	25
No. of students	6	28	34	15	2	4	1	20

3. The heights (in nearest cm) of 60 students of a certain school are given in the following frequency distribution table:
Find:
(i) median
(ii) lower quartile
(iii) upper quartile
(iv) inter quartile-range

4. The marks obtained by 200 students in an examination are given below: Using a graph paper, draw an ogive for the above distribution. Use your ogive to estimate:

Marks Obtained	0 – 10	10 – 20	20 – 30	30 – 40	40 – 50	50 – 60	60 – 70	70 – 80	80 – 90	90 – 100
No of students	5	10	11	20	27	38	40	29	14	6

(i) The median
(ii) The lower quartile
(iii) The number of students who obtained more than 80% marks in the examination and
(iv) The number of students who did not pass, if the pass percentage was 35.

5. The marks obtained by 120 students in a test are given below:
Draw an ogive for the given distribution on a graph sheet. Use a suitable scale for your ogive. Use the ogive to estimate the following:

Marks Obtained	0 – 10	10 – 20	20 – 30	30 – 40	40 – 50	50 – 60	60 – 70	70 – 80	80 – 90	90 – 100
No of students	5	9	16	22	26	18	11	6	4	3

(i) The median

(ii) The lower quartile
(iii) The upper quartile
(iv) The number of students who obtained more than 75% in the test
(v) The number of students who did not pass the test if the pass percentage was 40.

Class interval	30 – 39	40 – 49	50 – 59	60 – 69	70 – 79	80 – 89	90 – 99
Frequency	20	35	15	40	5	20	10

6. Draw an ogive of the following distribution:
Use the ogive to estimate the following:
(i) The median
(ii) The lower quartile
(iii) The upper quartile $\frac{Q_3-Q_1}{2}$
(iv) The number of variates below 55
(v) The number of variates above 75.

7. Attempt this question on a graph paper. The table below shows the distribution of marks gained by a group of students in an examination:

Marks less than	10	20	30	40	50	60	70	80	90	100
No. of Students	5	9	16	22	26	18	11	6	4	3

Using a scale of 2 cm to represent 10 marks and 2 cm to represent 50 students, plot these values and draw a smooth curve through the points. Estimate from the graph:
(i) The median marks
(ii) The quartile marks.

8. The following table shows the distribution of the heights of a group of factory workers:

Height (cm)	150 – 155	155 – 160	160 – 165	165 – 170	170 – 175	175 – 180	180 – 185
No. of workers	6	12	18	20	13	8	6

(i) Determine the cumulative frequencies.
(ii) Draw the cumulative frequency curve on a graph paper. Use 2 cm = 5 cm height on one axis and 2 cm = 10 workers on the other.
(iii) From your graph, write down the median height in cm.

9. The marks of 10 students of a class in an examination arranged in ascending order is as follows:
13, 35, 43, 46, x, $x + 4$, 55, 61, 71, 80. If the median marks are 48, find the value, of x. **(2017)**

10. Use Graph paper for this question.
A survey regarding height (in cm) of 60 boys belonging to Class 10 of a school was conducted. The following data was recorded: **(2018)**

Height in cm	135 – 140	140 – 145	145 – 150	150 – 155	155 – 160	160 – 165	165 – 170
No. of boys	4	8	20	14	7	6	1

Taking 2cm = height of 10 cm along one axis and 2 cm = 10 boys along the other axis draw an ogive of the above distribution. Use the graph to estimate the following:
(i) The median
(ii) Lower Quartile
(iii) If above 158 cm is considered as the tall boys of the class. Find the number of boys in the class who are tall.

11. 40 students enter for a game of short – put competition. The distance thrown (in meters) is recorded below:

Distance in m	12 – 13	13 – 14	14 – 15	15 – 16	16 – 17	17 – 18	18 – 19
No. of students	3	9	12	9	4	2	1

Use a graph paper to draw an ogive for the given distribution. **(2020)**
Use a scale of 2 cm = 1 m on one axis and 2 cm = 5 students on the other axis.
Hence using your graph find:

(i) The median
(ii) The upper quartile
(iii) Number of students who cover a distance which is above $16\frac{1}{2}$ m.

12. The mean of following numbers is 68. Find the value of 'x'. 45, 52, 60, x, 69, 70, 26, 81 and 94.
Hence estimate the median. **(2016)**

Answer key

Ans 1.	(i) 13	(ii) 6,	(iii) 17	(iv) 11	
Ans 2.	28.5				
Ans 3.	(i) 154.5	(ii) 153	(iii) 155	(iv) 2	
Ans 4.	(i) 58.5 marks	(ii) 42 marks	(iii) 20	(iv) 33	
Ans 5.	(i) 42 marks	(ii) 30 marks	(iii) 56 marks	(iv) 10	(v) 52
Ans 6	(i) 60.5	(ii) 45	(iii) 68.5	(iv) 63	(v) 32
Ans 7.	(i) 62	(ii) 49			
Ans 8.	166.5 cm				
Ans 9.	$x = 46$				
Ans 10.	(i) 148	(ii) 147	(iii) 10 boys		
Ans 11.	(i) 14.7 (approx.)	(ii) 1.6 (approx.)	(iii) 5		
Ans 12.	115.69				

Mode

1.11 Introduction: The data which appears most often in a set of data is called mode. Or number which has highest frequency is mode. Suppose there are 25 girls and 20 boys in a class, then **mode = girls**. A given data may have the same maximum frequency for more than one observation, then given data is **multimodal**.

1. Mode for raw data:

Example: Calculate the mean, the median and the mode of the following numbers: 3, 1, 5, 6, 3, 4, 5, 3, 7, 2. **(2000)**

In the given set of numbers 3 occurs most frequently so mode = 3

2. Mode for tabulated data (without class intervals):

Example: In a class of 40 students, marks obtained by the students in a class test (out of 10) are given below:

Marks	1	2	3	4	5	6	7	8	9	10
Number of students	1	2	3	3	6	10	5	4	3	3

Calculate the following for the given distribution:

(i) Mode
(ii) Median

In the given distribution variate 6 has the highest frequency i.e. 10 so mode in 6. **Ans.**

3. Mode for grouped data: In a continuous frequency distribution the mode can be determined from the **histogram** of the given (**continuous**) frequency distribution.

Steps to draw a histogram and find mode:

(i) Represent frequencies on the y – axis of the graph.
(ii) Represent continuous class intervals on the x – axis of the graph.
(iii) Draw columns on the x – axis equivalent to their respective frequencies.
(iv) Inside the highest rectangle (which represent the class with maximum frequency), join its lower limit to right side column's lower limit and join its upper limit to left side column's upper limit.
(v) From the point of intersection of two lines drawn in step (iv) draw a vertical line which meet the x – **axis**. This value of x axis is required **Mode**.

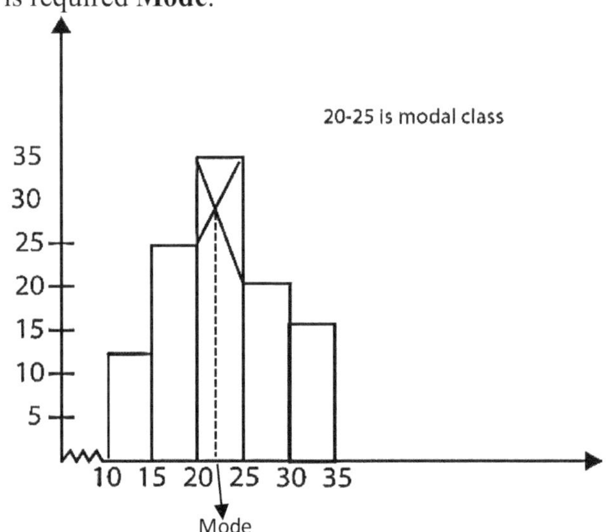

Remark: The class interval, to which the mode for the given data belongs, is called **Modal class**.

Practice Sheet - 3 (Based on Mode)

1. Find the mode of the following data:
2, 3, 5, 1, 3, 2, 4, 2, 3, 2, 6, 0, 2, 2, 5, 3, 4.

2. Find the mode for the following frequency distribution:

Marks Obtained	0	2	3	4	6	7	9	10
No of students	3	5	12	18	21	8	2	1

3. Find the following frequency distribution, draw, histogram. Hence calculate the mode:

Class Interval	0 – 5	5 – 10	10 – 15	15 – 20	20 – 25	25 – 30
Frequency	2	7	18	10	8	5

4. Find the mode of the following distribution by drawing a histogram:

Height (in cm)	30 – 40	40 – 50	50 – 60	60 – 70	70 – 80	80 – 90
No of plants	4	3	8	11	6	2

5. Find the mode of the following distribution by drawing a histogram:

Daily wages	31 – 36	37 – 42	43 – 48	49 – 54	55 – 60	61 – 66
No of workers	6	12	20	15	9	4

6. The marks of 20 students in a test were as follows: **(2002)**
5, 6, 8, 9, 10, 11, 11, 12, 13, 13, 14, 14, 15, 15, 15, 16, 16, 18, 19, 20.
Calculate:
(i) The Mean (iii) The Median
(ii) The Mode

7. Draw the histogram for the given data, using a graph paper: **[Boards 2020]**

Weekly wages (in)	3000 – 4000	4000 – 5000	5000 – 6000	6000 – 7000	7000 – 8000	8000 – 9000	9000 – 10000
No. of people	4	9	18	6	7	2	4

Answer key

Ans.1	2		
Ans.2	6		
Ans.3	13		
Ans.4	13		
Ans.5	46.5		
Ans.6	13	13.5	15
Ans.7	5400 (approx.)		

UNIT - 6

STATISTICS

CHAPTER

Probability

1.1 Introduction: The chances of happening of an **event** when measured quantitatively is called **probability**. This is a measure of uncertainty. **For example,** out of 1000 people, your chances to win a lottery, on rolling of a dice 6 will come on the top etc.

1.2 Terms related to probability:

1. Experiment: An operation which can produce some were defined results, is known as **experiment**. Sometimes the result is unique, like sum of interior angles of triangle is 180°. Such experiments are called **deterministic experiments**.

2. Random experiment: Sometimes the outcome may not be unique, like tossing a coin may have heads or tails on top. Such experiments are called **probabilistic** or **random** experiment.
An experiment is called **random** if it satisfies the following two conditions:

(i) It has more than one possible outcome.
(ii) It is not possible to predict the outcome in advance.

3. Sample space: The set of all possible outcomes in a random experiment is called **sample space**. **For example:**

(i) When a coin tossed, there are two possible outcomes, head (H) or tail (T).

$$\therefore \text{The sample space } S = \{H, T\}$$

(ii) When rolling an unbiased dice, 1, 2, 3, 4, 5, 6 are possible outcomes.

$$\therefore \text{The sample space } S = \{1, 2, 3, 4, 5, 6\}$$

4. Event (E): An event is something that happens. Like showing up head (H), when a coin is tossed, coming up an even number on the top when a dice is rolled, drawing a king of heart from a pack of cards randomly are all events. Let **E** be an event so Probability of an event is denoted by P(E) and is given by the formula:

$$P(E) = \frac{\text{Number of favourable outcomes}}{\text{Total number of outcomes}}$$

Probability of an even can never be less than 0 or more than 1. For an event E: $0 \leq P(E) \leq 1$

5. Sure and Impossible events: If the probability of an event = 1, it is a **sure or certain event**.
Let E is an event such that E = (Probability of getting a number less than 7) on throw of a die.
So when a die is thrown, all possible outcomes are 1, 2, 3, 4, 5, and 6
Since every number on die is less than 7 so number of favorable outcomes = 6
So P (getting a number less than 7) = $\frac{6}{6} = 1$
Therefore, getting a number less than 7 on rolling of a die is a **sure event**.
If Probability of an event = 0, it is an **impossible event**.
Let E is an event such that E = (Probability of getting 7) on throw of a dic.
So when a die is thrown, all possible outcomes are 1, 2, 3, 4, 5, and 6, so no face of the die has the number 7
Number of favorable outcomes = 0 and total number of outcomes = 6

So P(getting a number 7) = $\frac{0}{6} = 0$

6.Complimentary Event: If E is an event and $\bar{E}$ called its **complimentary** events then:

$$P(E) + P(\bar{E}) = 1$$

For example: on a single throw of a die an event E = getting a number less than 2 then its complimentary event $\bar{E}$ = getting a number not less than 2 (or getting a number more than or equal to 2.)

Practice Sheet - 1

1. A bag contains 5 red, 4 green and 6 white balls. If a ball is drawn at random from the bag, find the probability that it will be.

(i) White
(ii) Red
(iii) Green.

2. A box contains 7 blue, 8 white and 5 black marbles. If a marble is drawn at random from the box, what is the probability that it will be

(i) Black
(ii) Blue or black
(iii) Not black
(iv) Green

3. A letter is chosen from the word 'TRIANGLE'. What is the probability that it is a vowel?

4. A box contains 15 cards numbered 1, 2, 3, …., 15 which are mixed thoroughly. A card is drawn from the box at random. Find the probability that the number on the card is

(i) Odd
(ii) Prime
(iii) Divisible by 3
(iv) Divisible by 3 and 2 both
(v) Divisible by 3 or 2
(vi) A perfect square number

5. A die is thrown once. What is the probability that the:

(i) Number is even?
(ii) Number is greater than 2?

6. Two coins are tossed once. Find the probability of getting:

(i) head
(ii) At least 1 tail.

7. A die has 6 faces marked by the given numbers as shown below: **(2014)**
The die is thrown once. What is the probability of getting?

(i) A positive integer
(ii) An integer greater than –3.
(iii) The smallest integer.

1	2	3	-1	-2	-3

8. Cards bearing numbers 2, 4, 6, 8, 10, 12, 14, 16, 18 and 20 are kept in a bag. A card is drawn at random from the bag. Find the probability of getting a card which is : **(2018)**
   (i) A prime number
   (ii) A number divisible by 4
   (iii) A number that is a multiple of 6
   (iv) An odd number.

9. There are 25 discs numbered 1 to 25. They are put in a closed box and shake thoroughly. A disc is drawn at random from the box. Find the probability that the number on the disc is-
   (i) An odd number.
   (ii) Divisible by 2 and 3 both.
   (iii) A number less than 16.

10. Each of the letter of the word 'AUTHORIZES' is written on identical circular disks and put in a bag. They are well shuffled. If a disk is drawn at random from the bag, what is the probability that the letter is: **(2020)**
   (i) A vowel
   (ii) One of the first 9 letters of English alphabet which appears in the given word.
   (iii) One of the last 9 letters of English alphabet which appears in the given word.

11. A card is drawn from a well-shuffled pack of 52 cards. Find the probability of getting:
   (i) '2' of spades
   (ii) A jack
   (iii) A king of red colour
   (iv) A card of diamond
   (v) A king or a queen
   (vi) A non-face card
   (vii) A black face card
   (viii) A black card
   (ix) Neither a spade nor a jack
   (x) Non-face card of black colour
   (xi) Neither a spade nor a jack
   (xii) Neither a heart nor a red king

12. The king, queen and jack of club are removed from a deck of 52 playing cards and then shuffled. A card is drawn from the remaining cards. Find the probability of getting:
   (i) A heart (ii) A queen
   (iii) A club (iv) '9' of red color

13. Two players, Sania and Sonali, play a tennis match. It is known that the probability of Sania winning the match is 0.69. What is the probability of Sonali winning?

14. Two dice are thrown together. Represent the following events and find their probabilities:
   (i) The sum of the numbers shown is 7.
   (ii) The difference of the numbers shown is 2.
   (iii) The sum of the numbers shown is greater than 5.

15. 12 pens are defective in a lot of 120 pens. One pen is taken out at random from this lot Determine the probability that the pen taken out is not defective.

16. Find the probability of getting 53 Sundays in an ordinary year.

17. Find the probability of having 5 Sundays in the month of March in a leap year.

18. A game of chance consists of an arrow which comes to rest, pointing at one of the regions 1, 2 or 3. O is the centre of the circle, Find the probability that.

(i) Arrow is resting 3

(ii) Arrow is resting on 1

(iii) Arrow is not resting on 2

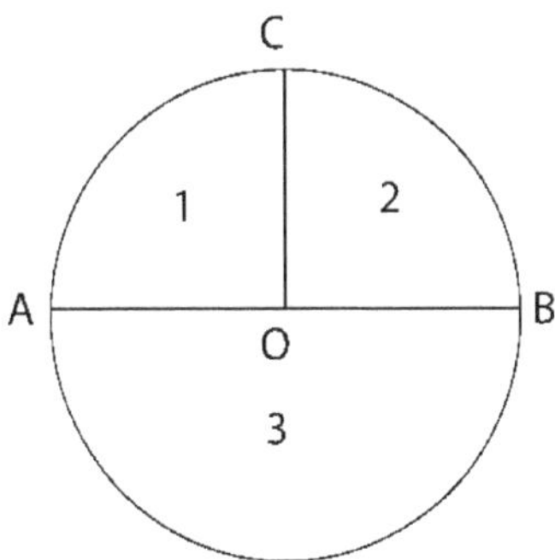

Answer key

Ans 1.	(i) $\frac{2}{5}$	(ii) $\frac{1}{3}$	(iii) $\frac{4}{15}$	
Ans 2.	(i) $\frac{1}{4}$	(ii) $\frac{3}{5}$	(iii) $\frac{3}{4}$	(iv) 0
Ans 3.	(i) $\frac{3}{8}$			
Ans 4.	(i) $\frac{8}{15}$	(ii) $\frac{2}{5}$	(iii) $\frac{1}{3}$	(iv) $\frac{2}{15}$
	(v) $\frac{2}{3}$	(vi) $\frac{3}{15}$		
Ans 5.	(i) $\frac{1}{2}$	(ii) $\frac{2}{3}$		
Ans 6.	(i) $\frac{1}{4}$	(ii) $\frac{3}{4}$		
Ans 7.	(i) $\frac{1}{2}$	(ii) $\frac{5}{6}$	(iii) $\frac{1}{6}$	
Ans 8.	(i) $\frac{1}{10}$	(ii) $\frac{1}{2}$	(iii) $\frac{3}{10}$	(iv) 0
Ans 9.	(i) $\frac{13}{25}$	(ii) $\frac{1}{25}$	(iii) $\frac{3}{5}$	
Ans 10.	(i) $\frac{1}{2}$	(ii) $\frac{2}{5}$	(iii) $\frac{1}{2}$	
Ans 11.	(i) $\frac{1}{52}$ (v) $\frac{2}{13}$ (ix) $\frac{4}{13}$	(ii) $\frac{1}{13}$ (vi) $\frac{10}{13}$ (x) $\frac{5}{13}$	(iii) $\frac{1}{26}$ (vii) $\frac{3}{26}$ (xi) $\frac{9}{13}$	(iv) $\frac{1}{4}$ (viii) $\frac{1}{2}$ (xii) $\frac{19}{26}$
Ans 12.	(i) $\frac{13}{49}$	(ii) $\frac{3}{49}$	(iii) $\frac{10}{49}$	(iv) $\frac{2}{49}$
Ans 13.	(i) 0.31			
Ans 14.	(i) $\frac{1}{6}$	(ii) $\frac{2}{9}$	(iii) $\frac{13}{18}$	
Ans 15.	(i) $\frac{9}{10}$			
Ans 16.	(ii) $\frac{1}{7}$			
Ans 17.	$\frac{3}{7}$			
Ans 18.	(i) $\frac{1}{2}$	(ii) $\frac{1}{4}$	(iii) $\frac{3}{4}$	

Practice Paper – 1 (Solved)
(MATHEMATICS)
(Time alloted: One and a half hour)

Answer to this paper must be written on the paper provided separately.
You will not be allowed to write during the first 10 minutes.
This time is to spent in reading the question paper.
Omission of essential working well result in loss of marks.
The intended marks for questions or part of questions are given in the brackets [ ].

Section A (10 Marks)
(Attempt all question from this section)

Question 1

Choose the correct answers to the questions from the given options. (Do not copy the questions. Write the correct options only.) [10]

(i) The point P (2, –4) is reflected about the line x = 0 to get the image Q. The co – ordinates of Q are:

(a) (–2, –4)
(b) (2, 4)
(c) (–2, 4)
(d) No change

Solution: Option (a) is correct.
Here $x = 0$ means y – axis (Equation of y – axis is $x = 0$)
When a point reflected in y – axis, sign of x – coordinate changes.

(ii) In the adjoining figure angle AOC = 110^0 calculate: (i) ∠ADC

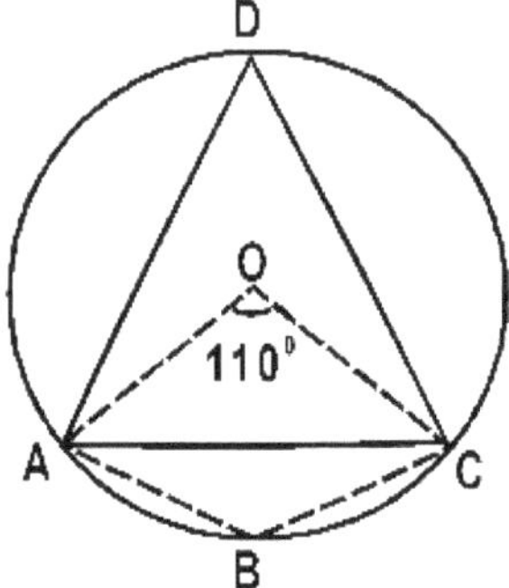

(a) 65°
(b) 55°
(c) 45°
(d) 220°

Solution: Option (b) is correct.

$\angle AOC = 2\,\angle ADC$ (Angle subtended by an arc at the centre is twice the angle at remaining part of the circle)

so $\angle ADC = \frac{1}{2}\angle AOC$

(iii) If the radius of the base of a right – circular cylinder is halved, keeping the height same, the ratio of the volume of the reduced cylinder to that of the original cylinder is:

(a) 2:3
(b) 3:4

(c) 1:4

(d) 4:1

Solution: Option (c) is correct.

Let original radius be x so new radius $= \frac{1}{2}x$

Ratio of volume of reduced cylinder to the original cylinder $= \dfrac{\pi\left(\frac{r}{2}\right)^2 h}{\pi r^2 h} = \dfrac{r^2 h}{4r^2 h} = \dfrac{1}{4}$

(iv) In what ratio is the join of (4, 3) and (2, –6) divided by the x – axis?

(a) 2: 1

(b) 1: 2

(c) 2 : 3

(d) 1 : 3

Solution: Option (b) is correct .

Let the ratio be $m_1 : m_2$

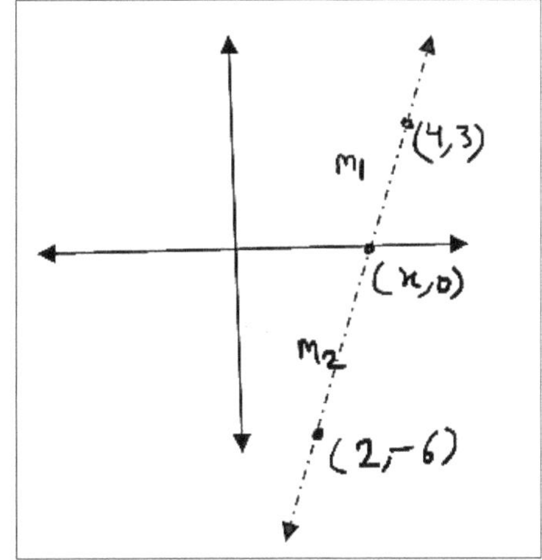

So using section formula: $y = \dfrac{m_1 y_2 + m_2 y_1}{m_1 + m_2}$

$$0 = \frac{m_1(-6) + m_2(3)}{m_1 + m_2}$$

$$-6m_1 + 3m_2 = 0$$

$$6m_1 = 3m_2 \Rightarrow \frac{m_1}{m_2} = \frac{1}{2}$$

(v) If cot A $= \frac{7}{8}$, then the value of $\dfrac{(1+\sin A)(1-\sin A)}{(1+\cos A)(1-\cos A)}$

(a) $\dfrac{64}{49}$

(b) $\dfrac{49}{64}$

(c) $\dfrac{49}{25}$

(d) $\dfrac{49}{36}$

Solution: Option (b) is correct

$$\frac{(1+\sin A)(1-\sin A)}{(1+\cos A)(1-\cos A)} = \frac{(1-\sin^2 A)}{(1-\cos^2 A)} = \frac{\cos^2 A}{\sin^2 A} = \cot^2 A$$

and $\cot A = \frac{7}{8}$

(vi) If the mean of 4, 5, a, 6, b, 9 and 11 is 10, then find the value of $(a + b)$

(a) 45

(b) 25

(c) 55

(d) 35

Solution: Option (d) is correct

$$\text{Mean} = \frac{\text{sum of observation}}{\text{number of observation}} \Rightarrow 10 = \frac{4+5+a+6+b+9+11}{7}$$

$$a + b = 70 - 35 = 35$$

(vii) The equation of a line passing through origin and coincident on x – axis.

(a) $x = 0$

(b) $y = 0$

(c) $x = y$

(d) $x + y = 0$

Solution: Option (b) is correct

Since the line is passes through origin and co – incident on x axis. So it is passes through x – axis or we can say that the line is x – axis itself. And equation of x – axis is $y = 0$

(viii) In a single throw of die, the probability of getting a multiple of 3 is

(a) $\frac{1}{2}$

(b) $\frac{1}{6}$

(c) $\frac{1}{3}$

(d) $\frac{2}{3}$

Solution: Option (c) is correct

In a single throw of dice any of the number among 1, 2, 3, 4, 5, 6 can come, so total number of outcomes are 6. Here 3 and 6 are multiple of 3, so number of possible outcomes are 2.

$$\text{So probability of an event} = \frac{\text{Number of possible outcomes}}{\text{total number of outcomes}} = \frac{2}{6} = \frac{1}{3}$$

(ix) The lateral surface area of a cylinder is equal to the curved surface area of a cone. If the radius be the same, find the ratio of the height of the cylinder and slant height of the cone.

(a) 2:1

(b) 1:2

(c) 2:3

(d) 3:1

Solution: Option (b) is correct

Let height of the cylinder be h and slant height of the cone is l.

So, $2\pi rh = \pi rl \Rightarrow 2h = l$

$$\frac{h}{l} = \frac{1}{2}$$

(x) What is the median class of the following data?

class intervals	10 – 20	20 – 30	30 – 40	40 – 50	50 – 60
Frequency	6	11	7	11	5

(a) 20 – 30
(b) 30– 40
(c) 40 – 50
(d) 50 – 60

Solution: Option (b) is correct

To find the median class, find cumulative frequency of this distribution

class intervals	10 – 20	20 – 30	30 – 40	40 – 50	50 – 60
Frequency	6	11	7	11	5
Cumulative frequencies	6	17	24	35	40

So N = 40, which is even so $\frac{N}{2} = 20$, which is less than or equal to 24. So median class is 30 – 40.

Section B (30 Marks)
(Attempt any three questions from this section)

Question 2

(i) In the adjoining figure, AT is a tangent to a circle at A. If $\angle CAB = 60°$ and $\angle TAB = 55°$ find $\angle ABC$. [2]

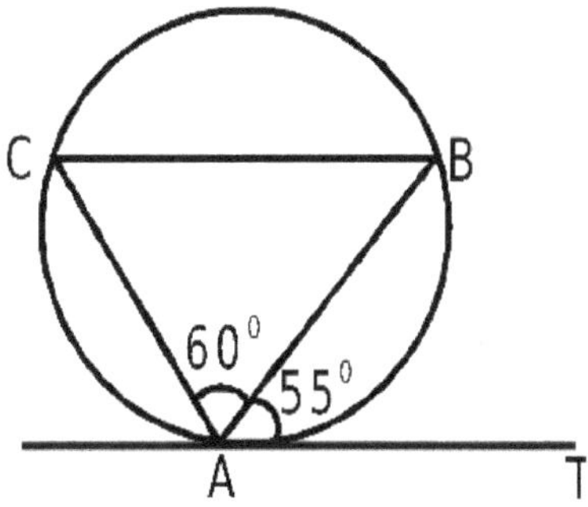

Solution:

$\angle ACB = \angle BAT$ (angles in alternate segment)

$\angle ACB = 55°$

In $\triangle$ ABC: $\angle ABC + \angle ACB + \angle CAB = 180°$ (angle sum property of triangle)

$\angle ABC + 55° + 60° = 180°$

$\angle ABC = 180 - 115°$

$\angle ABC = 65°$ **Ans.**

(ii) The area of curved surface of a right circular cylinder is 4400 cm^2 and the circumference of its base is 110 cm. Find the height of the cylinder. [2]

Solution:

Let radius of the cone be r cm and height = h cm.

Curved surface area of cone (CSA): $2\pi rh = 4400$ cm^2

Circumference $2\pi r = 110$ cm

$$\frac{2\pi rh}{2\pi r} = \frac{4400}{110}$$

$h = 40$ cm **Ans.**

(iii) From the top of a cliff 90 m high, the angles of depression of the top and bottom of *a* tower are observed to be 30° and 60° respectively. Find the height of tower. [3]

Solution:

In the adjacent diagram from the top A of a cliff AC the angle of depression of top and bottom of the tower E and D are 30° and 60° respectively.

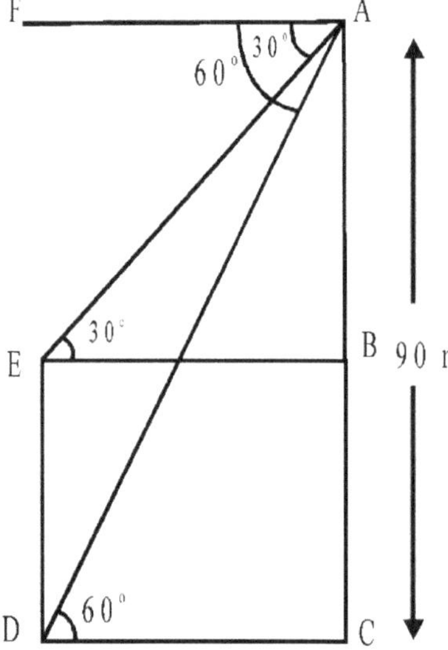

In ΔACD: $\tan 60^\circ = \frac{AC}{DC}\left(\tan\,\theta = \frac{\text{perpendicular}}{\text{base}}\right)$

$\sqrt{3} = \frac{90}{DC}$

$DC = \frac{90}{\sqrt{3}} = \frac{90\sqrt{3}}{\sqrt{3}\times\sqrt{3}} = \frac{90\sqrt{3}}{3} = 30\sqrt{3}$ m

In ΔABE $\tan\,30^\circ = \frac{AB}{BE}$

$\frac{1}{\sqrt{3}} = \frac{AB}{DC}$ (as BE = DC)

$\frac{1}{\sqrt{3}} = \frac{AB}{30\sqrt{3}}$

$AB\sqrt{3} = 30\sqrt{3} \Rightarrow AB = \frac{30\sqrt{3}}{\sqrt{3}}$

AB = 30 m

So BC = AC – AB = 90 – 30 = 60 m

So DE = BC = 60 m

Height of the tower = 60 m **Ans.**

(iv) Use graph paper for this question (Take 2 cm = 1 unit along both x and y axis). ABCD is a quadrilateral whose vertices are A(2, 2), B(2, –2), C(0, –1) and D(0, 1). [3]

(i) Reflect quadrilateral ABCD on the y-axis and name it as A'B'CD.

(ii) Write down the coordinates of A′ and B′.

(iii) Name two points which are invariant under the above reflection.

(iv) Name the polygon A'B'CD.

Solution:

(i) Co – ordinates of A′ (image of A under reflection

(a) In y – axis) = (–2, 2)

(b) Co – ordinates of B′ (image of B under reflection

(c) In y – axis) = (–2, –2)

(ii) Point C and D are invariants.

(iii) Name of polygon A'B'CD is isosceles trapezium.

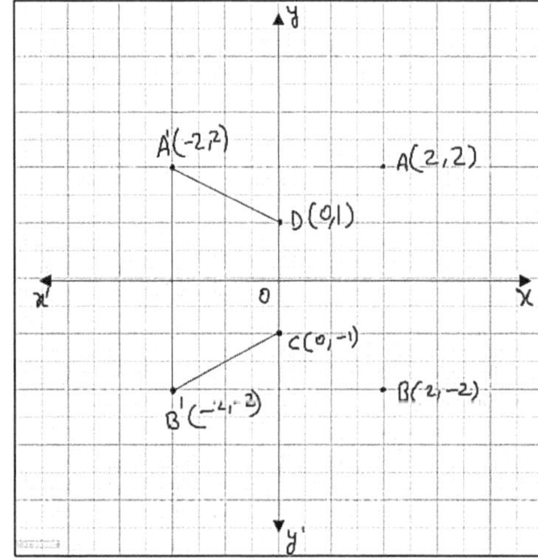

Question 3

(i) If $2x - 3y + 5 = 0$ and $px + 6y + 7 = 0$ are parallel lines, find the value of p. [2]

Solution:

Convert both lines in slope intercept ($y = mx + c$) form to find their slopes

$$2x - 3y + 5 = 0 \Rightarrow 2x + 5 = 3y$$

$$y = \frac{2}{3}x + \frac{5}{3} \qquad \text{so, slope of first line } m_1 = \frac{2}{3}$$

$$px + 6y + 7 = 0 \Rightarrow 6y = -px - 7$$

$$y = -\frac{p}{6}x - \frac{7}{6} \qquad \text{so slope of second line } m_2 = -\frac{p}{6}$$

Since lines are parallel so $m_1 = m_2$

$$\frac{2}{3} = -\frac{p}{6} \Rightarrow -3p = 12$$

$$p = -\frac{12}{3} \Rightarrow p = -4$$ **Ans.**

(ii) $1 + \frac{\cot^2 A}{1 + \text{cosec } A} = \text{cosec } A$ [2]

Solution:

L.H.S:

$$= 1 + \frac{\cot^2 A}{1 + \text{cosec } A}$$

$$= 1 + \frac{\text{cosec}^2 A - 1}{(1 + \text{cosec } A)} \qquad (\text{as } 1 + \cot^2 A = \text{cosec}^2 A)$$

$$= 1 + \frac{(\text{cosec } A - 1)(\text{cosec } A + 1)}{(1 + \text{cosec } A)} \qquad [a^2 - b^2 = (a + b)(a - b)]$$

$$= 1 + \text{cosec } A - 1$$

$$= \text{cosec } A$$

$$= \text{RHS}$$

(iii) The height of a right circular cone is 3.6 cm. and the radius of its base is 1.6 cm. It is melted and recast into a right circular cone with radius of its base as 1.2 cm., find its height. [3]

Solution:

Radius of cone is before melting (r) = 1.6 cm
Height of cone is before melting (h) = 3.6 cm
Radius of new cone after recast (R) = 1.2 cm
Let new height of the cone after recast is H cm
In melting volume remains same so

volume of cone before melting = volume of new cone recast

$$\pi r^2 h = \pi R^2 H$$

$$(1.6)^2 \times 3.6 = (1.2)^2 \times H$$

$$2.56 \times 3.6 = 1.44 \times H$$

$$H = \frac{2.56 \times 3.6}{1.44}$$

$$H = 6.4 \text{ cm}$$ **Ans.**

(iv) Use Graph paper for this question. [3]

A survey regarding height (in cm) of 60 boys belonging to Class 10 of a school was conducted. The following data was recorded:

Height in cm	135 – 140	140 – 145	145 – 150	150 – 155	155 – 160	160 – 165	165 – 170
No. of boys	4	8	20	14	7	6	1

Taking 2cm = height of 10 cm along one axis and 2 cm = 10 boys along the other axis draw an ogive of the above distribution. Use the graph to estimate the following:

(a) The median

(b) Lower Quartile

(c) If above 158 cm is considered as the tall boys of the class. Find the number of boys in the class who are tall.

Solution:

First construct a cumulative frequency table for the given distribution

Height in cm	**Number of boys**	**Cumulative frequency**
135 - 140	4	4
140 - 145	8	12
145 - 150	20	32
150 - 155	14	46
155 - 160	7	53
160 - 165	6	59
165 - 170	1	60
	N = 60	

Height (in cm) on x – axis with scale 2 cm = 5 cm

Number of boys on y – axis with scale 2 cm = 10 boys

Plot the points (140, 4), (145, 12), (150, 32), (155, 46), (160, 53), (165, 59) and (170, 60) on the graph paper. Draw a free hand curve passing through the points marked, starting from the lower limit of first class to the upper limit of the last class.

Since the sum of all frequencies N = 60 (even)

(i) Median = $\left(\frac{N}{2}\right)^{th}$ observation = $\left(\frac{60}{2}\right)$ th

= 30th observation = 149 cm (approximately)

(ii) Lower quartile (Q_1) = $\left(\frac{N}{4}\right)^{th}$ observation = $\left(\frac{60}{4}\right)^{th}$

= 15th observation = 146 cm (approximately)

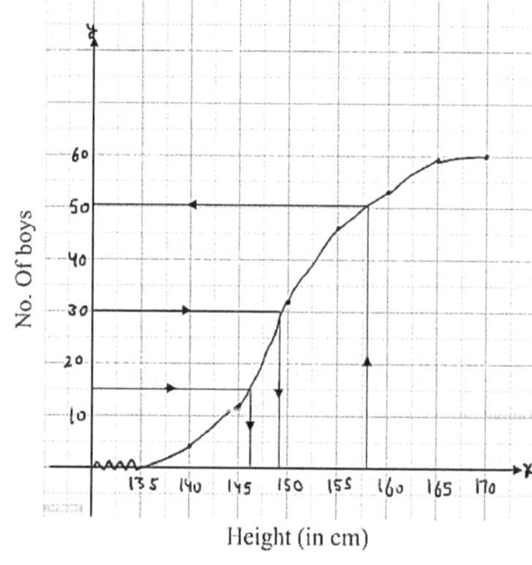

(ii) To find number of tall boys draw a vertical line through 158 cm (given), which meets the ogive at a point. Through this point draw a horizontal line which meets y – axis at the mark 51. This 51th student is also considered as tall boy. So number of tall boys = 60 – 50 = 10 boys.

Question 4

(i) Three consecutive vertices of a parallelogram ABCD are A (10, –6), B (2, –6) and C (–4, –2). Find the fourth vertex D. [2]

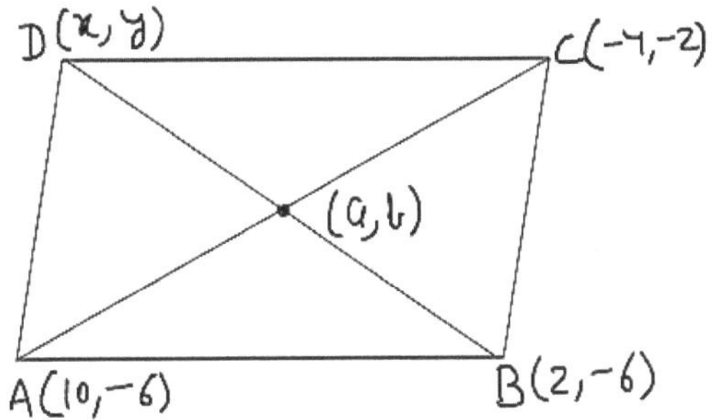

Solution:

Diagonals of a parallelogram bisect each other. So first find the midpoint of diagonal AC using Mid – point formula:

$$(a, b) = \left(\frac{x_1+x_2}{2}, \frac{y_1+y_2}{2}\right)$$

$$= \left(\frac{10 - 4}{2}, \frac{-6 - 2}{2}\right)$$

$$= \left(\frac{6}{2}, \frac{-8}{2}\right)$$

$$= (3, -4)$$

(a, b) = (3, –4) are also the co – ordinates of the mid – point of diagonal BD

Let (x, y) be the co – ordinates of point D.

$$a = \frac{x+2}{2} \qquad b = \frac{y-6}{2}$$

$$3 = \frac{x+2}{2} \qquad -4 = \frac{y-6}{2}$$

$$x + 2 = 6 \qquad y - 6 = -8$$

$$x = 6 - 2 \qquad y = -8 + 6$$

$$x = 4 \qquad y = -2$$

Co – ordinates of 4th vertex D = (4, –2) **Ans.**

(ii) In the figure, if PA = 16 cm, PC = 10 cm and PD = 8 cm, find AB. [2]

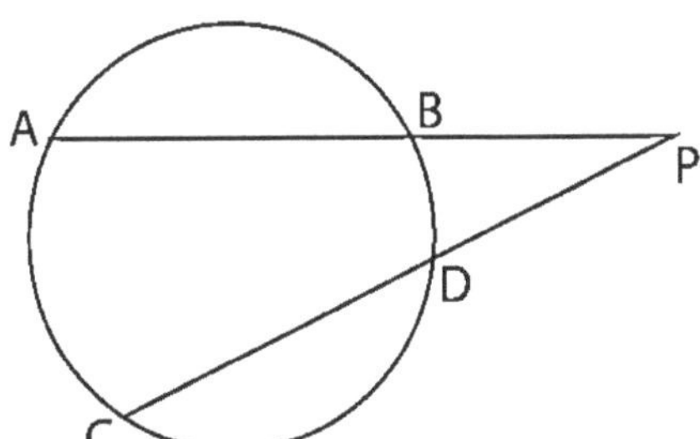

Solution:

Chord AB and CD intersect each other externally at point P

So PA × PB = PC × PD

16 × PB = 10 × 8

$$PB = \frac{80}{16} \Rightarrow 5 \text{ cm}$$

So, $AB = PA - PB \Rightarrow AB = 16 - 5 = 11$ cm **Ans.**

(iii) $(\text{cosec}^2\ A - 1)(\sec A + 1)(\sec A = 1) - 1$ [3]

Solution:

L.H.S

$= (\text{cosec}^2 A - 1)(\sec A + 1)(\sec A - 1)$

$= (\text{cosec}^2 A - 1)(\sec^2 A - 1)$

$= \cot^2 A \times \tan^2 A$ [as $1 + \tan^2 A = \sec^2 A$ and $1 + \cot^2 A = \text{cosec}^2 A$]

$= \frac{1}{\tan^2 A} \times \tan^2 A$

$= 1$

$=$ R.H.S

(iv) Find the mode of the following distribution by drawing a histogram: [3]

Height (in cm)	30 – 40	40 – 50	50 – 60	60 – 70	70 – 80	80 – 90
No of plants	4	3	8	11	6	2

Solution:

On x – axis heights of plants (in cm) plotted with the scale 2 cm = 10 cm

On y – axis number of plants plotted with the scale 2 cm = 2 plants.

Since the highest column is 60 – 70 so it is modal class.

Mode = 64 cm. **Ans.**

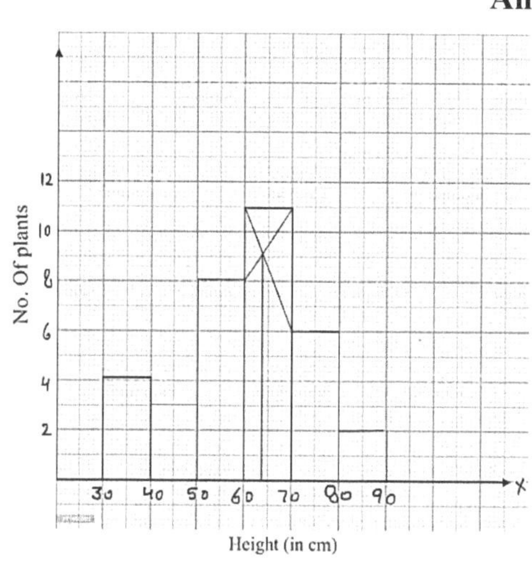

Question 5

(i) A letter is chosen from the word 'TRIANGLE'. What is the probability that it is a vowel? [2]

Solution:

Total Number of letters in the work 'TRIANGLE' = 8

Vowels present in the word = I, A, E

Number of vowels present in the word = 3

Probability of getting a vowel $= \frac{\text{Number of favorable outcomes}}{\text{Total number of outcomes}}$

$= \frac{3}{8}$ **Ans.**

(ii) The marks of 10 students of a class in an examination arranged in ascending order is as follows: 13, 35, 43, 46, $x, x + 4$, 55, 61, 71, 80 [2]

If the median marks are 48, find the value, of x.

Solution:

Since marks are arranged.

Number of observations = 10 (even)

$$\text{So Median} = \frac{1}{2}\left[\left(\frac{n}{2}\right)^{th} \text{term} + \left(\frac{n}{2}+1\right)^{th} \text{term}\right]$$

$$48 = \frac{1}{2}\left[\left(\frac{10}{2}\right)^{th} \text{term} + \left(\frac{10}{2}+1\right)^{th} \text{term}\right]$$

$$48 = \frac{1}{2}\left[5^{th} \text{ term} + 6^{th} \text{ term}\right]$$

$$48 = \frac{1}{2}[x + x + 4]$$

$$2x + 4 = 96$$

$$2x = 96 - 4 = 92$$

$$x = \frac{92}{2} \Rightarrow x = 46$$ **Ans.**

(iii) A (1, –5), B (2, 2) and C (–2, 4) are the vertices of triangle ABC. Find the equation of the altitude of the triangle through B. [3]

Solutions:

We have to find the equation of the altitude through B. Which is making 90° with AC.

So slope of AC (m_1) $= \frac{y_2-y_1}{x_2-x_1} = \frac{-5-4}{1+2} = \frac{-9}{3} = -3$

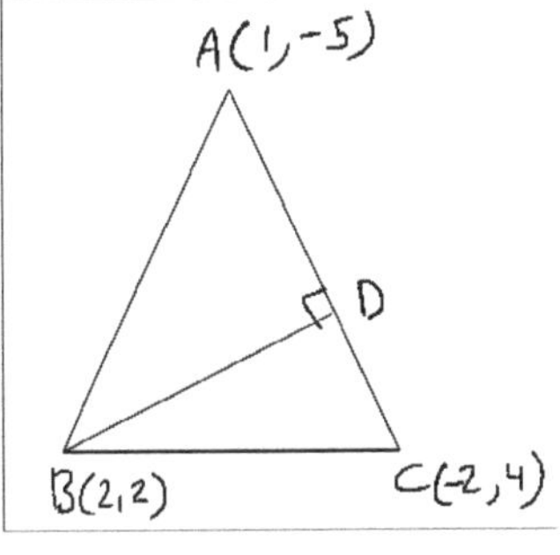

Let slope of BD is m_2,

$m_1 \times m_2 = -1$ (If two line are perpendicular then product of their slope = –1)

$$-3 \times m_2 = -1 \Rightarrow m_2 = \frac{1}{3}$$

And altitude passes through B(2, 2) = (x_1, y_1)

So equation of altitude passes through B is $(y - y_1) = m(x - x_1)$

$$x - 2 = \frac{1}{3}(x - 2)$$

$$x - 2 = 3y - 6$$

$$x - 3y = -6 + 2$$

$$x - 3y = -4$$ **Ans.**

(iv) In the figure, ∠DBC = 58°. BD is a diameter of the circle. [3]

Calculate: (i) ∠BDC (ii) ∠BEC (iii) ∠BAC

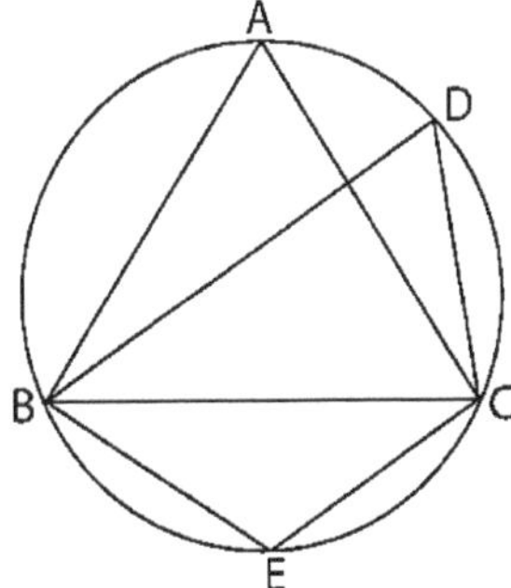

Solution:

BD is diameter given so $\angle BCD = 90°$(Angle on semi – circle)

∠DBC = 58° (given)

In ΔBDC,

$\angle BCD + \angle BDC + \angle DBC = 180^o$ (angle sum property of triangle)

$90^o + \angle BDC + 58^o = 180^o$
$\angle BDC + 148^o = 180^o$
$\angle BDC = 180^o - 148^o$
$\angle BDC = 32^o$ **Ans. (i)**
$\angle BAC = \angle BDC$ (angle in same segment)
$\angle BAC = 32^o$ **Ans. (iii)**

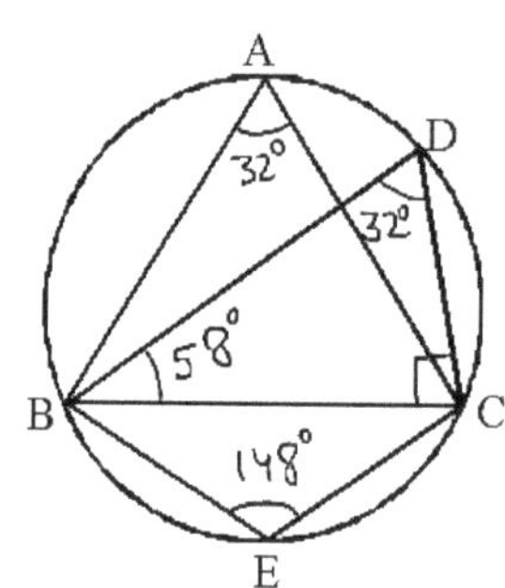

In ΔBDC,
$\angle BAC + \angle BEC = 180^o$ (Sum of opposite angles of cyclic quadrilateral $=180^o$)
$32^o + \angle BEC = 180^o$
$\angle BEC = 180^o - 32^o$
$\angle BEC = 148^o$ **(Ans. ii)**

Ans. (i) 32 (ii) 148° (iii) 32°

Question 6

(i) Two coins are tossed once. Find the probability of getting: [2]
(i) 2 head (ii) at least 1 tail.

Solution:

When two coins are tossed, following outcomes can come:
(HH, TT, HT, TH)
So total number of outcomes = 4
(i) getting two heads means (HH) is favorable
So total number of favorable outcomes = 1

So probability of getting two heads = $\frac{\text{Number of favorable outcomes}}{\text{Total number of outcomes}}$
$= \frac{1}{4}$ **(Ans.)**

(ii) Getting at least one tail means (HT, TT, TH) are favorable
So number of favorable outcomes = 3
So probability of getting at least one tail = $\frac{3}{4}$ **(Ans.)**

(iii) Given a line segment AB joining the points A(– 4, 6) and B(8, –3). Find: [2]
(a) The ratio in which AB is divided by the y-axis.
(b) Find the coordinates of the point of intersection.

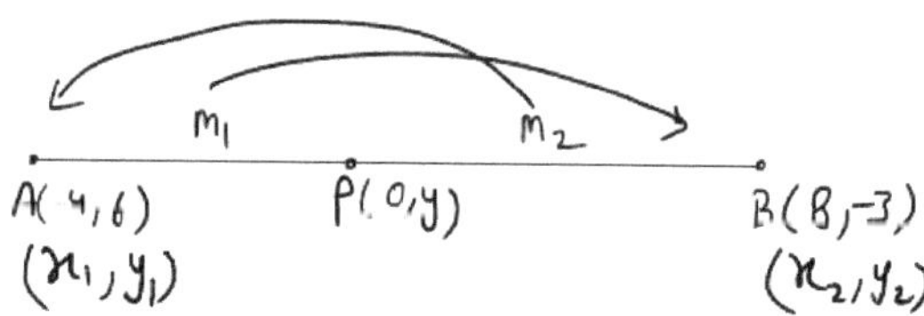

Solution:

Let point P(0, y) on y – axis which divide the

Join of A and B in $m_1 : m_2$
Using section formula:

$$x = \frac{m_1 x_2 + m_2 x_1}{m_1 + m_2}$$

$$0 = \frac{m_1 \times 8 + m_2 \times (-4)}{m_1 + m_2}$$

$$8m_1 - 4m_2 = 0$$

$$8m_1 = 4m_2$$

$$\frac{m_1}{m_2} = \frac{4}{8} \Rightarrow \frac{m_1}{m_2} = \frac{1}{2}$$ **Ans. (i)**

Now to find point of intersection

$$y = \frac{m_1 y_2 + m_2 y_1}{m_1 + m_2}$$

$$y = \frac{1 \times (-3) + 2 \times 6}{1 + 2}$$

$$y = \frac{-3 + 12}{3}$$

$$y = \frac{9}{3} \Rightarrow y = 3$$ **Ans: (0 , 3)**

(iii) From a point P on level ground, the angle of elevation of the top of a tower is 30°. If the tower is 100 m high, how far is P from the foot of the tower? [3]

Solution:

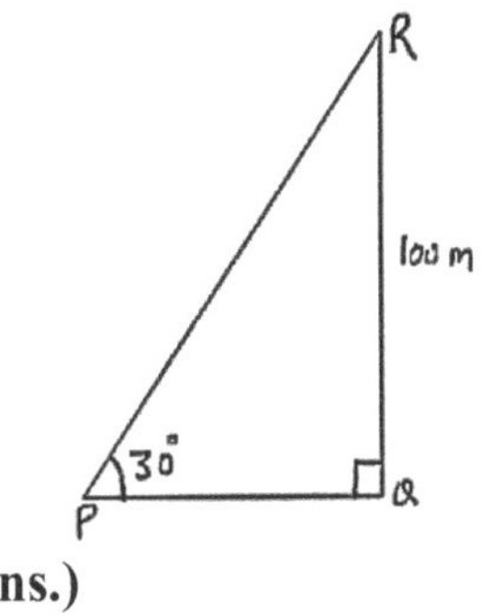

Given triangle PQR right angled at Q. height of tower = 30°

$$\tan 30^o = \frac{QR}{PQ} \qquad \left(\tan\theta = \frac{\text{perpendicular}}{\text{base}}\right)$$

$$\frac{1}{\sqrt{3}} = \frac{100}{PQ}$$

$$PQ = 100\sqrt{3}$$

$$PQ = 100 \times 1.732$$

$$PQ = 173.20 \text{ m}$$ **(Ans.)**

(iv) Find the mean of the following distribution. [3]

Class	0 – 10	10 – 20	20 – 30	30 – 40	40 - 50
Frequency	12	16	6	7	9

Solution:

Class	**class mark (x)**	**frequency (f)**	fx
0 – 10	5	12	60
10 – 20	15	16	240
20 – 30	25	6	150
30 – 40	35	7	245
40 – 50	45	9	405
		$\Sigma fx = 50$	$\Sigma fx = 1100$

$$\text{Mean} = \frac{\Sigma fx}{\Sigma f}$$

$$= \frac{1100}{50}$$

$$= 22$$ **Ans.**

Practice Paper – 2 (Solved)
(MATHEMATICS)
(Time alloted: One and a half hour)

Answer to this paper must be written on the paper provided separately.
You will not be allowed to write during the first 10 minutes.
This time is to spent in reading the question paper.

Omission of essential working well result in loss of marks.
The intended marks for questions or part of questions are given in the brackets [].

Section A (10 Marks)
(Attempt all question from this section)

Question 1

Choose the correct answers to the questions from the given options. (Do not copy the questions. Write the correct options only.) [10]

(i) A point P is its own image under the reflection in a line l. Describe the position of the point P with respect to the line l.

(a) on x – axis
(b) on y – axis
(c) on line l
(d) on origin

Solution: Option (c) is correct
When a point lies on a line and reflected in the same line it will be invariant.

(ii) 9 $\sec^2$ A – 9 $\tan^2$ A is equal to:

(a) 1
(b) 9
(c) 8
(d) 0

Solution: Option (b) is correct
$1 + \tan^2 A = \sec^2 A$
$\sec^2 A - \tan^2 A = 1$

(iii) Given M is the mid – point of AB, the co – ordinates of A; if M = (1, 7) and B = (–5, 10).

(a) (4, 8)
(b) (4, 7)
(c) (7, 4)
(d) (4, 3)

Solution: Since M(1, 7) is the mid-point.
Let coordinates of A = (x, y)

1 M 1
A(x,y) (1,7) B(-5,10)

Using midpoint formula:

$$x = \frac{x_1 + x_2}{2} \qquad y = \frac{y_1 + y_2}{2}$$

$$1 = \frac{x - 5}{2} \qquad 7 = \frac{y + 10}{2}$$

$$x - 5 = 2 \qquad y + 10 = 14$$

$x = 2 + 5$ $\quad\quad$ $y = 14 - 10$

$x = 7$ $\quad\quad$ $y = 4$

(iv) In the adjoining figure AB is a diameter of the circle with centre O. Angle BOC = 120°, the measure of angle ADC.

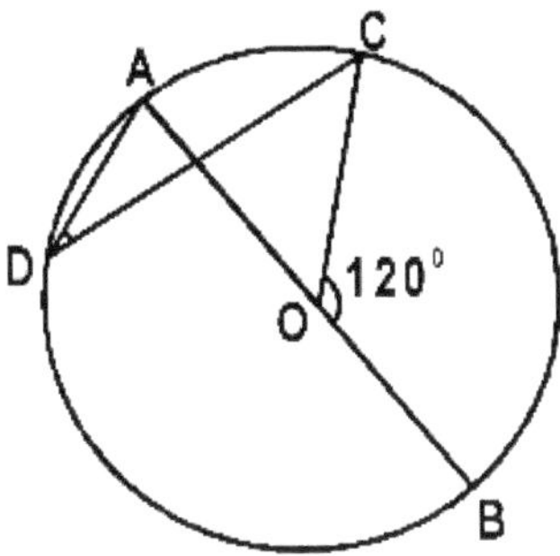

(a) 25°
(b) 50°
(c) 30°
(d) 60°

Solution: Option (c) is correct

$\angle AOC = 2\angle ADC$ (angle subtended by an arc at the center is double the angle at remaining part of the circle)

and $\angle AOC = 180^o - 120^o = 60^o$ (Linear pair)

so $\angle ADC = \frac{60^o}{2}$

(v) The volume of a right circular cylinder is 345 cm^3. Then the volume of a right circular cone whose radius of the base and height is same as of circular cylinder, will be

(a) 345 cm^3
(b) 690 cm^3
(c) 115 cm^3
(d) 230 cm^3

Solution: Option (c) is correct

Since radii and height of both is same

Volume of cylinder $\pi r^2 h = 345$

Volume of cone $= \frac{1}{3}\pi r^2 h = \frac{1}{3} \times 345$

(vi) The area of the curved surface of a right circular cone of diameter 14 cm is 550 cm^2. The height of the cone is

(a) 25 cm
(b) 22 cm
(c) 23 cm
(d) 24 cm

Solution: Option (d) is correct

Radius of cone = 7 cm

curved surface area of cone $= \pi r l$

$\pi r l = 550$

$l = \frac{550 \times 7}{22 \times 7} = 25\text{cm}$

Since $l^2 = h^2 + r^2$ so h = 24 cm

(vii) The median of a given frequency distribution is found graphically with the help of :
(a) Histogram
(b) Frequency curve
(c) Frequency polygon
(d) Ogive
Solution: Option (d) is correct

(viii) If a digit chosen at random from the digits 1, 2, 3, 4, 5, 6, 7, 8, 9, then the probability that it is odd, is
(a) $\frac{4}{9}$
(b) $\frac{5}{9}$
(c) $\frac{1}{9}$
(d) $\frac{2}{3}$
Solution: Option (b) is correct
Here among the given numbers odd numbers are: 1, 3, 5, 7, and 9 total 5 favorable outcomes

$$\text{Total number of outcomes} = 9$$

$$\text{Probability} = \frac{\text{Number of favorable outcomes}}{\text{Total number of outcomes}} = \frac{5}{9}$$

(ix) Which of the following points lie on the line $x - 2y + 5 = 0$
(a) (0, 5)
(b) (1, 3)
(c) (3, 7)
(d) (–2, –4)
Solution: Option (b) is correct
Points which lie on the line will satisfy the equation
Substitute $x = 1$ and y = 3 in the equation its left hand will be equals to right hand side (Satisfied)

(x) If the arithmetic means of $x, x+3, x+6, x+9$ and $x+12$ is 10, then x =?
(a) 1
(b) 2
(c) 6
(d) 4
Solution: Option (d) is correct

$$\text{mean} = \frac{\text{sum of observation}}{\text{number of observation}}$$

$$\frac{x+x+3+x+6+x+9+x+12}{5} = 10$$

$$5x + 30 = 50$$

$$5x = 50 - 30 = 20$$

$$x = \frac{20}{5} = 4$$

Section B (30 Marks)
(Attempt any three questions from this section)

Question 2

(i) $\tan^2 A - \frac{1}{\cos^2 A} + 1 = 0$

Solution:

$$\begin{aligned} \text{LHS.} &= \tan^2 A - \frac{1}{\cos^2 A} + 1 \\ &= \tan^2 A - \sec^2 A + 1 \\ &= \sec^2 A - \sec^2 A \, [1 + \tan^2 A = \sec^2 A] \\ &= 0 \\ &= \text{RHS.} \end{aligned}$$

(ii) The line given by the equation $\frac{y}{2} = x - p$ passes through the point (– 4, 4). Find p.

Solution:

Since equation of line $\frac{y}{2} = x - p$ passes through the point (–4, 4) so co – ordinates of the point will satisfy the equation of the line

$$\frac{y}{2} = x - p$$

$$\frac{4}{2} = -4 - p$$

$$2 = -4 - p \Rightarrow p = -4 - 2$$

$$p = -6$$ **Ans.**

(iii) In the given figure AB is a diameter of the circle with centre O. If BCD = 120°, find (a)∠BAD (b) ∠DBA

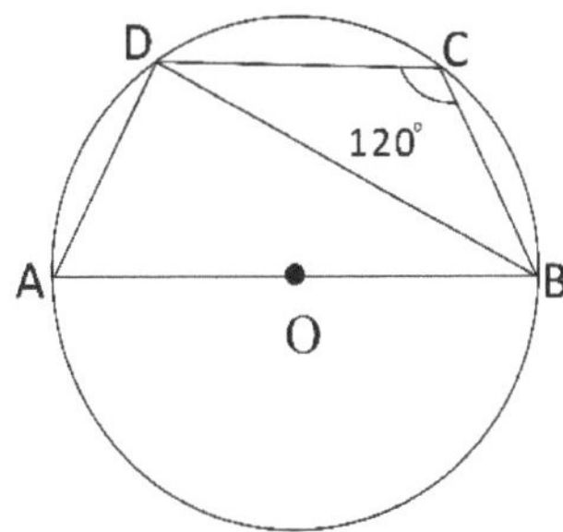

Solution:

Given $\angle BCD = 120°$

(a) $\angle BAD + \angle BCD = 180°$ (Opposite angles of cyclic quadrilateral are supplementary)

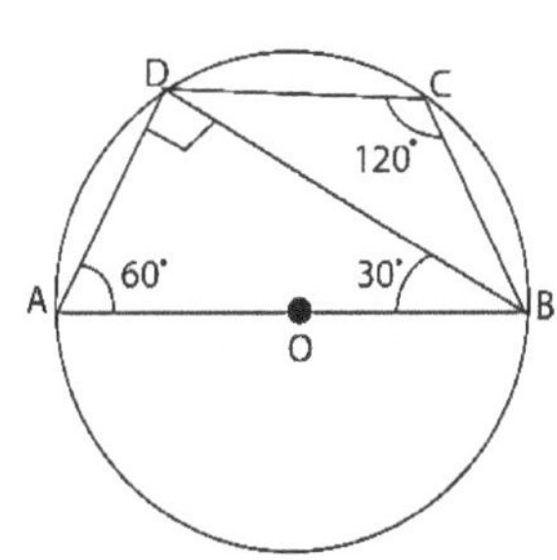

$$\angle BAD + 120^o = 180^o$$

$$\angle BAD = 180^o - 120^o$$

$$\angle BAD = 60^o$$ **Ans.**

(b) $\angle ADB = 90°$[angle on diameter is 90°]

In ΔABD

$\angle ADB + \angle DBA + \angle BAD = 180^o$ [angle sum property of triangle]

$$90^o + \angle DBA + 60^o = 180^o$$

$$\angle DBA + 150^o = 180^o$$

$$\angle DBA = 180^o - 150^o$$
$$\angle DBA = 30^o \qquad \textbf{Ans.}$$

(iv) The marks obtained (out of 50) by 100 students in a test are given below. Find the median marks.

Marks	20	29	28	33	42	38	43	25
No. of students	6	28	34	15	2	4	1	20

Solution:

To calculate median first create a cumulative frequency table from the given distribution

Marks	**No. of students (f)**	**cumulative frequency**
20	6	6
29	28	34
28	34	68
33	15	83
42	2	85
38	4	89
43	1	90
25	20	110
	N = 110	

Sum of frequency N = 110 (even)

$$\text{so median} = \frac{1}{2}\left[\left(\frac{N}{2}\right)^{\text{th}} \text{term} + \left(\frac{N}{2}+1\right)^{\text{th}} \text{term}\right]$$
$$= \frac{1}{2}\left[\left(\frac{110}{2}\right)^{\text{th}} \text{term} + \left(\frac{110}{2}+1\right)^{\text{th}} \text{term}\right]$$
$$= \frac{1}{2}\left[55^{\text{th}} \text{ term} + 56^{\text{th}} \text{ term}\right]$$

From the cumulative frequencies values just less than or equals to 55 and 56 is 68 and value of variant from that cumulative frequency is 28

$$= \frac{1}{2}[28 + 28]$$
$$= \frac{1}{2} \times 56 \Rightarrow 28 \qquad \textbf{Ans.}$$

Question 3

(i) Two vertices of a triangle are (3, –5) and (–7, 4). If its centroid is (2, –1). Find the third vertex.

Solution:

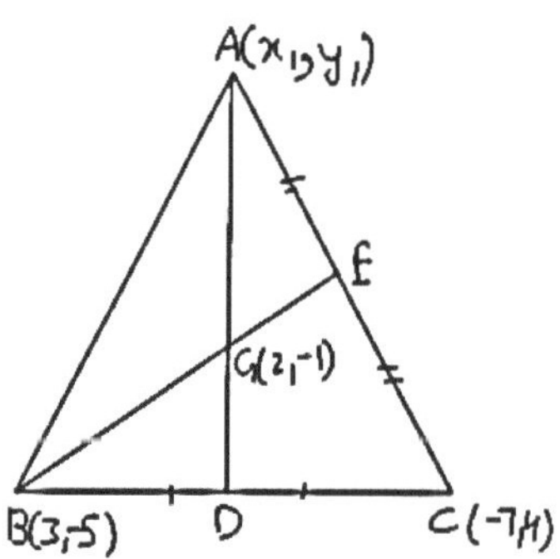

Let the co – ordinates of the third vertex is (x_1, y_1)

Co – ordinates of centroid

$$G(x, y) = \left(\frac{x_1 + x_2 + x_3}{3}, \frac{y_1 + y_2 + y_3}{3}\right)$$

$$x = \frac{x_1 + x_2 + x_3}{3} \qquad y = \frac{y_1 + y_2 + y_3}{3}$$

$$2 = \frac{x_1 + 3 - 7}{3} \qquad -1 = \frac{y_1 - 5 + 4}{3}$$

$$x_1 - 4 = 6 \qquad y_1 - 1 = -3$$

$$x_1 = 6 + 4 \qquad y_1 = -3 + 1$$

$$x_1 = 10 \qquad y_1 = -2$$

So co – ordinates of third vertex = (10, –2) **Ans.**

(ii) A bag contains 5 red, 4 green and 6 white balls. If a ball is drawn at random from the bag, find the probability that it will be.

(a) white

(b) not red

Solution:

Number of red ball = 5

Number of green ball = 4

Number of white ball = 6

Total number of balls = 5 + 4 + 6 = 15 balls

(a) Probability of getting white ball = $\frac{\text{Number of favorable outcomes}}{\text{Total number of outcomes}} = \frac{6}{15} \Rightarrow \frac{2}{5}$ **Ans.**

(b) Not red means either white or green

Number of favorable outcomes = 4 + 6 =10

P(not red) = $\frac{10}{15} \Rightarrow \frac{2}{3}$ **Ans.**

(iii) In a class test, the marks obtained by 11 students are

13,17, 20, 5, 3, 19, 7, 6, 11, 15, 17. Find:

(a) median (b) lower quartile (c) upper quartile

Solution:

To find median first arrange the marks in ascending order:

3, 5 ,6, 7, 11, 13, 15, 17, 17, 19, 20

Number of observations = 11 (odd)

(a) median $= \left(\frac{n+1}{2}\right)^{th}$ term

$= \left(\frac{11+1}{2}\right)^{th}$ term = 6th term

=13 **Ans.**

(b) Lower quartile $(Q_1) = \left(\frac{n+1}{4}\right)^{th}$ term

$= \left(\frac{11+1}{4}\right)^{th}$ term = 3rd term

= 6 **Ans.**

(c)Upper quartile $(Q_3) = \frac{3}{4}(n + 1)$th term

$= \frac{3}{4}(11 + 1)$th term = 9th term

=17 **Ans.**

(iv) From the top of a cliff 90 m high, the angles of depression of the top and bottom of a tower are observed to be 30° and 60° respectively. Find the height of tower.

Solution:

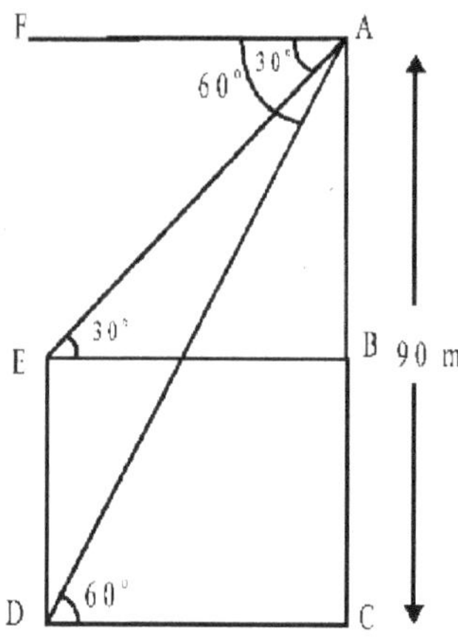

In the adjacent diagram from the top A of a cliff AC the angle of depression of top and bottom of the tower E and D are 30° and 60° respectively.

In ΔACD: $\tan 60° = \frac{AC}{DC}$

$$\left(\tan\theta = \frac{\text{perpendicular}}{\text{base}}\right)$$

$$\sqrt{3} = \frac{90}{DC}$$

$$DC = \frac{90}{\sqrt{3}} = \frac{90\sqrt{3}}{\sqrt{3}\times\sqrt{3}} = \frac{90\sqrt{3}}{3} = 30\sqrt{3}\text{m}$$

In ΔABE: $\tan 30° = \frac{AB}{BE}$

$$\frac{1}{\sqrt{3}} = \frac{AB}{DC} \qquad \text{(As BE = DC)}$$

$$\frac{1}{\sqrt{3}} = \frac{AB}{30\sqrt{3}}$$

$$AB\sqrt{3} = 30\sqrt{3} \Rightarrow AB = \frac{30\sqrt{3}}{\sqrt{3}}$$

AB = 30 m

So BC = AC – AB = 90 – 30 = 60 m

So DE = BC = 60 m

Height of the tower = 60 m **Ans.**

Question 4

(i) The height of a right circular cylinder is 21 cm, and its radius is 14 cm. Find:

(a) Volume (b) Curved surface area

Solution:

Height of cylinder = 21 cm

Radius of cylinder = 14 cm

(a) Volume of cylinder = $\pi r^2 h$

$$= \frac{22}{7} \times 14 \times 14 \times 21$$

$$= 22 \times 14 \times 14 \times 3$$

$$= 12{,}936 \text{ cm}^3$$ **Ans.**

(b) Curved surface area of cylinder = $2\pi rh$

$$= 2 \times \frac{22}{7} \times 14 \times 21$$

$$= 2 \times 22 \times 14 \times 3$$

$$= 1{,}848 \text{ cm}^2$$ **Ans.**

(ii) In the figure given: from an external point P, tangents PA and PB are drawn to a circle. CE is a tangent to the circle at D. If AP = 15 cm, find the perimeter of the triangle PEC.

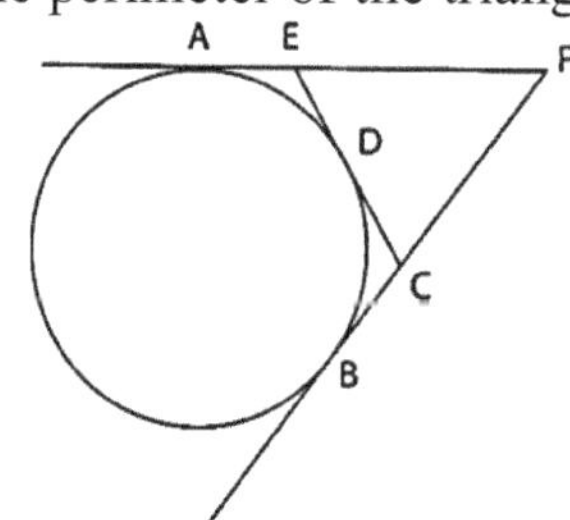

Solution:

Tangent PA= 15 cm (given)

PA = PB [Tangents from an external point to a circle are equal]

Perimeter of triangle PEC = PE + EC + PC

= PE + ED + CD + PC [EC = ED + CD]

= PE + EA + CB + PC [ED = EA and CD= CB]

= PA + PB

= 15 + 15

= 30 cm **Ans.**

(iii) $(\cot A - \operatorname{cosec} A)^2 = \frac{1-\cos A}{1+\cos A}$

Solution:

L.H.S.

$$= (\cot A - \operatorname{cosec} A)^2$$

$$= \left(\frac{\cos A}{\sin A} - \frac{1}{\sin A}\right)^2$$

$$= \left(\frac{\cos A - 1}{\sin A}\right)^2$$

$$= \frac{(1 - \cos A)^2}{\sin^2 A}$$

$$= \frac{(1 - \cos A)(1 - \cos A)}{1 - \cos^2 A} \quad [(a - b)^2 = (b - a)^2]$$

$$= \frac{(1 - \cos A)(1 - \cos A)}{(1 + \cos A)(1 - \cos A)} \quad [a^2 - b^2 = (a + b)(a - b)]$$

$$= \frac{(1 - \cos A)}{(1 + \cos A)} \quad \text{R.H.S}$$

(iv) Use graph paper for this question. The point P (5, 3) was reflected in the origin to get the image P′.

(a) Write down the coordinates of P′.

(b) If M is the foot of the perpendicular from P to the x-axis, find the coordinates of M.

(c) If N is the foot of the perpendicular from P′ to the x – axis, find the coordinates of N.

(d) Name the figure PMP'N.

(e) Find the area of the figure PMP'N.

Solution:

(a) P′ is the image of P (5, 3) when reflected in origin so P′ = (–5, –3)

(b) Co – ordinates of M (5, 0)

(c) Co – ordinates of N (–5, 0)

(d) Parallelogram

(e) area of parallelogram PMP’N = base × height

= PM × MN

= 3 × 10

= 30 unit^2

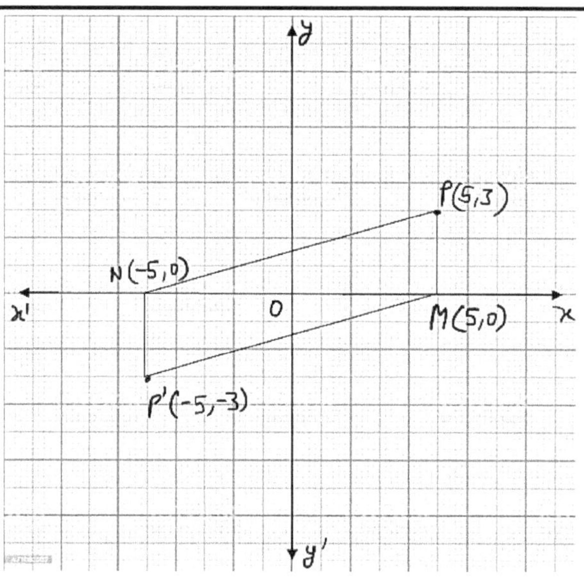

Question 5

(i) Calculate the arithmetic mean of first five prime numbers.

Solution:

First five prime number are: 2, 3, 5, 7, 11

$$\text{Mean} = \frac{\text{sum of observations}}{\text{number of observations}}$$

$$= \frac{2 + 3 + 5 + 7 + 11}{5}$$

$$= \frac{28}{5}$$

$$= 5.6$$ **Ans.**

(ii) M and N are two points on the X axis and Y axis respectively. P (3, 2) divides the line segment MN in the ratio 2:3. Find:

(a) The coordinates of M and N.

(b) Slope of the line MN

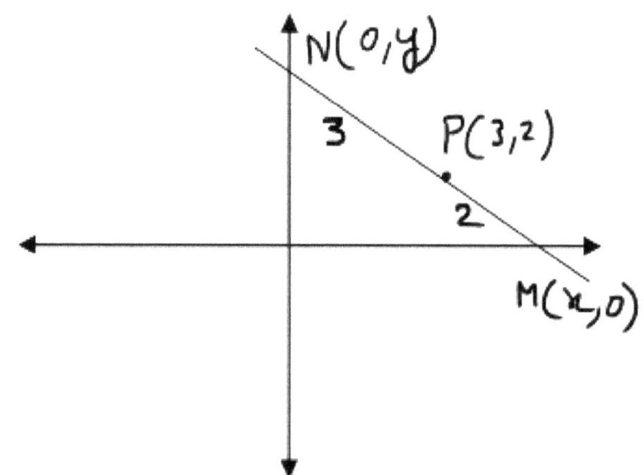

Solution:

Let co – ordinates of M on x – axis = $(x, 0)$

Let co – ordinates of N on y – axis = (0, y)

Ratio $m_1 : m_2 = 2 : 3$

(a) Using section formula:

$$x = \frac{m_1x_2 + m_2x_1}{m + n} \qquad y = \frac{m_1y_2 + m_2y_1}{m + n}$$

$$3 = \frac{2\times 0 + 3x}{2 + 3} \qquad 2 = \frac{2y + 3\times 0}{2 + 3}$$

$$15 = 3x \qquad 10 = 2y$$

$$x = \frac{15}{3} \qquad y = \frac{10}{2}$$

$$x = 5 \qquad y = 5$$

So co – ordinates of M = (5, 0) and co – ordinates of N = (0, 5) **Ans.**

(b) Let M(5, 0) = (x_1, y_1) and N(0, 5) = (x_2, y_2)

$$\text{Slope of MN} = \frac{y_2 - y_1}{x_2 - x_1}$$

$$= \frac{5 - 0}{0 - 5}$$

$$= \frac{5}{-5} = -1$$ **Ans.**

(iii) A solid right circular copper cone of height 15 cm and radius 6 cm is melted, and smaller copper cones of height 3 cm and radius 2 cm are made. How many smaller cones can be made?

Solution:

Radius of cone (R) = 6 cm

Height of come (H) = 15 cm

$$\text{Volume of cone} = \frac{1}{3}\pi R^2 H$$

$$= \frac{1}{3} \times \pi \times 6 \times 6 \times 15$$

$$= 180\,\pi\ \text{cm}^2$$

Radius of small cone (r) = 2 cm

Height of small cone (h) = 3 cm

$$\text{Volume of small cone} = \frac{1}{3}\pi r^2 h$$

$$= \frac{1}{3} \times \pi \times 2 \times 2 \times 3$$

$$= 4\,\pi\ \text{cm}^2$$

$$\text{Volume of small cone} = \frac{1}{3}\pi r^2 h$$

$$= \frac{1}{3} \times \pi \times 2 \times 2 \times 3$$

$$= 4\,\pi\ \text{cm}^2$$

(iv) A tower is 64 m tall. A man standing erect at a distance of 36 m from the tower observes the angle of elevation of the top of the tower to be 60°. Find the height of the man.

Solution:

AB is a tower = 64 m

CD is a man which is at a distance of 36 m from the tower.

In triangle AED

$$\tan 60^o = \frac{AE}{DE} \qquad [\tan\theta = \frac{\text{perpendicular}}{\text{base}}]$$

$$\sqrt{3} = \frac{AE}{DE}$$

$\sqrt{3} = \frac{AE}{BC}$ [DE = BC]

$\sqrt{3} = \frac{AE}{36}$

AE = $36\sqrt{3}$

$= 36 \times 1.732$

$= 62.352$ m

CB = BE = AB – AE

= 64 – 62.352

= 1.648 m = 1.7 m (approximately)

Height of the man = 1.7 m (approximately)

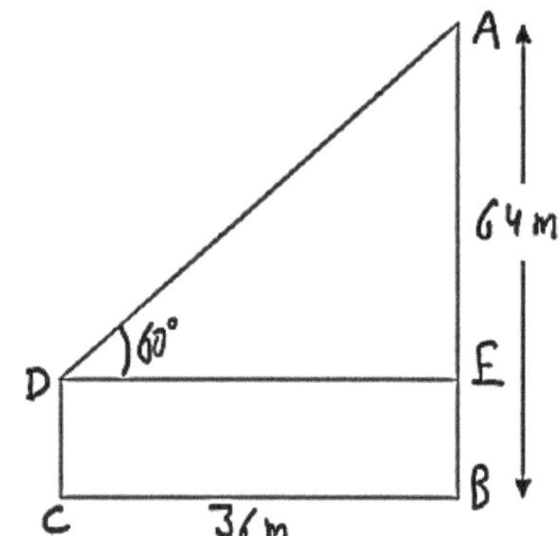

Question 6

(i) A box contains 7 blue, 8 white and 5 black marbles. If a marble is drawn at random from the box, what is the probability that it will be

(a) black (b) blue or black

Solution:

Number of blue marble = 7

Number of white marble = 8

Number or black marble = 5

Total number of marbles = 7 + 8 + 5 = 20

(a) Probability of drawing black marble $= \frac{\text{Number of black marble}}{\text{Total number of marble}}$

$= \frac{5}{20} = \frac{1}{4}$ **Ans.**

(b) Probability of blue or black marble, means the drawn marble should be blue or black

Number or favourable outcomes (either blue or black marble) = 7 + 5 = 12

P (blue or black) $= \frac{12}{20}$

$= \frac{3}{5}$ **Ans.**

(ii) In the given figure, AB is a diameter. The tangent at C meets AB produced at Q, ∠CAB = 34°. Find

(a) ∠CBA (b) ∠CQA.

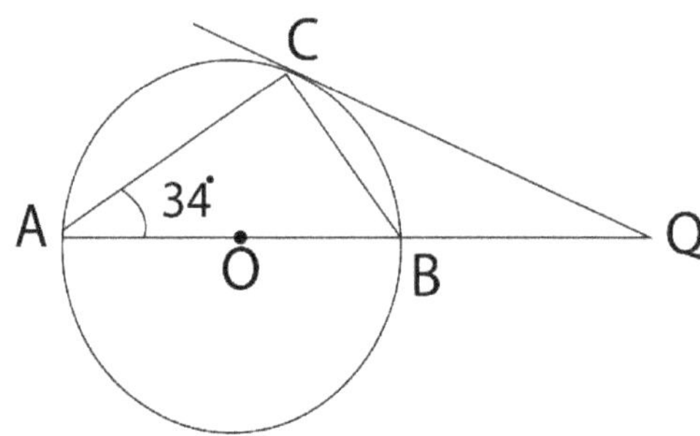

Solution:

(a) ∠ACB = 90° [Angle on diameter]

In ΔABC,

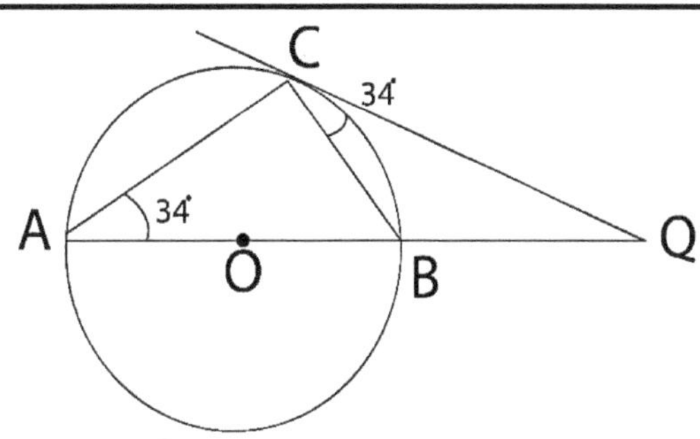

$\angle ACB + \angle CBA + \angle CAB = 180^\circ$ [Angle sum property of a triangle]

$90^\circ + \angle CBA + 34^\circ = 180^\circ$

$\angle CBA + 124^\circ = 180^\circ$

$\angle CBA = 180^\circ - 124^\circ$

$\angle CBA = 56^\circ$ **Ans.**

(b) In ΔACQ,

$\angle CAQ + \angle ACQ + \angle CQA = 180^\circ$ [Angle sum property of a triangle]

$34^\circ + (90^\circ + 34^\circ) + \angle CQA = 180^\circ$ [$\angle BCQ = \angle CAB$ – angles in alternate segment]

$\angle CQA + 158^\circ = 180^\circ$

$\angle CQA = 180^\circ - 158^\circ$

$\angle CQA = 22^\circ$ **Ans.**

(iii) A line through (5, 3) whose inclination is 45°, intersects y – axis at Q.

(a) Write the slope of the line.

(b) Write the equation of the line.

(c) Find the co – ordinates of Q.

Solution:

(a) Inclination $\theta = 45^0$

Slope m = $\tan\theta = 1$ 

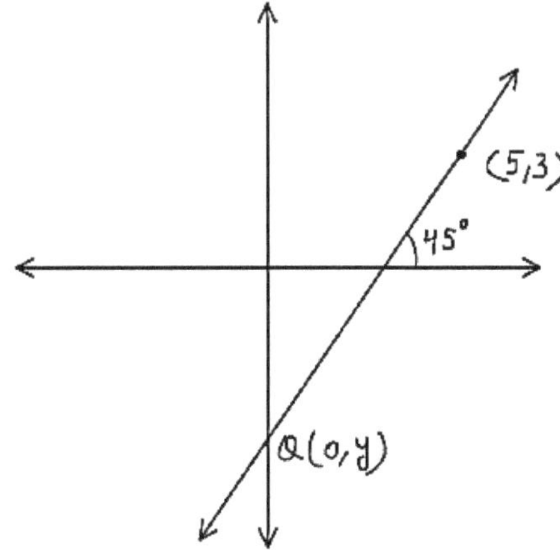

(b) The required line passes through (5, 3) $\rightarrow (x_1, y_1)$

The equation of the line is $(y - y_1) = m(x - x_1)$

$y - 3 = 1(x - 5)$

$y - 3 = x - 5$

$x - y = 2$ **Ans.**

(c) Since the equation of line obtained in (ii) passes through Q(0, y), so co – ordinates of Q will satisfy the equation of the line $x - y = 2$

$0 - y = 2$

$y = -2$

Co – ordinates of Q = (0, –2) **Ans.**

(iv). Find the following frequency distribution, draw, histogram. Hence calculate the mode:

Class Interval	0 – 5	5 – 10	10 – 15	15 – 20	20 – 25	25 – 30
Frequency	2	7	18	10	8	5

Solution:

Scale:

On x – axis: 2 cm = 5 units

On y – axis 2 cm = 2 units

Mode = 13 **Ans.**

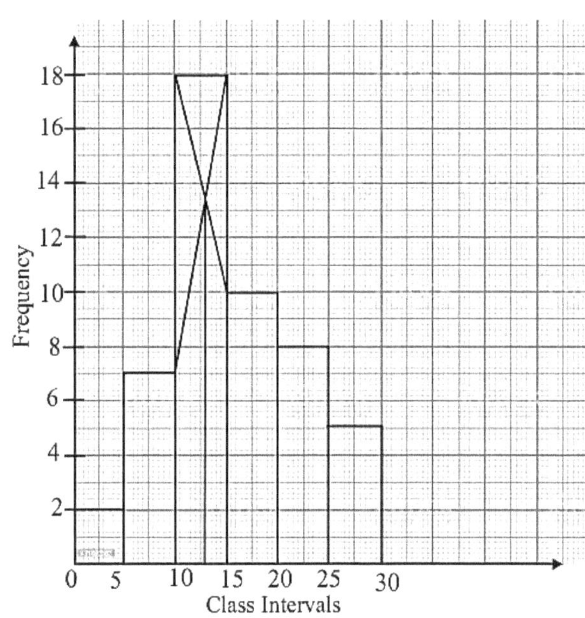

Practice Paper – 3 (Solved)
(MATHEMATICS)
(Time alloted: One and a half hour)

Answer to this paper must be written on the paper provided separately.
You will not be allowed to write during the first 10 minutes.
This time is to spent in reading the question paper.

Omission of essential working well result in loss of marks.
The intended marks for questions or part of questions are given in the brackets [ ].

Section A (10 Marks)
(Attempt all question from this section)

Question 1
Choose the correct answers to the questions from the given options. (Do not copy the questions. Write the correct options only.) [10]

(i) State the co – ordinates of the point (–6, 4) under reflection in the line $x = 0$.

(a) (–6, –4)
(b) (6, 4)
(c) (6, –4)
(d) No change

Solution: Option (b) is correct
$x = 0$ is the equation of y – axis. When a point reflected in y – axis, sign of x – coordinate changes.

(ii) In the adjoining figure, C and D are points on the circumference of the semicircle described on AB as diameter. Given angle $BAD = 70°$ and angle $DBC = 30°$ calculate angle ADB.

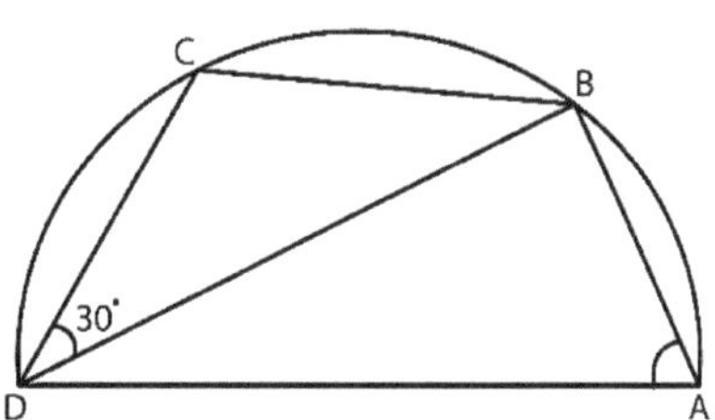

(a) 35°
(b) 25°
(c) 30°
(d) 20°

Solution: Option (d) is correct

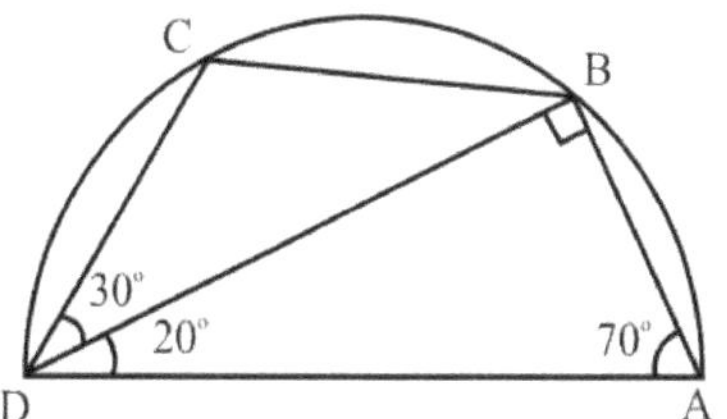

$\angle ABD = 90°$ (angle on diameter)

In ΔABD

$\angle ABD + \angle ADB + \angle BAD = 180°$

$\angle ADB = 180° - 160° = 20°$

(iii) $\frac{1+\tan^2 A}{1+\cot^2 A}$ is equal to:

(a) $\sec^2 A$
(b) -1
(c) $\cot^2 A$

(d) $\tan^2 A$

Solution: Option (d) is correct

$$= \frac{1 + \tan^2 A}{1 + \cot^2 A}$$

$$= \frac{\sec^2 A}{\text{cosec}^2 A}$$

$$= \frac{\sin^2 A}{\cos^2 A} = \tan^2 A$$

(iv) What is radius of a cylinder whose volume and curved surface area are numerically equal?

(a) 2 unit

(b) 3 unit

(c) 4 unit

(d) 1 unit

Solution: Option (a) is correct

Let radius be r unit and height be h unit

Volume of cylinder = curved surface area

$$\pi r^2 h = 2\pi rh$$

$$r = 2 \text{ units}$$

(v) P (–3, 2) is the mid – point of line segment AB as shown in the given figure. Find the co – ordinates of point A.

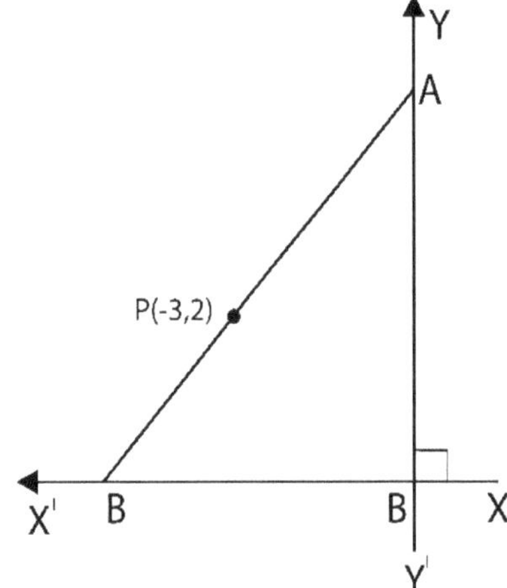

(a) (0, 4)

(b) (0, 5)

(c) (4, 0)

(d) (0, 3)

Solution: Option (a) is correct

Since A lies on y-axis, let co – ordinates of A = (0, y)

Since B lies on x – axis, let co – ordinates of A = $(x, 0)$

Using midpoint formula $\left(\frac{x_1 + x_2}{2}, \frac{y_1 + y_2}{2}\right)$

$$y = \frac{y_1 + y_2}{2}$$

$$2 = \frac{0 + y}{2}$$

$$y = 4$$

(vi) If the mean of 6, 7, $x, 8, y,$ 14 is 9, then:

(a) $x+\ y=21$

(b) $x+y=19$

(c) $x-y=19$

(d) $x-y=21$

Solution: Option (b) is correct

$$\text{mean} = \frac{\text{sum of observation}}{\text{number of observation}}$$

$$9 = \frac{6+7+x+8+y+14}{6}$$

$$x+y+35=54$$

$$x+y=19$$

(vii) The probability of winning a race by a boy is $\frac{x}{12}$ If the probability of not winning the race by the boy is $\frac{2}{3}$, then x =

(a) 2

(b) 3

(c) 4

(d) 6

Solution: Option (C) is correct

$$\text{The probability of winning the race P(E)} = \frac{x}{12}$$

$$\text{The probability of not winning the race P'(E)} = \frac{2}{3}$$

$$P(E)+P'(E)=1$$

$$\frac{x}{12}+\frac{2}{3}=1$$

$$x=4$$

(viii) The line $y=mx+8$ contains the point (–4, 4), calculate the value of m.

(a) 2

(b) –1

(c) 1

(d) –2

Solution: Option (c) is correct

Since the point (–4, 4) lie on the line y = mx + 8, so we can substitute the co – ordinates of the points in the equation

$$4 = -4m + 8$$

$$m = 1$$

(ix) If the mode of the data: 16, 15, 17, 16, 15, x, 19, 17, 14 is 15, then $x+2$ =?

(a) 15

(b) 16

(c) 17

(d) 19

Solution: Option (c) is correct

Since mode is 15 and frequency of 16 and 15 = 2

mode is the value of highest frequency. So, $x = 15$ and $x + 2 = 17$.

(x) Two cones A and B have their base radii in the ratio of 4:3 and their heights in the ratio 3:4. The ratio of volume of cone A to that of cone B is:

(a) 4:3

(b) 3:4

(c) 4:5

(d) 2:3

Solution: Option (a) is correct

Let radii of cones A and B are $4x$ and $3x$ respectively.

Let heights of cone A and B are $3y$ and $4y$ respectively.

$$\frac{\text{Volume of cone A}}{\text{Volume of cone B}} = \frac{\frac{1}{3}\pi(4x)^2 \times 3y}{\frac{1}{3}\pi(3x)^2 \times 4y} \qquad \left(\text{volume of cone} = \frac{1}{3}\pi r^2 h\right)$$

$$= \frac{16x^2 \times 3}{9x^2 \times 4} = \frac{4}{3}$$

Section B (30 Marks)

(Attempt any three questions from this section)

Question 2

(i) Find the volume of a circular cone whose height is 3 cm and slant length is 5 cm.

Solution:

Let radius of the cone is r cm

$$r^2 + h^2 = l^2$$

$$r^2 = 5^2 - 3^2$$

$$r^2 = 16 \Rightarrow r = \sqrt{16} = 4 \text{ cm}$$

$$\text{Volume of cone} = \frac{1}{3}\pi r^2 h$$

$$= \frac{1}{3} \times \frac{22}{7} \times 4 \times 4 \times 3$$

$$= 50.29 \text{ cm}^3$$ **Ans.**

(ii) Find the ratio in which the point (2, a) divides the join of (– 4, 3) and (6, 3). Hence find a.

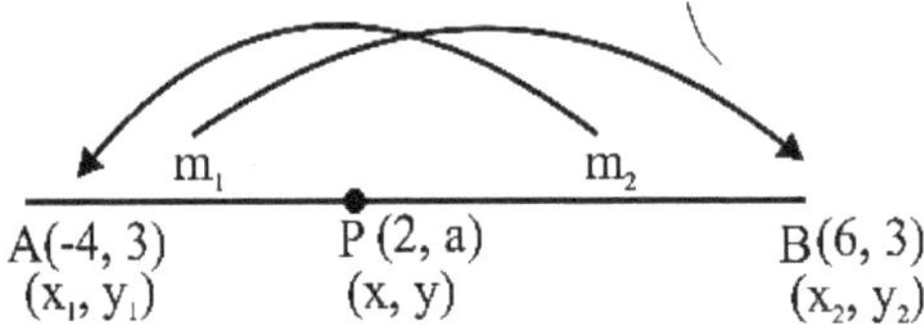

Solution:

Let A (–4, 3) as (x_1, y_1) and B (6, 3) as (x_2, y_2)

Let P(2, a) as (x, y) divide the join of A and B in the ratio $m_1 : m_1$.

Using section formula for x

$$x = \frac{m_1x_2 + m_2x_1}{m_1 + m_2}$$

$$2 = \frac{6m_1 - 4m_2}{m_1 + m_2}$$

$$6m_1 - 4m_2 = 2m_1 + 2m_2$$

$$6m_1 - 2m_1 = 2m_2 + 4m_2$$

$$4m_1 = 6m_2$$

$$\frac{m_1}{m_2} = \frac{6}{4} = \frac{3}{2}$$

$$m_1 : m_2 = 3 : 2$$ **Ans.**

Using section formula for y

$$y = \frac{m_1 y_2 + m_2 y_1}{m_1 + m_2}$$

$$a = \frac{3 \times 3 + 2 \times 3}{3 + 2}$$

$$= \frac{9 + 6}{5}$$

$$= \frac{15}{5} \Rightarrow 3$$

$$a = 3$$ **Ans.**

(iii) $\frac{1}{\tan A + \cot A} = \cos A \cdot \sin A$

Solution:

L.H.S.

$$= \frac{1}{\tan A + \cot A}$$

$$= 1 \div \left(\frac{\sin A}{\cos A} + \frac{\cos A}{\sin A}\right)$$

$$= 1 \div \left(\frac{\sin^2 A + \cos^2 A}{\cos A \,.\, \sin A}\right)$$

$$= 1 \div \left(\frac{1}{\cos A \,.\, \sin A}\right) \qquad [\sin^2 A + \cos^2 A = 1]$$

$$= 1 \times \frac{\cos A \,.\, \sin A}{1}$$

$$= \cos A \,.\, \sin A$$ R.H.S.

(i) Calculate the mean of the distribution, given below, using the short cut method:

Class intervals	1 - 5	6 - 10	11 - 15	16 – 20	21 - 25
Frequency	20	50	46	22	12

Solution:

class intervals	class marks (x)	d = x - A	frequency (f)	fd
1 – 5	3	-10	20	-200
6 – 10	8	-5	50	-250
11 - 15	13 = A	0	46	0
16 - 20	18	5	22	110
21 - 25	23	10	12	120
			$\Sigma f = 150$	$\Sigma f = -220$

Assumed mean A = 13

$$\text{Mean} = A + \frac{\Sigma fd}{\Sigma f}$$
$$= 13 + \frac{-220}{150}$$
$$= \frac{13}{1} - \frac{22}{15}$$
$$= \frac{195 - 22}{15}$$
$$= \frac{173}{15} = 11.53$$ **Ans.**

Question 3

(i) A letter is chosen from the word 'TRIANGLE'. What is the probability that it is not a vowel?

Solution:

Total number of letters in triangle = 8

Number of Not vowel (i.e. consonant) = 5

$$\text{P(not a vowel)} = \frac{\text{No. of consonant}}{\text{Total no. of letters}} = \frac{5}{8}$$ Ans.

(ii) In the adjoining figure, a circle is inscribed in the quadrilateral ABCD. Given that BC = 38 cm, QB = 27 cm and DC = 25 cm and that AD is perpendicular to DC, find the radius of the circle.

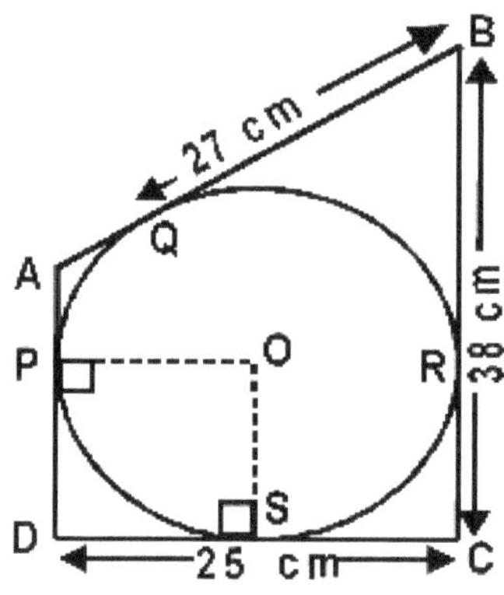

Solution:

It is given that AD is perpendicular to BC and OP ⊥ AD and OS ⊥ DC, OPDS is a rectangle.

OP = OS [radii]

So, OPDS is a square.

BQ = BR = 27 cm [tangents from an external point to a circle]

CR = CB – BR = 38 – 27 = 11 cm

SC = CR = 11 cm [tangents from an external point to a circle]

DS = DC – SC = 25 – 11 = 14 cm

DS = DP = OP = OS [sides are square]

So radius of circle OS = 14 cm **Ans.**

(iii) Point (3, 0) and (–1, 0) are invariant points under reflection in the line L_1; point (0,–3) and (0, 1) are invariant points on reflection on line L_2.

(a) Name or write equation for the lines L_1 and L_2

(b) Write down the images of point P (3, 4) and Q (–5, –2) on reflection on L_1. Name the images as P′ and Q′ respectively:

(c) Write down the images of P and Q on reflection in L_2. Name the images a P″ and Q″ respectively.

(d) State or describe a single Transformation that maps P′ into P″.

Solution:

(a) Since the points (3, 0) and (–1, 0) are invariant points under reflection in the line L_1, So the line L_1 is the x – axis.
The points (0, –3) and (0, 1) are invariants points under reflection in the line L_2, so the line L_2 is the y – axis.

(b) The images of point P(3, 4) and Q(–5, –2) in reflection on the line L_1 (i.e. x – axis) are P′(3, –4) and Q′(–5, 2) respectively.

(c) The images of point P(3, 4) and Q(–5, –2) in reflection on the line L_2 (i.e. y – axis) are P″ (–3, 4) and Q″ (5, –2) respectively.

(d) The single transformation that maps P′ onto P″ is the reflection in the origin. **Ans.**

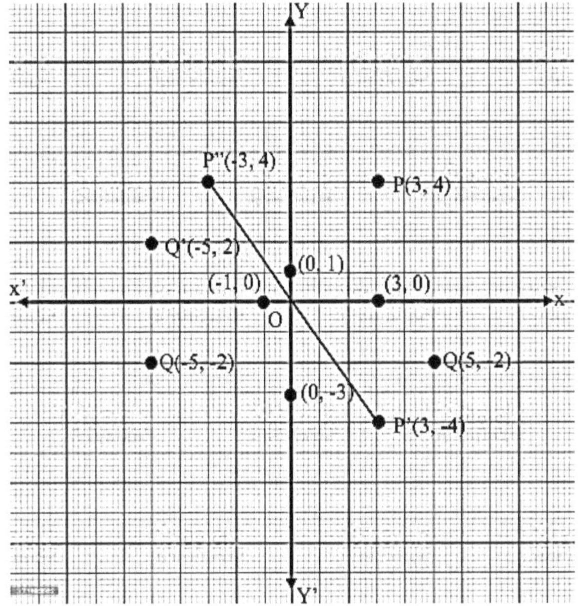

(iv) Draw a histogram and hence estimate the mode for the following frequency distribution.

Class	0 - 10	10 – 20	20 - 30	30 - 40	40 – 50	50 - 60
Frequency	2	8	10	5	4	3

Solution:

Scale on x – axis: 2 cm = 10 units
Scale on y – axis: 2 cm = 1 unit
Mode = 23 Modal class: 20 – 30

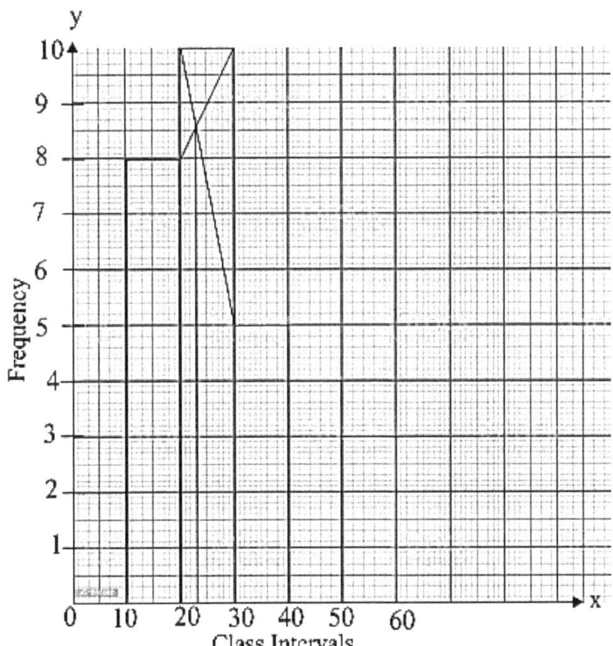

Question 4. $\frac{\sec A-1}{\sec A+1}=\frac{1-\cos A}{1+\cos A}$

Solution:

LHS.

$$= \frac{\sec A - 1}{\sec A + 1}$$

$$= \left(\frac{1}{\cos A} - 1\right) \div \left(\frac{1}{\cos A} + 1\right)$$

$$= \left(\frac{1 - \cos A}{\cos A}\right) \div \left(\frac{1 + \cos A}{\cos A}\right)$$

$$= \frac{1 - \cos A}{\cos A} \times \frac{\cos A}{1 + \cos A}$$

$$= \frac{1 - \cos A}{1 + \cos A} \quad \text{RHS.}$$

(ii) A box contains 15 cards numbered 1, 2, 3, …., 15 which are mixed thoroughly. A card is drawn from the box at random. Find the probability that the number on the card is

(a) Prime

(b) Divisible by 3 and 2 both.

Solution:

Total number of cards = 15

(a) Prime numbered cards = 2, 3, 5, 7, 11, 13

number of prime numbered cards = 6

$$P(\text{prime}) = \frac{\text{Number of prime numbered cards}}{\text{Total number of cards}} = \frac{6}{15} = \frac{2}{5}$$ **Ans.**

(b) Number which are divisible by 2 and 3 are those number which are divisible by 6 So among these numbers 6 and 12 are those numbers which are divisible by 2 and 3.

Number of cards which are divisible by 2 and 3 = 2

$$P(\text{divisible by 2 and 3}) = \frac{2}{15}$$ **Ans.**

(iii) In the diagram given alongside, AC is the diameter of the circle, with centre O. CD and BE are parallel. Angle

$\angle AOB = 80°$ and angle $\angle ACE = 10°$

Calculate: (a) ∠BEC (b) ∠BCD (c) ∠CED

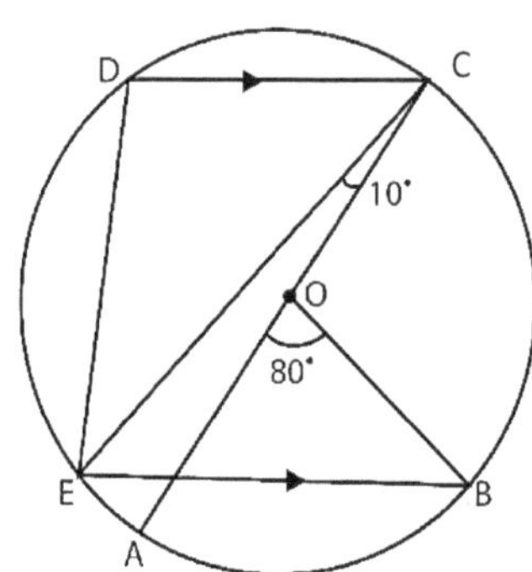

Solution:

(a) $\angle BOC = 180° - 80° = 100°$ [linear pair]

$\angle BEC = \frac{1}{2}\angle BOC$ [angle subtended by arc at the center is double of the angle at remaining part of the circle.]

∠BEC = 50° **Ans.**

(b) Join BC

$\angle BCD = \frac{1}{2}\angle BOA$ [angle subtended by arc at the center is double of the angle at remaining part of the circle.]

$\angle BCA = 40°$

So $\angle BCD = \angle BCA + \angle ACE + \angle ECD$

$= 40° + 10° + 50°$ [$\angle ECD = \angle BEC$, alternate angle]

$= 100°$ **Ans.**

(c) $\angle BCD + \angle BED = 180°$ [Opposite angles of cyclic quadrilateral are supplementary]

$100° + \angle BEC + \angle CED = 180°$

$100° + 50° + \angle CED = 180°$

$\angle CED = 180° - 150°$

$\angle CED = 30°$ **Ans.**

(iv) Find the equation of a straight line which cuts an intercept -2 units from y-axis and equally inclined with positive x – axis and negative y-axis.

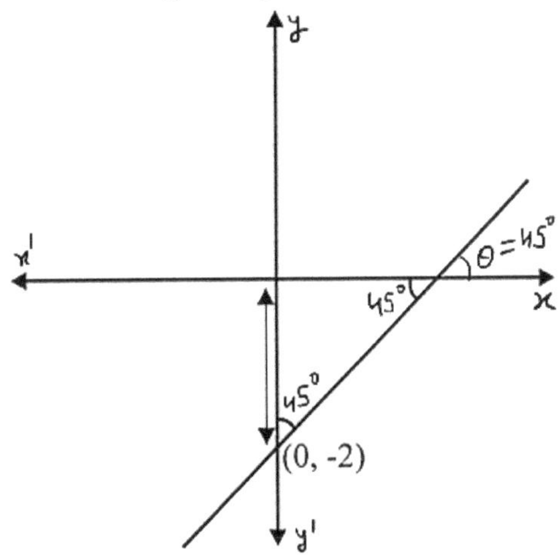

Solution:

Since line cuts equal intercept on positive x – axis and –ve y – axis

So, it looks like the given picture alongside. Since it is equally inclined to both the axes so inclination will be 45°.

slope m = tan θ = tan 45° = 1

y intercept is c = –2

So, equation of the line is $y = mx + c$

$y = 1x + (-2)$

$y = x - 2$

$x - y - 2 = 0$ **Ans.**

Question 5

(i) M is the mid–point of the line segment joining the points A (0, 4) and B (6, 0). M also divides the line segment OP in the ratio 1:3, where O is the origin. Find:

(a) Co – ordinates of M.

(b) Co – ordinates of P.

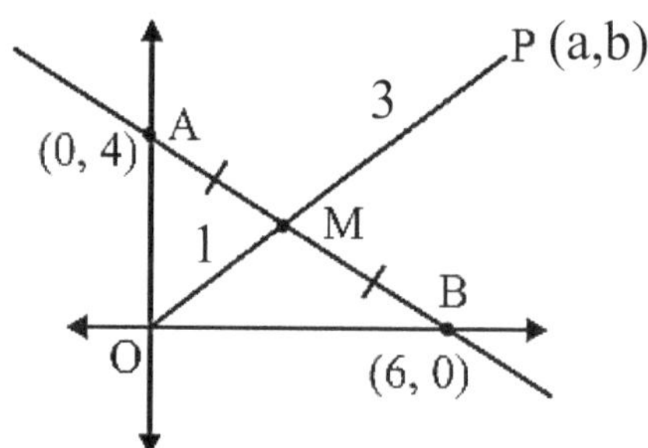

Solution:

(a) Let M = (x, y) are the co – ordinates of the midpoint of line segment joining AB.

A(0, 4) as (x_1, y_1) and B(6, 0) as (x_2, y_2)

Using midpoint formula $\left(\frac{x_1+x_2}{2}, \frac{y_1+y_2}{2}\right)$

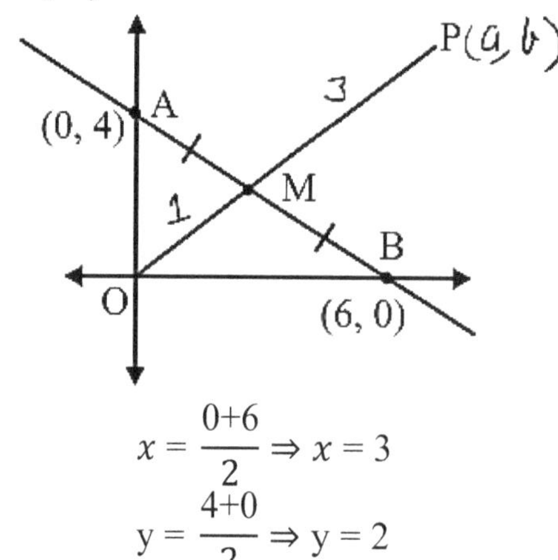

$$x = \frac{0+6}{2} \Rightarrow x = 3$$

$$y = \frac{4+0}{2} \Rightarrow y = 2$$

So co – ordinates of M = (3, 2) **Ans.**

(b) Let co – ordinates of P = (a, b)

OM: MP = 1:3 = $m_1 : m_2$

O(0, 0) as (x_1, y_1)) and P (a, b) as (x_2, y_1)

Using section formula M(3,2) = $\left(\frac{m_1x_2+m_2x_1}{m_1+m_2}, \frac{m_1y_2+m_2y_1}{m_1+m_2}\right)$

$$3 = \frac{1\times a + 3\times 0}{1+3}, \quad 2 = \frac{1\times b + 3\times 0}{1+3}$$

$$3 = \frac{a + 0}{4}, \quad 2 = \frac{b + 0}{4}$$

$$a = 12, \quad b = 8$$

So co – ordinates of P = (12, 8) **Ans.**

(ii) The mean of following numbers is 68. Find the value of 'x'.

45, 52, 60, x, 69, 70, 26, 81 and 94 Hence estimate the median.

Solution:

$$3 = \frac{1 \times a + 3 \times 0}{1+3} \qquad 2 = \frac{1 \times b + 3 \times 0}{1+3}$$

$$3 = \frac{a + 0}{4} \qquad 2 = \frac{b + 0}{4}$$

$$a = 12 \qquad b = 8$$

To find median arrange the numbers is ascending order

26, 45, 52, 60, 69, 70, 81, 94, 115

Number of terms n = 9 (odd)

$$\text{Median} = \left(\frac{n+1}{2}\right)^{th} term$$

$$= \left(\frac{9+1}{2}\right)^{th} term$$

$$= \text{5th term} = 69$$ **Ans.**

(iii) If the diameter of the cross-section of a wire is decreased by 5%, how much percent will the length is increased so that the volume remains the same.

Solution:

A wire can be treated like a cylinder.

Let original diameter of a wire is $2x$ units. So original radius R = x units

Original length of the wire is l units.

If diameter is decreased by 5% then new diameter = $2x - \frac{5}{100} \times 2x = 1.90\ x$ New radius $r = 1.90x/2 = 0.95x$ units

Since volume remain the same, let new length be L units

$$\pi r^2 L = \pi R^2 l$$

$$(0.95x)^2 L = x^2 l$$

$$L = \frac{x^2 l}{0.95 \times 0.95x^2}$$

$$L = \frac{10000l}{95 \times 95}$$

$$L = \frac{400}{361} l$$

So increased length = New length – original length

$$= \frac{400}{361} l - l = \frac{39l}{361}$$

$$\% \text{ increased} = \frac{\text{increased length}}{\text{original length}} \times 100$$

$$= \frac{\text{increased length}}{\text{original length}}$$

$$= \left(\frac{39l}{361} \div l\right) \times 100$$

$$= \left(\frac{39l}{361} \times \frac{1}{l}\right) \times 100$$

$$= 10\frac{290}{361}\%$$ **Ans.**

(iv) From a point on the ground 40 m away from the foot of a tower, the angle of elevation of the top of the tower is 30°. The angle of elevation to the top of a water tank (on the top of the tower) is 45°. Find the

(a) Height of the tower

(b) The depth of the tank

Solution:

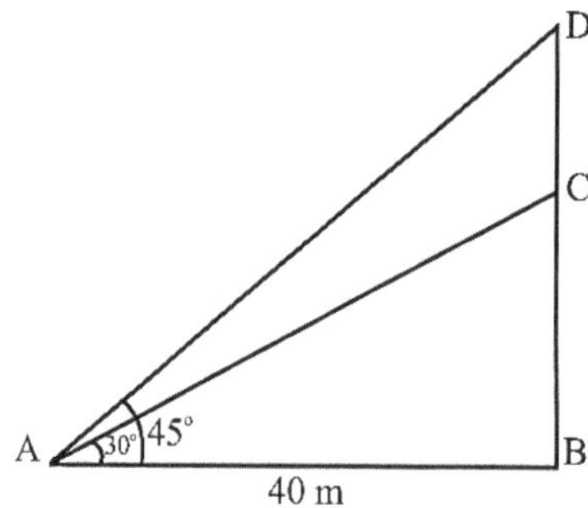

In the adjacent diagram C is the top of the tower and D is the water tank on the top of the tower.

(a) In $\triangle$ ABC tan 30° $= \frac{BC}{AB} \left(\tan\theta = \frac{\text{Perpendicular}}{\text{Base}}\right)$

$$\frac{1}{\sqrt{3}} = \frac{BC}{40}$$

$\sqrt{3}$ BC = 40

$$BC = \frac{40 \times \sqrt{3}}{\sqrt{3} \times \sqrt{3}} = \frac{40\sqrt{3}}{3} = \frac{40 \times 1.732}{3} = 23.09\ m = 23\ m$$

Height of the tower is 23 m **Ans.**

(b) In ΔABD = tan 45° $= \frac{BD}{AB}$

$$1 = \frac{BD}{40}$$

BD = 40 m

The depth of the tank is CD = BD – BC = 40 – 23 = 17 m **Ans.**

Question 6

(i) In the following figure O is the centre of the circle and AB is a tangent to it at point B. ∠BDC = 65°.

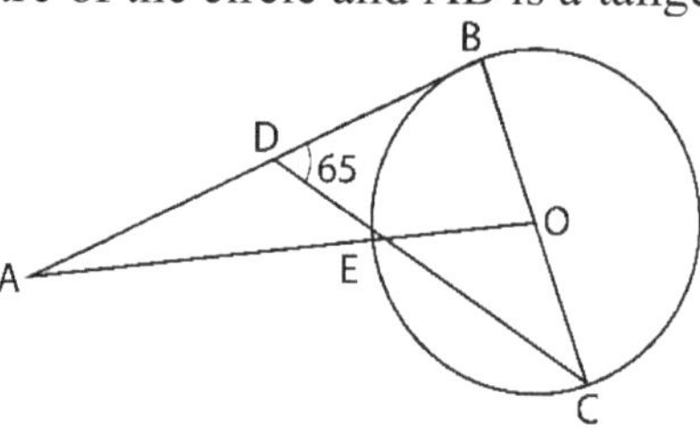

Find ∠BAO.

Solution:

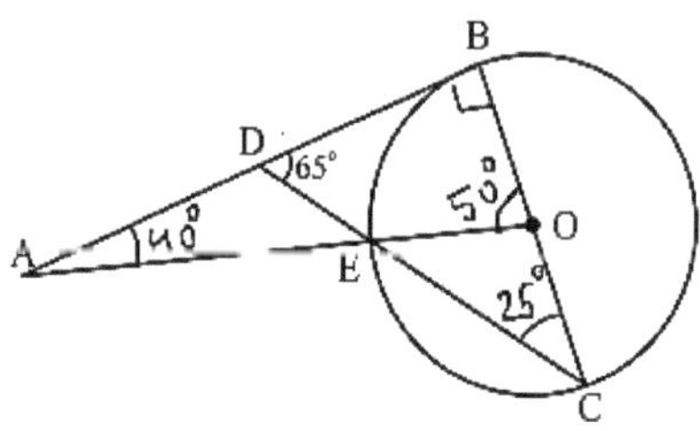

$\angle DCB = 90°$ [Line drawn from centre to the point of contact of tangent make 90°]

In ΔDBC

$$\angle DBC + \angle BDC + \angle DCB = 180^\circ$$ [angle sum prop. Of triangle]

$$90^\circ + 65^\circ + \angle DCB = 180^\circ$$

$$\angle DCB + 155^\circ = 180^\circ$$

$$\angle DCB = 180^\circ - 155^\circ = 25^\circ$$

$$\angle BOE = 2\angle BCE$$ [angle made be an arc at the center is double the angle at the remaining part of the circle]

[angle at the remaining part of the circle]

$$BOE = 2 \times 25^\circ = 50^\circ$$

Now In $\triangle ABO$

$\angle ABO + \angle AOB + \angle BAO = 180^\circ$ [angle sum prop. Of triangle]

$$90^\circ + 50^\circ + \angle BAO = 180^\circ$$

$$\angle BAO = 180^\circ - 140^\circ = 40^\circ$$

(ii) The line passing through (–4, –2) and (2, –3) is perpendicular to the line passing through (a, 5) and (2, –1), find a.

Solution:

Slope of the line passes through (–4, –2) and (2, –3) $m_1 = \frac{y_2-y_1}{x_2-x_1} = \frac{-3+2}{2+4} = -\frac{1}{6}$

Slope of the line passes through (a, 5) and (2, –1) $m_2 = \frac{y_2-y_1}{x_2-x_1} = \frac{-1-5}{2-a} = \frac{-6}{2-a}$

$m_1 \times m_2 = -1$ (Product of slopes of two perpendicular lines = –1)

$$-\frac{1}{6} \times \left(\frac{-6}{2-a}\right) = -1$$

$$\frac{1}{2-a} = -1$$

$$-2 + a = 1$$

$$a = 1 + 2$$

$$a = 3$$ **Ans.**

(iii) The angle of elevation of the top Q of a vertical tower PQ from a point X on the ground is 60°. At a point Y, 40 m vertically above X, the angle of elevation is 45°. Find the height of the tower PQ.

Solution:

In ΔQRY

$$\tan 45^\circ = \frac{QR}{YR} \quad \left(\tan\theta = \frac{\text{perpendicular}}{\text{base}}\right)$$

$$1 = \frac{QR}{YR}$$

$$QR = YR = x \text{ (let)} \qquad \text{(i)}$$

In ΔXPQ

$$\tan 60^\circ = \frac{PQ}{XP}$$

$$\sqrt{3} = \frac{PR + RQ}{YR}$$

$$\sqrt{3}x = 40 + x$$ [from (i) and PR = YX]

$$\sqrt{3}x - x = 40$$

$$x(\sqrt{3} - 1) = 40$$

$$x = \frac{40}{\sqrt{3}-1} \times \frac{\sqrt{3}+1}{\sqrt{3}+1}$$

$$= \frac{40(\sqrt{3}+1)}{2}$$

$$= 20 \times 2.732 = 54.64 \text{ m}$$

So, height of the tower PQ = PR + RQ

= 54.64 + 40 = 94.64 m **Ans.**

(iv) The following table shows the distribution of the heights of a group of factory workers:

Height (cm)	150 – 155	155 – 160	160 – 165	165 – 170	170 – 175	175 – 180	180 – 185
No. of workers	6	12	18	20	13	8	6

(a) Determine the cumulative frequencies.

(b) Draw the cumulative frequency curve on a graph paper. Use 2 cm = 5 cm height on one axis and 2 cm = 10 workers on the other.

(c) From your graph, write down the median height in cm.

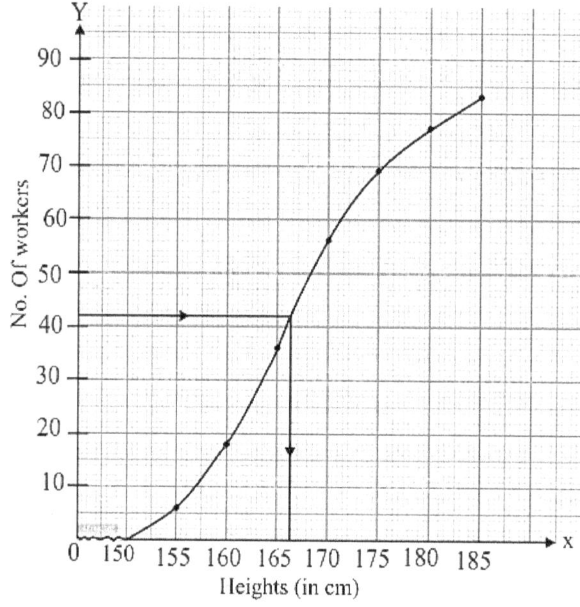

Solution:

(a) Following is the cumulative frequency distribution table from the given distribution:

Heights (in cm)	**No. of workers**	**cumulative frequency**
150 - 155	6	6
155 - 160	12	18
160 - 165	18	36
165 - 170	20	56
170 - 175	13	69
175 - 180	8	77
180 - 185	6	83
	N = 83	

(b) Take heights on x – axis and number of workers on y – axis according to the given scale. Plot (155, 6), (160, 18), (165, 36), (170, 56) , (175, 69) , (180, 77) , (185, 83) on the graph. Join each marked point from lower limit of first class to the upper limit of last class intervals. This is the required cumulative frequency curve.

(c) Sum of workers N = 83 (odd)

Median height = $\left(\frac{N+1}{2}\right)^{th}$ term

$= \left(\frac{83+1}{2}\right)^{th}$ term

= 42nd term

= 166.5 cm (approximately) **Ans.**

Unsolved Questions paper

Practice Paper – 1 (Unsolved)
(MATHEMATICS)
(Time alloted: One and a half hour)

Answer to this paper must be written on the paper provided separately.
You will not be allowed to write during the first 10 minutes.
This time is to spend in reading the question paper.

Omission of essential working well result in loss of marks.

The intended marks for questions or part of questions are given in the brackets [ ].

Section A (10 Marks)

(Attempt all question from this section)

Question 1

Choose the correct answers to the questions from the given options. (Do not copy the questions. Write the correct options only.) [10]

(i) A point P is reflected in the x – axis. Co – ordinate of its image is (–4, 5). Co – ordinates of P?

(a) (4, 5)
(b) (4, –5)
(c) (–4, –5)
(d) (–4, 5)

(ii) The radius of the base and the height of a right circular cone are 7 cm and 24 cm respectively. The slant height of the cone is:

(a) 26 cm
(b) 25 cm
(c) 23 cm
(d) 24 cm

(iii) Using the following figure, the value of x is:

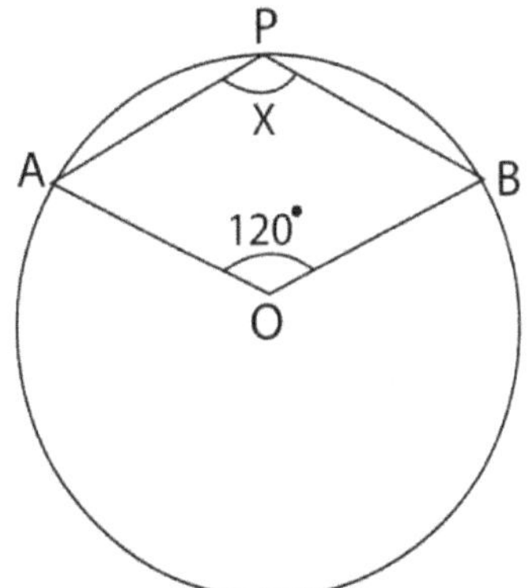

(a) 20°
(b) 60°
(c) 240°
(d) 110°

(iv) The value of $\sin^2 45 + \cos^2 45$ is:

(a) –1
(b) 1

(c) 0.5

(d) $\frac{2}{\sqrt{2}}$

(v) One end of the diameter of a circle is (– 2, 5). The co – ordinates of the other end of it, if the centre of the circle is (2, –1).

(a) (5, –7)

(b) (–7, 6)

(c) (6, –7)

(d) (6, 7)

(vi) If the mean of observations $x_1, x_2, x_3, \ldots\ldots, x_n$ is $\bar{x}$, then the mean of $x_1 + a_2x_2 + a_3 \ldots, x_n + a$ is:

(a) $a\overline{X}$

(b) $\overline{X} - a$

(c) $\overline{X} + a$

(d) $\frac{\bar{x}}{a}$

(vii) A number is selected at random from the numbers 3, 5, 5, 7, 7, 7, 9, 9, 9, 9. The probability that the selected number is their average is

(a) $\frac{1}{10}$

(b) $\frac{3}{10}$

(c) $\frac{7}{10}$

(d) $\frac{9}{10}$

(viii) A solid consists of a circular cylinder with an exact fitting right circular cone placed at the top. The height of the cone is 'h'. If the total volume of the solid is 3 times the volume of the cone, then the height of the circular cylinder is

(a) $2h$

(b) $\frac{2h}{3}$

(c) $\frac{3h}{2}$

(d) $4h$

(ix) Mode is:

(a) Least frequent value

(b) Middle most value

(c) Most frequent value

(d) None of these

(x) The slope of the line passing through (– 2, – 3) and (1, 2)

(a) $\frac{3}{5}$

(b) $\frac{5}{7}$

(c) $\frac{5}{3}$

(d) $\frac{5}{2}$

Section B (30 Marks)
(Attempt any three questions from this section)

Question 2

(i) Prove the identity: $1 + \frac{\cot^2 A}{1+\operatorname{cosec} A} = \operatorname{cosec} A$

(ii) The diameter of a garden roller is 1.4 m and it is 2 cm long. How much area will it cover in 5 revolutions?

(iii) Use graph paper for this. Write down the coordinates of the image of the point (3, –2) when:

(a) Reflected in the x-axis,

(b) Reflected in the y-axis,

(c) Reflected in the x-axis followed by reflection in the y-axis.

(d) Reflected in the origin.

(iv) Find the image of the point (1, 2) in the line $x - 2y - 7 = 0$.

Question 3

(i) Find the slope and y-intercept of the following line $\frac{x}{3} + \frac{y}{4} = 1$.

(ii) A box contains 15 cards numbered 1, 2, 3, …., 15 which are mixed thoroughly. A card is drawn from the box at random. Find the probability that the number on the card is:

(a) Divisible by 3 or 2

(b) A perfect square numbers

(iii) In the figure given below, O is the centre of the circle and SP is a tangent. If ∠SRT = 65°, find the value of x, y and z.

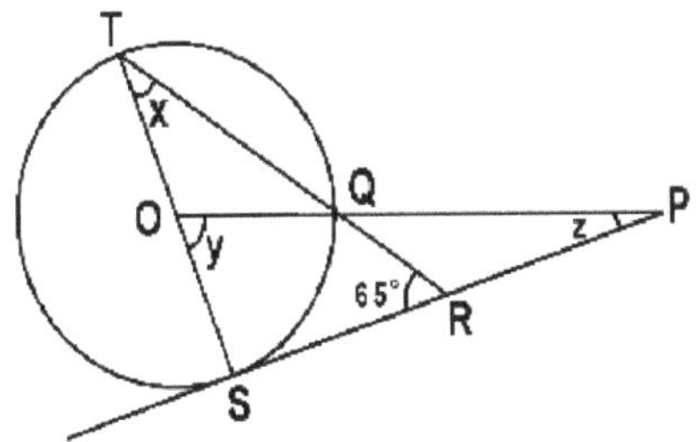

(iv) Find the mode of the following distribution by drawing a histogram:

Daily wages	31-36	37-42	43-48	49-54	55-60	61-66
No. of workers	6	12	20	15	9	4

Question 4

(i) Calculate the ratio in which the line joining A (– 4, 2) and B (3, 6) is divided by point P (x, 3). Also find x:

(ii) In the given figure, the angle A of the triangle ABC is a right angle. The circle on AC as diameter cuts BC at D. If BD = 9 cm, and DC = 7 cm, calculate the length of AB.

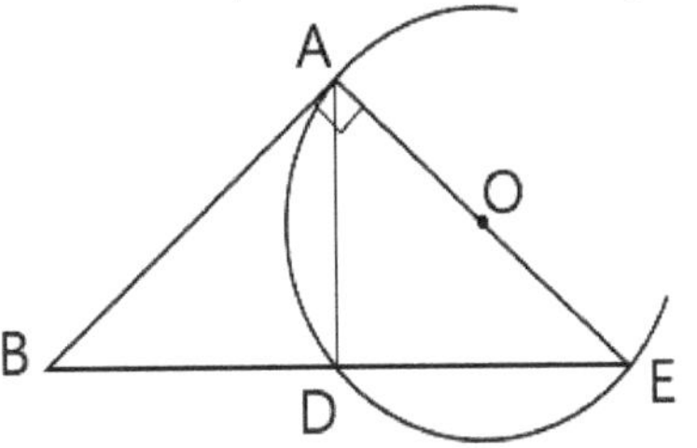

(iii) The volume of a conical tent is 1232 m^3 and the area of the bare floor is 154 m^2. Calculate the:

(a) radius of the floor.

(b) height of the tent.

(c) length of the canvas required to cover this conical tent if its width is 2m.

(iv) From the top of a tower, a man finds that the angle of depression of a car on the ground is 30°. If the car is at a distance 40 m away from the tower, find the height of the tower in nearest meter.

Question 5

(i) A die is thrown once. What is the probability that the?

(a) Number is even?

(b) Number is greater than 2?

(ii) The mean of the following data is 16. Calculate the value of f.

Marks	5	10	15	20	25
No. of Students	3	7	f	9	6

(iii) Write down the equation of a line parallel to the line $3x + 2y = 8$ and passing through the point (0, 1).

(iv) Prove the identity: $\frac{\sin^3 A - \cos^3 A}{\sin A - \cos A} - \sin A \cdot \cos A = 1$

Question 6

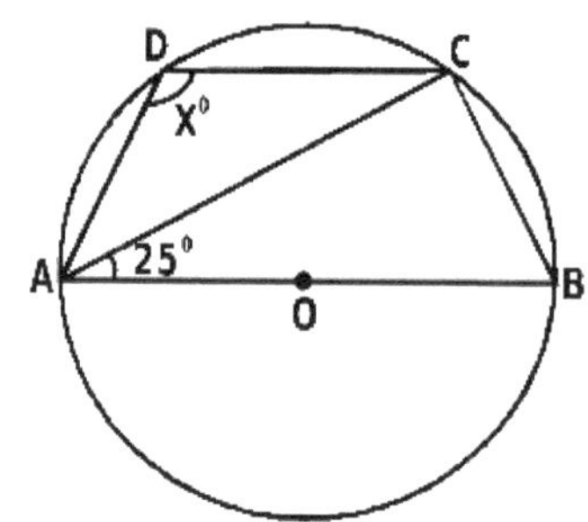

(i) In the following figures find the values of x:

(ii) The slope of a line joining P(6, k) and Q (1–3k, 3) is $\frac{1}{2}$. Find.

(a) k

(b) Midpoint of PQ, using the value of 'k' found in (i).

(iii) The angle of elevation of a cloud from a point h meter above a lake is 30° and the angle of depression of the reflection of cloud in the lake is 45°. If the height of the cloud be 200 m. find h.

(iv) Attempt this question on a graph paper. The table below shows the distribution of marks gained by a group of students in an examination:

Marks less than	10	20	30	40	50	60	70	80	90	100
No.of Students	5	9	16	22	26	18	11	6	4	3

Using a scale of 2 cm to represent 10 marks and 2 cm to represent 50 students, plot these values and draw a smooth curve through the points. Estimate from the graph:

Practice Paper – 2 (Unsolved)
(MATHEMATICS)
(Time alloted: One and a half hour)

Answer to this paper must be written on the paper provided separately.
You will not be allowed to write during the first 10 minutes.
This time is to spend in reading the question paper.

Omission of essential working well result in loss of marks.
The intended marks for questions or part of questions are given in the brackets [ ].

Section A (10 Marks)
(Attempt all question from this section)

Question 1

Choose the correct answers to the questions from the given options. (Do not copy the questions. Write the correct options only.) [10]

(i) The point A (–3, 2) is reflected in the x – axis to the point A′. Point A′ is then reflected in the origin to point A". Co – ordinates of A".

(a) (3, 2)
(b) (3, –2)
(c) (–3, –2)
(d) (2, –3)

(ii) Which of the following cannot be the probability of occurrence of an event?

(a) 0.2
(b) 0.4
(c) 0.8
(d) 1.7

(iii) Point A (–5, x), B (–2, 7) and C (1, –3) are collinear (i.e. lie on the same straight line) such that AB = BC. Calculate the value of x.

(a) 16
(b) 17
(c) 15
(d) –17

(iv) In the given figure the value of angle ∠BCD is:

(a) 95°
(b) 75°
(c) 210°
(d) 52.5°

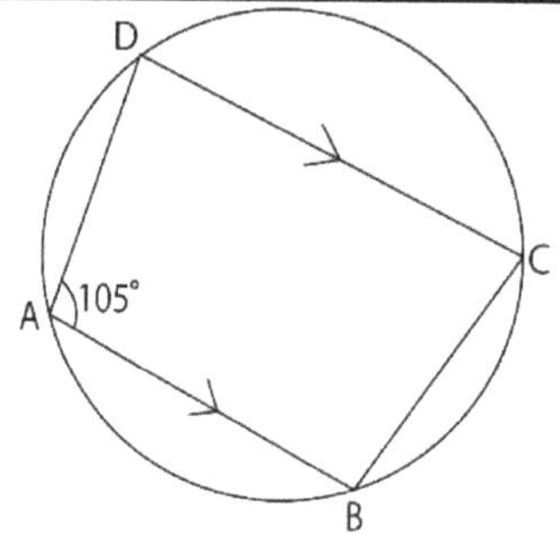

(v) The curved surface area of a right circular cone of height 15 cm and base diameter 16 cm is:
(a) $60\pi cm^2$
(b) $68\pi cm^2$
(c) $120\pi cm^2$
(d) $136\pi cm^2$

(vi) If tan A + cot A = 2, (A is acute) the value of $\tan^2 A + \cot^2 A$ is
(a) 0
(b) 1
(c) 2
(d) 4

(vii) The line passing through (0, 2) and (–3, –1) is parallel to the line passing through (–1, 5) and (4, a). The value of a.
(a) –10
(b) 10
(c) 9
(d) 11

(viii) The mean of 20 numbers is 13. The new mean if each observation is increased by 5, is:
(a) 13
(b) 18
(c) 65
(d) 8

(ix) A semi – circular sheet of metal of radius 14 cm is folded so that the two bounding radii are joined together to form a cone. The radius of the cone is
(a) 7 cm
(b) 14 cm
(c) 3.5 cm
(d) 44 cm

(x) Find the modal class of the following distribution:

Class intervals	10 – 20	20 – 30	30 – 40	40 – 50	50 – 60
Frequency	12	10	25	15	8

(a) 20 – 30
(b) 30 – 40
(c) 40 – 50
(d) 10 – 20

Section B (30 Marks)
(Attempt any three questions from this section)

Question 2

(i) The point (k, 3), (2, -4) and $(-k + 1, -2)$ are collinear. Find k.

(ii) Find the value of x.

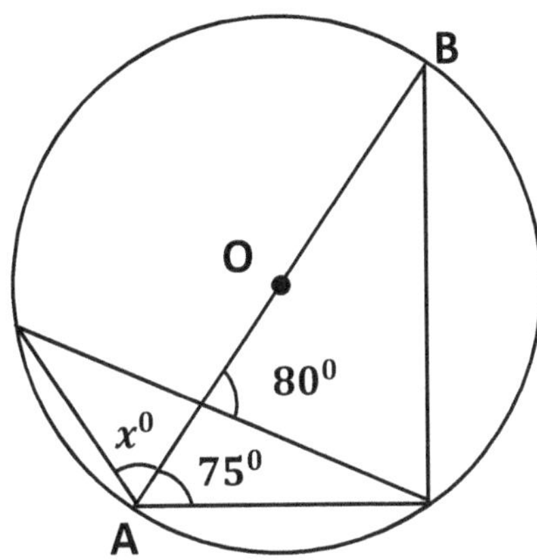

(iii) Prove the identity: $(\text{cosec}^2 A - 1)(\sec A + 1)(\sec A - 1) = 1$

(iv) The data on the number of patients attending a hospital in the morning are given below. Find the average (mean) number of patients attending the hospital in a month by using the shortcut method.

No. of patients	10 – 20	20 - 30	30 – 40	40 – 50	50 – 60	60 – 70
No. of days	5	2	7	9	2	5

Take the assumed mean as 45. Give your answer correct to 2 decimal places.

Question 3

(i) In what ratio is the line joining P (5, 3) and Q (-5, 3) divided by the y – axis? Also, find the co – ordinates of point of intersection.

(ii) A cylinder has a diameter of 14 cm and the area of its curved surface is 220 sq cm. Find the volume of the cylinder.

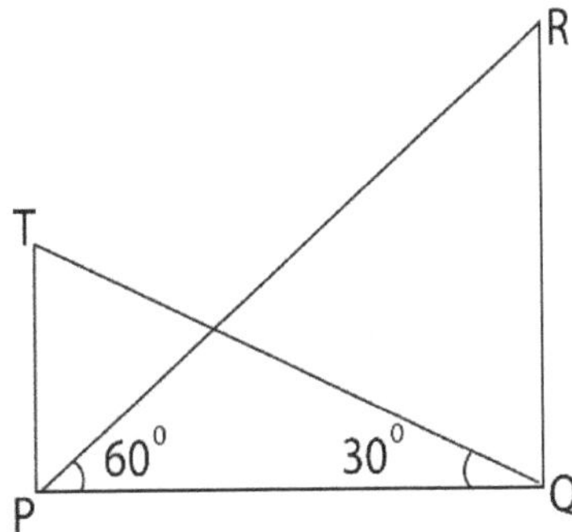

(iii) The angle of elevation from a point P of the top of a tower QR, 50m high is 60° and that of the tower PT from a point Q is 30°. Find the height of the tower PT, correct to the nearest meter.

(iv) The marks obtained by 120 students in a test are given below:

Marks Obtained	0 – 10	10 – 20	20 – 30	30 – 40	40 – 50	50 – 60	60 – 70	70 – 80	80 – 90	90 – 100
No of students	5	9	16	22	26	18	11	6	4	3

Draw an ogive for the given distribution on a graph sheet. Use a suitable scale for your ogive. Use the ogive to estimate the following:

(a) The median
(b) Lower Quartile
(c) The number of students who did not pass the test if the pass percentage was 40.

Question 4

(i) Prove the identity: $\sqrt{\sec^2 A + \text{cosec}^2 A} = \tan A + \cot A$
(ii) In the figure, if PA = 16 cm, PC = 10 cm and PD = 8 cm, find AB.

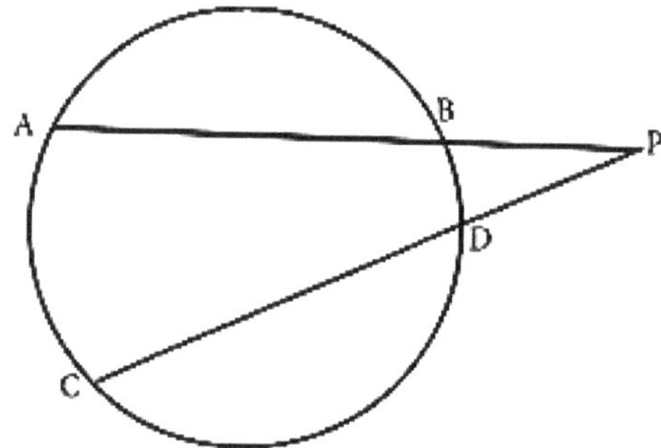

(iii) If the image of the point (2, 1) with respect to a line l be (5, 2). Find:
(a) The slope of the line l.
(b) The equation of the line l.
(iv) Draw the histogram for the given data, using a graph paper:

Weekly wages (in')	3000 – 4000	4000– 5000	5000–8000	6000–7000	7000–8000	8000–9000	9000–10000
No. of people	4	9	18	6	7	2	4

Question 5

(i) Two coins are tossed once. Find the probability of getting:
(a) head
(b) at least 1 tail.

(ii) The mean of following numbers is 68. Find the value of 'x'.
45, 52, 60, x, 69, 70, 26, 81 and 94. Hence estimate the median.
(iii) A circus tent is in the shape of a cylinder surmounted by a right cone. The height of the cylindrical part is 11 meters. The base of the tent has a diameter of 24 meters and the total height of the tent is 16 meters. Find the area of the canvas required to make the tent.
(iv) Use a graph paper for this question (Take 2 cm = 1 unit along both x and y – axis):
(a) The point P (2, –4) is reflected about the line $x = 0$ to get the image Q. Find the co-ordinates of Q.
(b) Point Q is reflected about the line y = 0 to get the image R. Find the co-ordinates of R.
(c) Name the figure PQR.
(d) Find the area of figure PQR.

Question 6

(i) A die has 6 faces marked by the given numbers as shown below:

1	2	3	-1	-2	-3

The die is thrown once. What is the probability of getting?
(a) An integer greater than –3.
(b) The smallest integer.

(ii) The co-ordinates of A and B are (–3, a) and (1, a+4). The mid-point of AB is (–1, 1). Find the value of a.

(iii) In the figure given, O is the centre of the circle. $\angle DAE = 70°$. Find giving suitable reasons, the measure of:

(a) $\angle BCD$
(b) $\angle BOD$
(c) $\angle OBD$

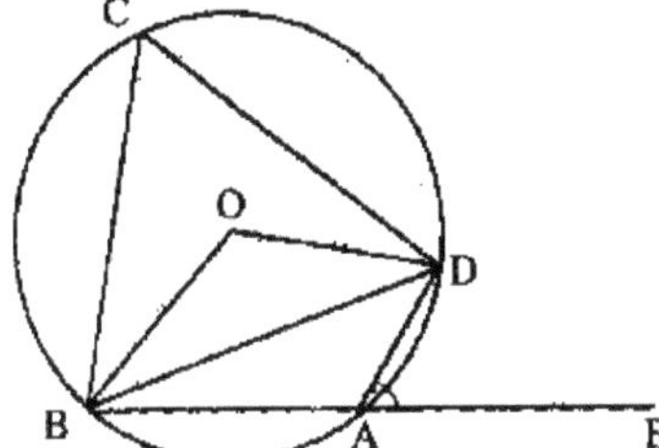

(iv) The angle of elevation of the top of a tower from two points P and Q at distances a and b respectively, from the base and in the same straight line with it, are complementary. Prove that the height of the tower is $\sqrt{ab}$.

Practice Paper – 3 (Unsolved)
(MATHEMATICS)
(Time alloted: One and a half hour)

Answer to this paper must be written on the paper provided separately.
You will not be allowed to write during the first 10 minutes.
This time is to spend in reading the question paper.

Omission of essential working well result in loss of marks.

The intended marks for questions or part of questions are given in the brackets [ ].

Section A (10 Marks)

(Attempt **all** question from this section)

Question 1

Choose the correct answers to the questions from the given options. (Do not copy the questions. Write the correct options only.) [10]

(i) Point (3, 0) is invariant point under reflection in the line l. Name the line l.

(a) $y - axis$
(b) $x - axis$
(c) $y = 3$
(d) $x = 3$

(ii) The height of the largest cone that can be carved out from a cylinder whose curved surface area is 4400 cm^2 and the circumference of its base is 110 cm.

(a) 44 cm
(b) 40 cm
(c) 35 cm
(d) 17.5 cm

(iii) Find the length of the tangent drawn to a circle of radius 3 cm, from a point distant 5 cm from the centre.

(a) 3 cm
(b) 4 cm
(c) 6 cm
(d) 2.5 cm

(iv) Calculate the co – ordinates of the centroid of the triangle ABC, if A = (7, -2), B = (0, 1) and C = (-1, 4).

(a) (2, 2)
(b) (1, 2)
(c) (2, 3)
(d) (2, 1)

(v) If the probability of an event is 0.65, then the probability of not happening of that event is:

(a) 0.35
(b) 0.035
(c) 1.25
(d) 3

(vi) The value of $(\sin A + \cos A)^2 + (\sin A - \cos A)^2$ is:
(a) 2
(b) 1
(c) 4
(d) –2

(vii) Which measure of central tendency can be calculated using the following picture:

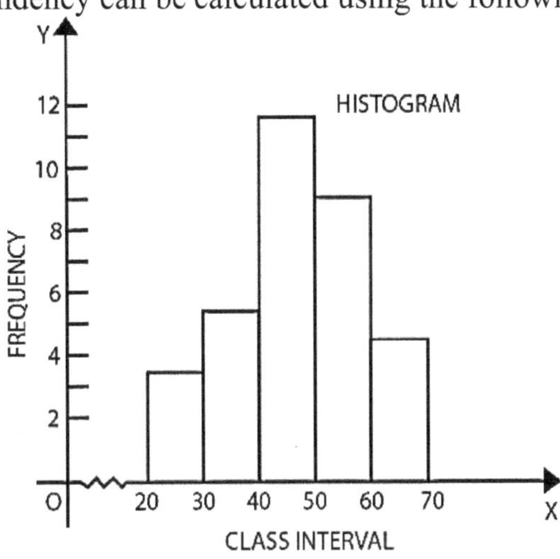

(a) median
(b) mode
(c) mean
(d) None

(viii) If the radius of a right circular cone is 4 cm and height of cone is 3 cm, then the curved surface area is:
(a) 16π
(b) 12π
(c) 20π
(d) 4π

(ix) The line passing through (–4, –2) and (2, –3) is perpendicular to the line passing through (a, 5) and (2, –1). The value of a.
(a) –3
(b) 2
(c) 3
(d) –2

(x) If the median of the data 6, 7, $x - 2, x$, 17, 20 written in ascending order is 16, then x =?
(a) 15
(b) 16
(c) 17
(d) 18

Section B (30 Marks)
(Attempt any three questions from this section)

Question 2

(i) Cards bearing numbers 2, 4, 6, 8, 10, 12, 14, 16, 18 and 20 are kept in a bag. A card is drawn at random from the bag. Find the probability of getting a card which is:

(a) A prime number.

(b) A number that is a multiple of 6.

(ii) Find the points of trisection of the line segment joining the points (–4, 2) and (3, 7).

(iii) In the figure, $\angle DBC = 58°$ BD is a diameter of the circle.

Calculate: (i) $\angle BDC$ (ii) $\angle BEC$ (iii) $\angle BAC$

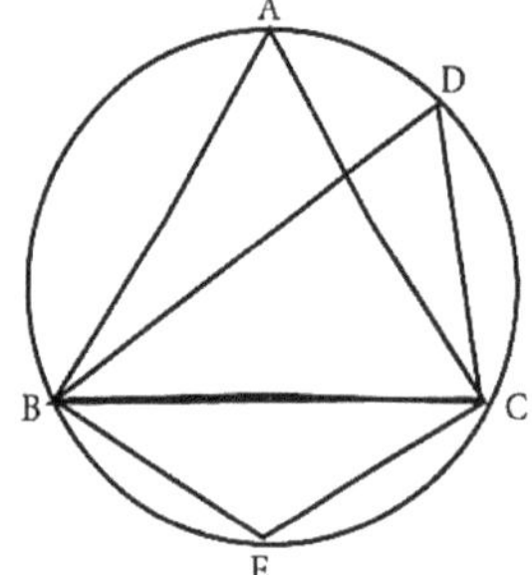

(iv) Find the following frequency distribution, draw, histogram. Hence calculate the mode:

Class Interval	0 – 5	5 – 10	10 – 15	15 – 20	20 – 25	25 – 30
Frequency	2	7	18	10	8	5

Question 3

(i) In the figure given below, diameter AB and chord CD of a circle meet at P. PT is a tangent to the circle at T. CD = 7.8 cm, PD = 5 cm, PB = 4 cm. Find:

(a) AB (b) the length of tangent PT.

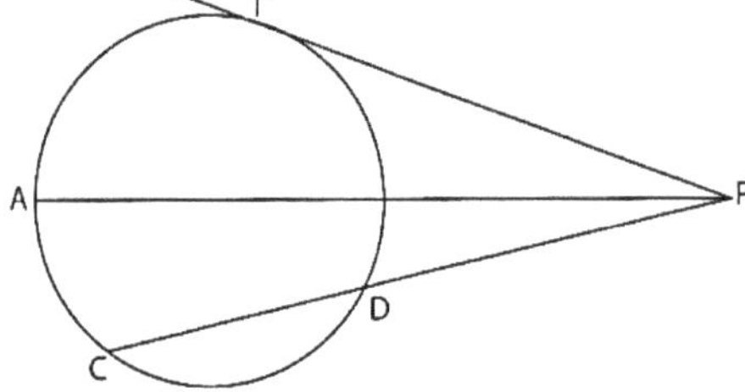

(ii) Three consecutive vertices of a parallelogram ABCD are A (10, –6), B (2, –6) and C (–4, –2). Find the fourth vertex D.

(iii) An exhibition tent is in the form of a cylinder surmounted by a cone. The height of the tent above the ground is 85 m and the height of the cylindrical part is 50 m. If the diameter of the base is 168 m, find the quantity of canvas required to make the tent. Allow 20% extra for folds and for stitching. Give your answer to the nearest m^2.

(iv) From the top of a cliff, the angle of depression of the top and bottom of a tower are observed to be 45° and 60° respectively. If the height of the tower is 20 m. Find:

(a) The height of the cliff.

(b) The distance between the cliff and the tower.

Question 4

(i) There are 25 discs numbered 1 to 25. They are put in a closed box and shake thoroughly. A disc is drawn at random from the box. Find the probability that the number on the disc is-

(a) divisible by 2 and 3 both.

(b) a number less than 16.

(ii) In the given circle with centre O, $\angle ABC = 100°, \angle ACD = 40°$, and CT is a tangent to the circle at C. Find $\angle ADC$ and $\angle DCT$.

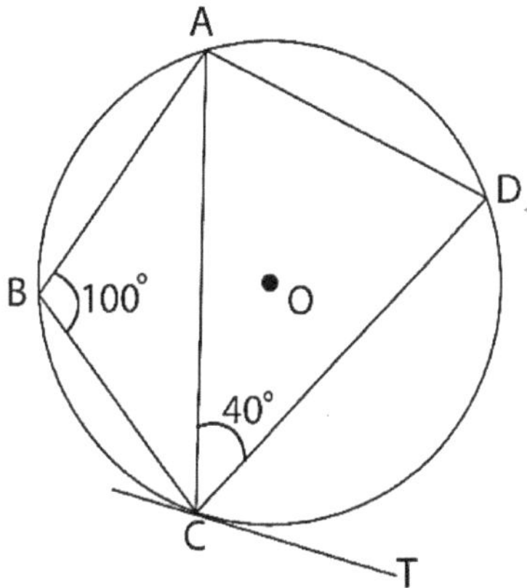

(iii) Prove the identity: $\frac{\sin A}{1+\cot A} - \frac{\cos A}{1+\tan A} = \sin A - \cos A$

(iv) A point P is reflected to P' in the $x - axis$. The co-ordinates of its image are (2,–3) find

(a) The co-ordinates of P.

(b) The co-ordinates of the image P under reflection in the $y - axis$.

(c) The co-ordinates of the image Q' of the point Q (1, 2) in the line PP'.

Question 5

(i) Find the mean and median of the following distribution: 8, 10, 7, 6, 10, 11, 6, 13, 10

(ii) A (5, 4), B (-3, -2) and C (1, -8) are the vertices of a triangle ABC. Find:

(a) The slope of AB

(b) The slope of the altitude of AB.

(iii) The angle of elevation of a jet plane from a point A on the ground is 60°. After flight of 15 seconds, the angle of elevation changes to 30°. If the jet plane is flying at a constant height of 1500 m, find the speed of the jet plane.

(iv) The marks obtained by 200 students in an examination are given below:

Marks Obtained	0 – 10	10 – 20	20 – 30	30 – 40	40 – 50	50 – 60	60 – 70	70 – 80	80 – 90	90 – 100
No of students	5	10	11	20	27	38	40	29	14	6

Using a graph paper, draw an ogive for the above distribution. Use your ogive to estimate:

(a) The median

(b) the lower quartile

(c) The number of students who obtained more than 80% marks in the examination and

(d) the number of students who did not pass, if the pass percentage was 35.

Question 6

(i) Prove the identity: $\sin A(1 + \tan A) + \cos A(1 + \cot A) = \sec A + \text{cosec } A$

(ii) A conical tent requires 264 m^2 of canvas. If the slant height is 12 m, find the vertical height.

(iii) A line AB meets x – axis at A and y – axis at B. P (4, –1) divides AB in the ratio 1: 2. Find:

(a) The co – ordinates of A and B.

(b) The equation of the line through P and perpendicular to AB.

(iv) The data on the number of patients attending a hospital in the morning are given below. Find the average (mean) number of patients attending the hospital in a month by using the shortcut method.

No. of patients	10 – 20	20 – 30	30 – 40	40 – 50	50 – 60	60 – 70
No. of days	5	2	7	9	2	5

Take the assumed mean as 45. Give your answer correct to 2 decimal places.

Practice Paper – 4 (Unsolved)
(MATHEMATICS)
(Time alloted: One and a half hour)

Answer to this paper must be written on the paper provided separately.
You will not be allowed to write during the first 10 minutes.
This time is to spend in reading the question paper.

Omission of essential working well result in loss of marks.
The intended marks for questions or part of questions are given in the brackets [ ].

Section A (10 Marks)
(Attempt all question from this section)

Question 1

Choose the correct answers to the questions from the given options. (Do not copy the questions. Write the correct options only.) [10]

(i) The point P (4, 1) is reflected in the line $y = 3$ to become P′. Find the co – ordinates of P′.

(a) (– 4, 5)
(b) (4, –1)
(c) (4, –5)
(d) (4, 5)

(ii) In the figure given, O is the centre of the circle. AB is a diameter, TPT' is a tangent to the circle at P. If ∠BPT = 30°. The value of angle ∠BAP is:

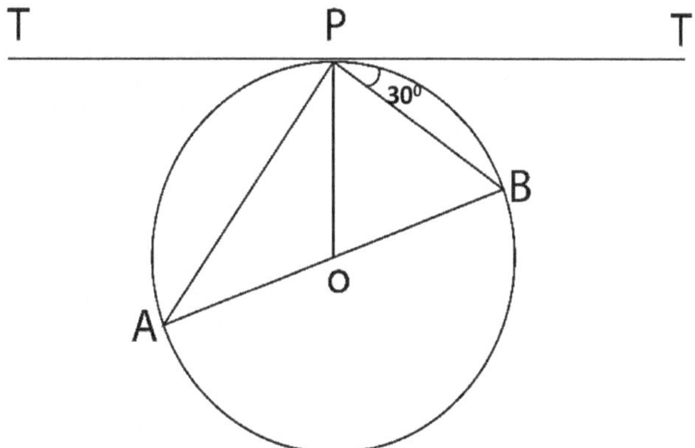

(a) 30°
(b) 60°
(c) 15°
(d) 45°

(iii) The co – ordinates of the centroid of a triangle PQR are (2, – 5). If Q = (– 6, 5) and R = (11, 8); calculate the co – ordinates of vertex P.

(a) (1, –28)
(b) (1, 28)
(c) (2, –28)
(d) (–1, 28)

(iv) The radius of the largest cylinder formed when a rectangular piece of paper 22 cm by 15 cm is rolled along its longer side:

(a) 4.5 cm
(b) 7.5 cm
(c) 3.5 cm
(d) 7 cm

(v) The value of sec A (1 – sin A) (sec A + tan A) is:

(a) 2
(b) 1
(c) –1
(d) –2

(vi) The arithmetic mean, and mode of a data are 24 and 12 respectively, then its median is:

(a) 25
(b) 18
(c) 20
(d) 22

(vii) The points (–3, 2), (2, –1) and (a, 4) are collinear. The value of a.

(a) $-5\frac{1}{3}$
(b) $6\frac{1}{3}$
(c) $-3\frac{1}{3}$
(d) $-6\frac{1}{3}$

(viii) Find the mode of the following items 0, 1, 6, 7, 2, 3, 7, 6, 6, 2, 6, 0, 5, 6, 0

(a) 6
(b) 2
(c) 0
(d) 7

(ix) The probability of getting a bad egg from a lot of 400 eggs is 0.035. The number of bad eggs in the lot is:

(a) 7
(b) 14
(c) 21
(d) 28

(x) The diameters of the two cones are equal. If their slant heights are in the ratio 5 : 4, find the ratio of their curved surface area.

(a) 4: 5
(b) 16: 25
(c) 5: 4
(d) 3: 4

Section B (30 Marks)

(Attempt any three questions from this section)

Question 2

(i) Each of the letter of the word 'AUTHORIZES' is written on identical circular disks and put in a bag. They are well shuffled. If a disk is drawn at random from the bag, what is the probability that the letter is:

(a) A vowel

(b) One of the first 9 letters of English alphabet which appears in the given word.

(ii) The line joining the points A (4, –5) and B (4, 5) is divided by the point P such that $\frac{AP}{AP} = \frac{4}{5}$, find the coordinates of P.

(iii) In the figure given below, AD is a diameter. O is the centre of the circle. AD is parallel to BC and ∠CBD = 32°. Find (I) ∠OBD (ii) ∠AOB (iii) ∠BED.

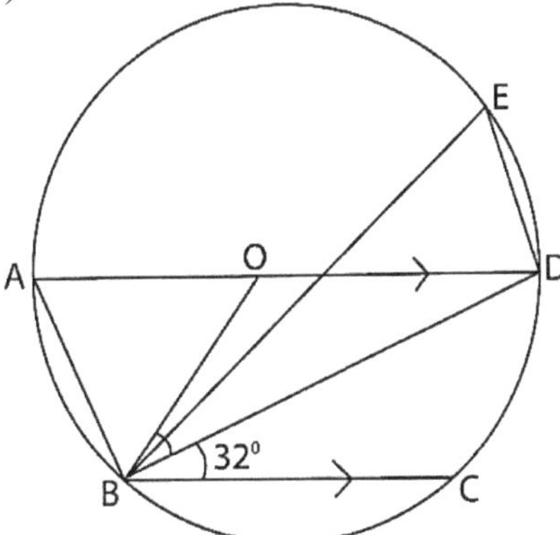

(iv) The daily profits in Rupees of 100 shops in a department store are distributed as follows:

Profit	0 – 100	100 – 200	200 – 300	300 – 400	400 – 500	500 – 60
No. of shops	12	18	27	20	17	6

Draw a histogram of the data given above on graph paper and estimate the mode.

Question 3

(i) The volume of a cone is the same as that of a cylinder whose height is 9 cm and diameter 40 cm. Find the radius of the base of cone if its height is 108 cm. (take $\pi = \frac{22}{7}$)

(ii) Find the unknown length x in each of the following figures:

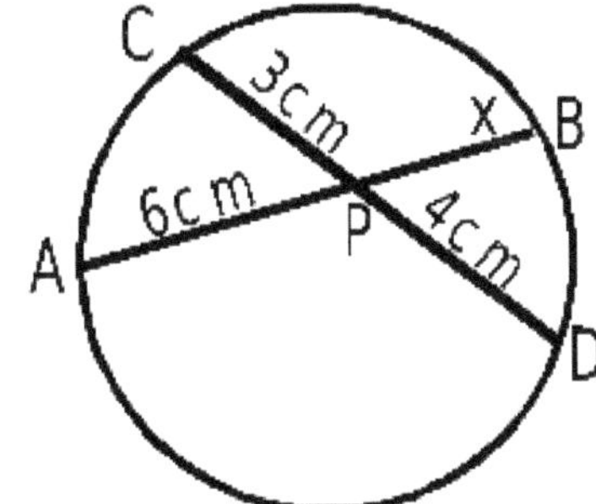

(iii) Use graph paper for this question. Take 1 cm = 1 unit on both x and y axis.

(a) Plot the following points on your graph sheets; A (-4, 0), B (-3, 2), C (0, 4), D (4, 1) and E (7, 3).

(b) Reflect the point B, C, D, E on x – axis and name them as B′, C′, D′ and E′ respectively.

(c) Join the points A, B, C, D, E, E′, D′, C′, B′ and A in order.

(d) Name the closed figure formed.

(iv) From the top of a cliff 150 m high, the angles of depression of two boats are 60° and 30°. Find the distance between the boats, if the boats are

(a) on the same side of the cliff
(b) on the opposite sides of the cliff

Question 4

(i) Prove the identity: $\tan^4 A + \tan^2 A = \sec^4 A - \sec^2 A$

(ii) A card is drawn from a well-shuffled pack of 52 cards. Find the probability of getting:
(a) A king of red color
(b) Non-face card of black color.

(iii) Write down the equation of the line whose gradient is $\frac{3}{2}$ and which passes through P, where P divides the line segment joining A (–2, 6) and B (3, – 4) in the ratio 2 : 3.

(iv) Draw an ogive of the following distribution:

Class interval	30 – 39	40 – 49	50 – 59	60 – 69	70 – 79	80 – 89	90 – 99
Frequency	20	35	15	40	5	20	10

Use the ogive to estimate the following:
(a) the median
(b) the upper quartile
(c) the number of variants below 55

Question 5

(i) Find the value of p, if the mean of the following distribution is 20.

x	15	17	19	20 + p	23
f	2	3	4	5p	6

(ii) The centre O, of a circle has the co-ordinates (4, 5) and one point on the circumference is (8, 10). Find the co-ordinates of the other end of the diameter of the circle through this point.

(iii) From a solid wooden cylinder of height 28 cm and diameter 6 cm, two conical cavities are hollowed out. The diameter of the cones are also of 6 cm and height 10.5 cm. Taking $\pi = \frac{22}{7}$), find the volume of remaining solid.

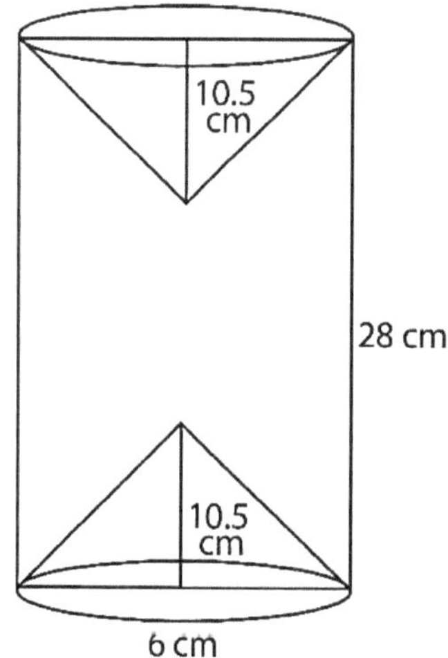

(iv) Prove the identity: $\sqrt{\frac{1-\cos A}{1+\cos A}} = \operatorname{cosec} A - \cot A$

Question 6

(i) In the given figure, O is the centre of the circle, OM ⊥ AB. If ∠ABC = 42°, calculate:
(a) ∠AOC (b) ∠ODC

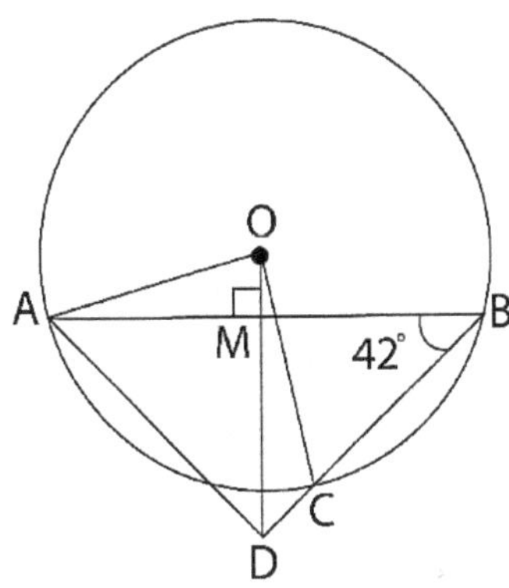

(ii) For what value of k will the point (3, –k) lie on the line $9x + 4y = 3$?

(iii) The angle of elevation of a jet plane from a point A on the ground is 60°. After flight of 15 seconds, the angle of elevation changes to 30°. If the jet plane is flying at a constant height of 1500 m, find the speed of the jet plane.

(iv) Calculate the mean of the distribution, given below, using the short cut method:

Marks	11–20	21–30	31–40	41–50	51–60	61–70	71–80
No. of students	2	6	10	12	9	7	4

Practice Paper – 5 (Unsolved)
(MATHEMATICS)
(Time alloted: One and a half hour)

Answer to this paper must be written on the paper provided separately.
You will not be allowed to write during the first 10 minutes.
This time is to spend in reading the question paper.

Omission of essential working well result in loss of marks.
The intended marks for questions or part of questions are given in the brackets [ ].

Section A (10 Marks)
(Attempt all question from this section)

Question 1

Choose the correct answers to the questions from the given options. (Do not copy the questions. Write the correct options only.) [10]

(i) The point P (5, 3) was reflected in the origin to get the image P′. Co – ordinates of P′.
(a) (–5, 3)
(b) (5, –3)
(c) (–5, –3)
(d) No change

(ii) In a throw of a pair of dice, the probability of getting a doublet is:
(a) $\frac{1}{2}$
(b) $\frac{1}{3}$
(c) $\frac{1}{6}$
(d) $\frac{5}{6}$

(iii) A (5, x), B (–4, 3) and C(–1, –2) are the vertices of the triangle ABC whose centroid is the origin. Calculate the value of x.
(a) –2
(b) –1
(c) 1
(d) 2

(iv) In the figure, chords AB and CD when extended meet at X. Given AB = 4cm, BX = 6cm, XD = 5cm, calculate the length of CD.

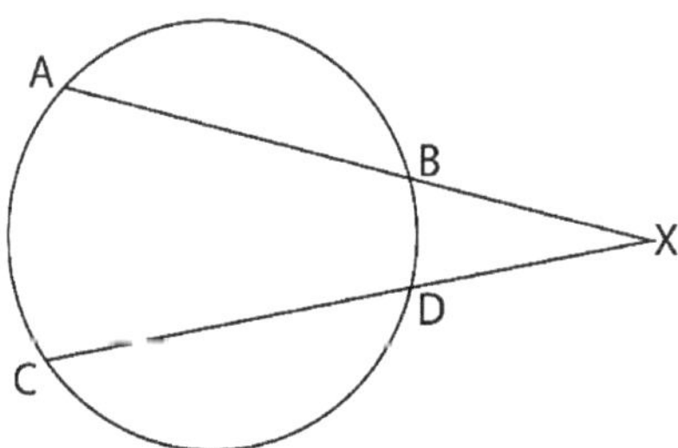

(a) 5 cm
(b) 6 cm

(c) 7 cm
(d) 7.5 cm

(v) The volume of a conical tent is 1232 m^3 and the area of the base floor is 154 m^2. The radius of the floor is:
(a) 7 m
(b) 7.5 m
(c) 3.5 m
(d) 5 m

(vi) Value of $\sec^2 A + \text{cosec}^2 A$ is equal to:
(a) $\cos^2 A$
(b) $\sin^2 A$
(c) $\sec^2 A \times \text{cosec}^2 A$
(d) tan A

(vii) If the mode of the data: 64, 60, 48, x, 43, 48, 43, 34 is 43, then $x + 3 =$
(a) 44
(b) 45
(c) 46
(d) 48

(viii) The equation of a line is $x - y = 4$. Its slope is:
(a) 2
(b) –1
(c) 1
(d) –2

(ix) The value of k if the points A (2, 3), B(4, k) and C(6, –3) are collinear is
(a) 0
(b) 2
(c) –2
(d) 1

(x) Which measure of central tendency can be measured on sorted data only.
(a) mean
(b) mode
(c) median
(d) mean and median

Section B (30 Marks)
(Attempt any three questions from this section)

Question 2

(i) In figure given below, triangle ABC is circumscribed, find x.

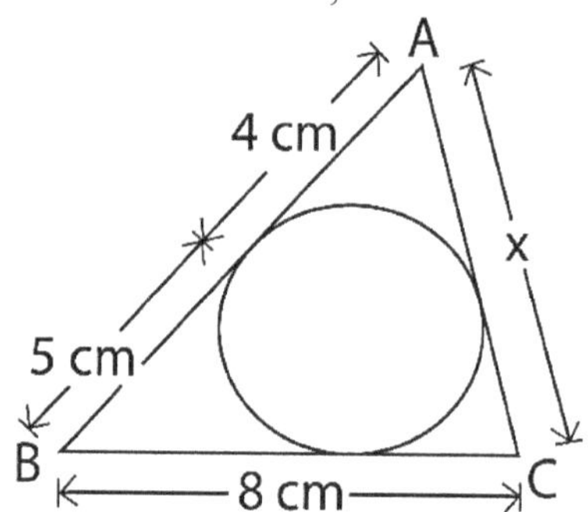

(ii) Calculate the ratio in which the line joining A (6, 5) and B (4, –3) is divided by the line $y = 2$.

(iii) A tower is 100 m high. Find the angle of elevation of its top from a point 100 m away from its foot.

(iv) The mean of the following frequency table is 50. But the frequencies f_1 and f_2 in class 20-40 and 60-80 are missing. Find the missing frequencies:

Class-interval	0 – 20	20 – 40	40 – 60	60 – 80	80 – 100	Total
Frequency	17	f_1	32	f_2	19	120

Question 3

(i) In the given figure, the side of the quadrilateral touches the circle. Prove that AB + CD = BC + DA.

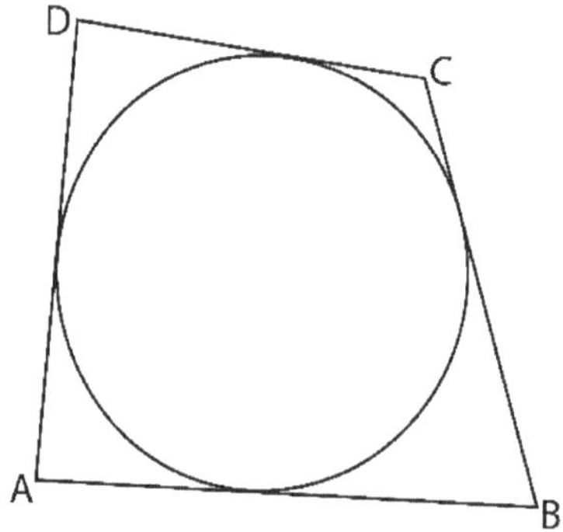

(ii) Find the value of 'p' for which the line $5x - 3y + 2 = 0$ and $6x - py + 7 = 0$ are perpendicular to each other.

(iii) A kite flying at a height of 75 m from the level ground is attached to a straight string inclined at 60° to the horizontal ground. Find the length of the string to the nearest meter.

(iv) Attempt this question on a graph paper. The table shows the distribution of the daily wages, earned by 160 workers in a building site.

Wages	0 – 10	10 – 20	20 – 30	30 – 40	40 – 50	50 – 60	60 – 70	70 – 80
No. of workers	12	20	30	38	24	16	12	8

Using a scale of 2 cm to represent 10 and 2 cm to represent 20 workers, plot these values, and draw a smooth Ogive, through the points. Estimate from the graph.

(a) The Median wage

(b) The upper and lower quartile wage earned by the workers.

Question 4

(i) A semi-circular sheet of metal of diameter 70 cm is bent into an open conical cup by joining two of its radii. Find the radius of the cone so formed.

(ii) The mid-point of the line joining A (2, p) and B (q, 4) is (3, 5). Calculate the numerical values of p and q.

(iii) Prove the identity: $\frac{1+\sec A-\tan A}{1+\sec A+\tan A}=\frac{1-\sin A}{\cos A}$

(iv) Find the mode of the following distribution by drawing a histogram:

Daily wages	31 – 36	37 – 42	43 – 48	49 – 54	55 – 60	61 – 66
No. of workers	6	12	20	15	9	4

Question 5

(i) Prove the identity: (sin A + cos A) (tan A + cot A) = sec A + cosec A

(ii) The king, queen and jack of club are removed from a deck of 52 playing cards and then shuffled. A card is drawn from the remaining cards. Find the probability of getting:

(a) A heart

(b) '9' of red color

(iii) The triangle OAB is reflected in the origin O to triangle OA′B′. A′ and B′ have co – ordinates (−3, −4) and (0, – 5) respectively.

(a) Find the co – ordinates of A and B.

(b) Draw a diagram to represent the given information.

(c) What kind of figure is the quadrilateral ABA′B′?

(iv) From a solid cylinder of height 36 cm and radius 14 cm, a conical cavity of radius 7 cm and height 24 cm is drilled out. Find the volume and the total surface area of the remaining solid.

Question 6

(i) If the numbers 25, 22, 21, $x + 6$, $x + 4$, 9, 8, 6 are in order and their median is 16, find the value of x.

(ii) Two players, Sania and Sonali, play a tennis match. It is known that the probability of Sania winning the match is 0.69. What is the probability of Sonali winning?

(iii) Find the equation of a line passing through the point (2, -5) and making an intercept of – 3 on the y-axis.

(iv) In the given figure, O is the centre of the circle and AB is a diameter. If AC = BD and ∠AOC = 72°, find:

(a) ∠ABC

(b) ∠BAD

(c) ∠ABD

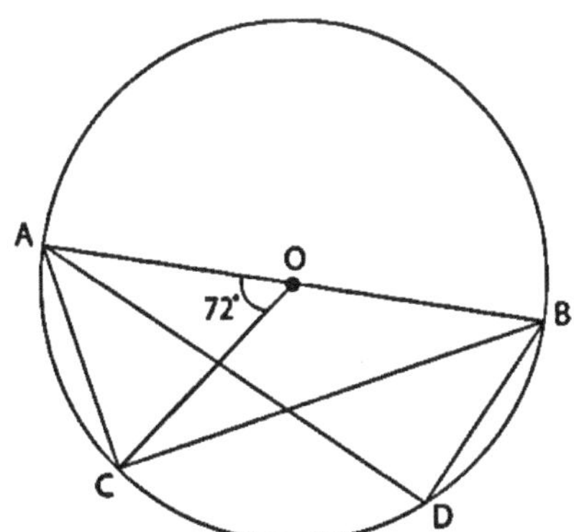

Practice Paper – 6 (Unsolved)
(MATHEMATICS)
(Time alloted: One and a half hour)

Answer to this paper must be written on the paper provided separately.
You will not be allowed to write during the first 10 minutes.
This time is to spend in reading the question paper.

Omission of essential working well result in loss of marks.

The intended marks for questions or part of questions are given in the brackets [ ].

Section A (10 Marks)

(Attempt all question from this section)

Question 1

Choose the correct answers to the questions from the given options. (Do not copy the questions. Write the correct options only.) [10]

(i) P (0, 5) is invariant when reflected in an axis. Name the axis.

(a) $x - axis$

(b) both a and b $axis$

(c) $y - axis$

(d) $None$

(ii) In the class test, the marks scored by 11 students are: 13, 17, 20, 5, 3, 19, 7, 6, 11, 15 and 17. Find lower quartile:

(a) 6

(b) 13

(c) 17

(d) None

(iii) In the given figure find TP if AT = 16 cm and AB = 12 cm.

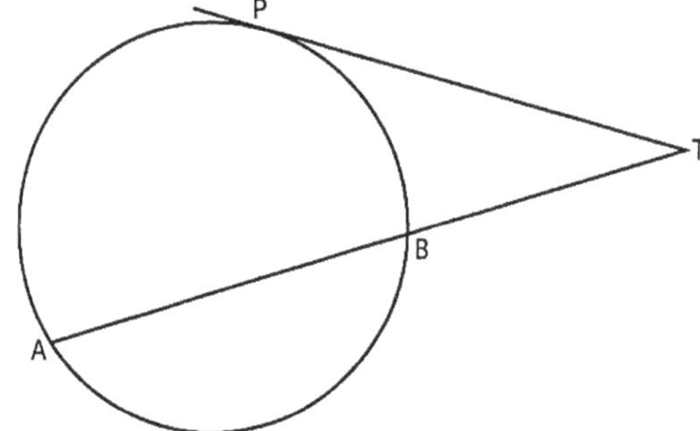

(a) 8 cm

(b) 7 cm

(c) 6 cm

(d) 12 cm

(iv) The probability that the month of January may have 5 Mondays in a leap year:

(a) $\frac{2}{7}$

(b) $\frac{3}{7}$

(c) $\frac{1}{7}$

(d) $\frac{5}{31}$

(v) AB is a diameter of a circle with centre C = (–2, 5). If A = (3, –7), the co – ordinates of B.

(a) $(6, 17)$

(b) $(-7, -17)$

(c) $(-7, 17)$

(d) $(7, 17)$

(vi) The volume of a conical tent is 1232 m^3 and the area of the base floor is 154 m^2. The height of the tent is:

(a) 17.5 m

(b) 24 m

(c) 13.5 m

(d) 14 m

(vii) If a line cuts equal positive intercept on both axes, then its slope is:

(a) 0

(b) 1

(c) –1

(d) 2

(viii) In the given graph, the modal class is:

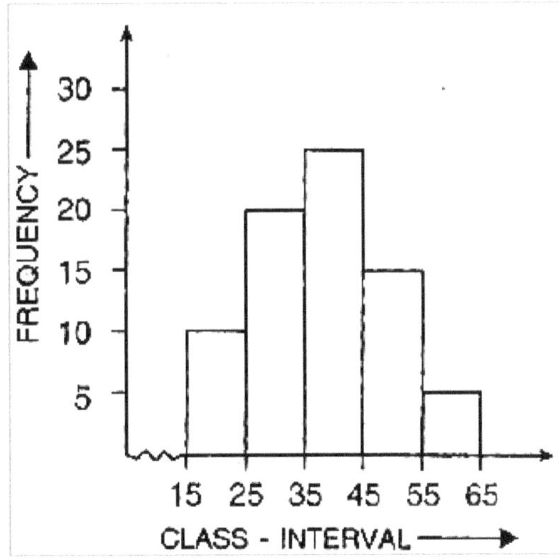

(a) 45 – 55

(b) 35 – 45

(c) 25 – 35

(d) 30 – 40

(ix) The line $4x - 3y + 12 = 0$ meets x – $axis$ at A. Write the co – ordinates of A.

(a) (3, 0)

(b) (–3, 0)

(c) (–4, 0)

(d) (0, –3)

(x) If the height and length of the shadow of a man are the same, then the angle of elevation of the sun is:

(a) 30°
(b) 60°
(c) 45°
(d) 15°

Section B (30 Marks)
(Attempt any three questions from this section)

Question 2

(i) Find the equation of a line which is perpendicular bisector of the line segment joining the points A (3, 2) and B (1, 6).

(ii) Prove the identity: $\frac{\sin A}{1+\cos A} = \operatorname{cosec} A - \cot A$

(iii) Use the information given in the histogram; calculate the mean correct to one decimal place.

(iv) Use a graph paper for this question. (Take 10 small divisions = 1 unit on both axes). P and Q have co-

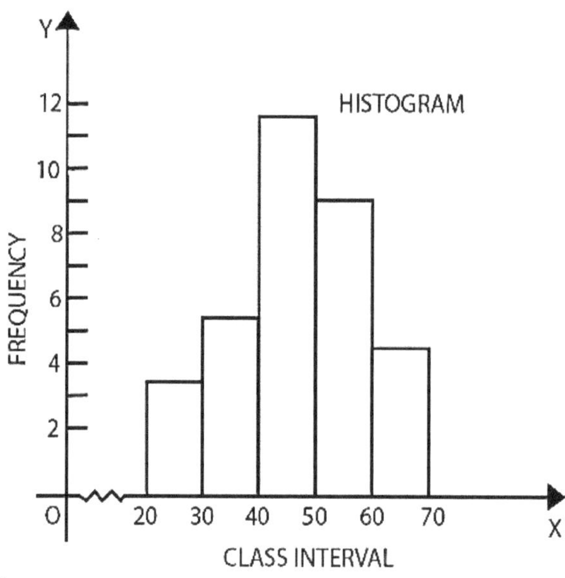

ordinates (0, 5) and (–2, 4).

(a) P is invariant when reflected in an axis. Name the axis.
(b) Find the image of Q on reflection in the axis found in (i).
(c) (0, k) on reflection in the origin is invariant. Write the value of k.

Question 3

(i) Two dice are thrown together. Represent the following events and find their probabilities:
(a) The sum of the numbers shown is 7.
(b) Number on the top of both dice should be same.

(ii) In the following figures, PAB is a secant and PT is tangent to the circle. Find unknown length x in each.

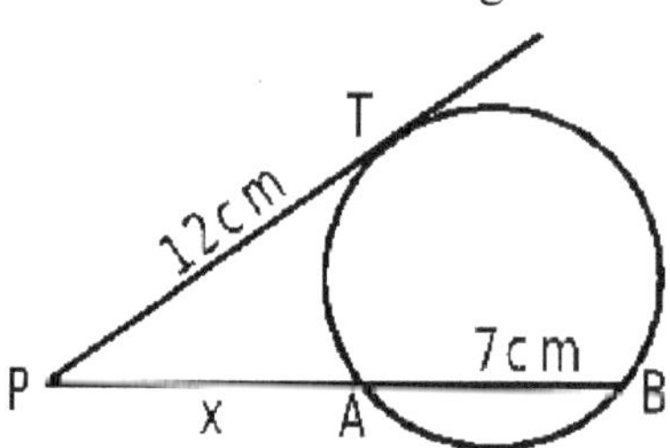

(iii) Find the equation of the perpendicular from the point P (–1, –2) on the line $3x + 4y - 12 = 0$. Also find the co-ordinates of the foot of the perpendicular.

(iv) A kite flying at a height of 75 m from the level ground is attached to a straight string inclined at 60° to the horizontal ground. Find the length of the string to the nearest meter.

Question 4

(i) A solid cone of height 8 cm and base radius 6 cm is melted and recast into identical cones, each of height 2 cm and diameter 1 cm. Find the number of cones formed.

(ii) Given a line segment AB joining the points A (– 4, 6) and B (8, –3). Find:

(a) The ratio in which AB is divided by the $y-axis$.

(b) Find the coordinates of the point of intersection.

(iii) Prove the identity: $\sin^6 A + \cos^6 A = 1 - 3\sin^2 A \cdot \cos^2 A$

(iv) In the given figure, QAP is the tangent at point A and PBD is a straight line. If $\angle ACB = 36°$ and $\angle APB = 42°$, find:

(a) $\angle BAP$

(b) $\angle ABD$

(c) $\angle QAD$

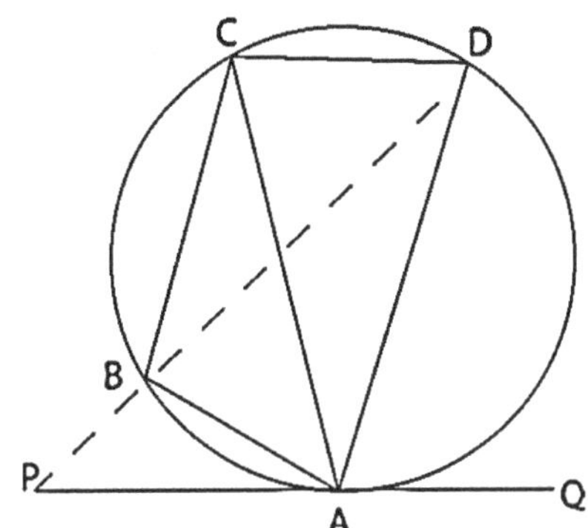

Question 5

(i) 12 pens are defective in a lot of 120 pens. One pen is taken out at random from this lot. Determine the probability that the pen taken out is not defective.

(ii) If $2x - 3y + 5 = 0$ and $px + 6y + 7 = 0$ are parallel lines, find the value of p.

(iii) Draw ogive for the following distribution.

Monthly Income	600 – 700	700 – 800	800 – 900	900 – 1000	1000 – 1100	1100 – 1200	1200 – 1300
No. of employees	40	68	86	120	90	40	26

Hence determine:

(a) The median income

(b) The number of employees whose income exceeds Rs. 1180

(c) The lower and upper quartiles

(d) The interquartile range.

(iv) From a point P on level ground, the angle of elevation of the top of a tower is 30°. If the tower is 100 m high, how far is P from the foot of the tower?

Question 6

(i) The mid-point of the line segment AB shown in the diagram is (4, – 3). Write down the coordinates of A, B.

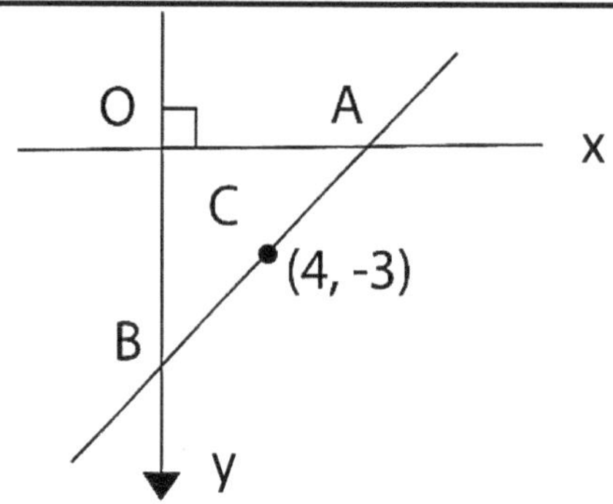

(ii) In the figure, ABF is a straight line and BE || DC. If ∠DAB = 92°, find (i) ∠BCD (ii) ∠ADC

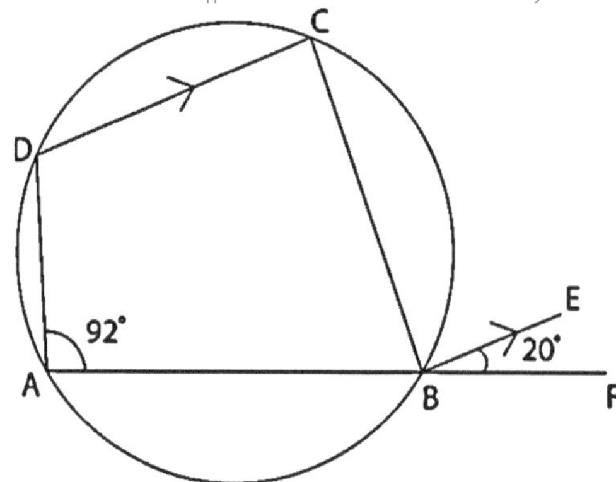

(iii) A cylindrical pillar of temple is shown in the figure which is conical at the top. There are 14 such pillars in the temple. Find the cost of polishing their curved surface area at the rate of Rs. 1.50 per m^2.

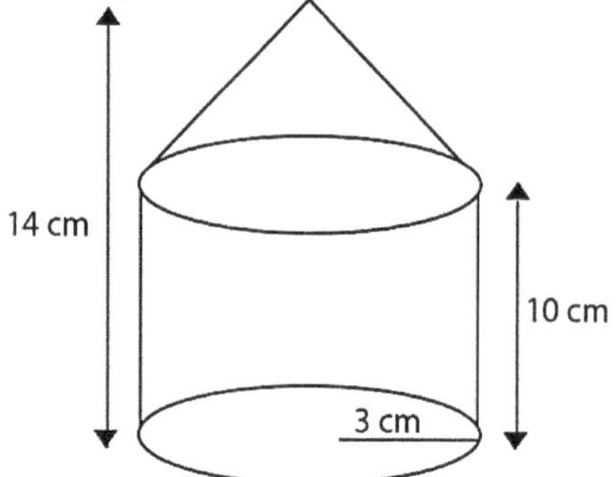

(iv) Find the following frequency distribution, draw histogram. Hence calculate the mode:

Class Interval	0 – 5	5 – 10	10 – 15	15 – 20	20 – 25	25 – 30
Frequency	2	7	18	10	8	5

Practice Paper – 7 (Unsolved)
(MATHEMATICS)
(Time alloted: One and a half hour)

Answer to this paper must be written on the paper provided separately.
You will not be allowed to write during the first 10 minutes.
This time is to spend in reading the question paper.

Omission of essential working well result in loss of marks.
The intended marks for questions or part of questions are given in the brackets [ ].

Section A (10 Marks)
(Attempt all question from this section)

Question 1

Choose the correct answers to the questions from the given options. (Do not copy the questions. Write the correct options only.) [10]

(i) The point P (5, -3) is reflected in the point Q (2, 2) to become point R. Co – ordinates of R.
(a) (2, 0)
(b) (5, 2)
(c) (1, 7)
(d) (–1, 7)

(ii) From the following distribution, state the modal class.

Mid Value	12	18	24	30	36	42	48
Frequency	20	12	8	24	16	8	12

(a) 30 – 40
(b) 27 – 33
(c) 33 – 39
(d) 30 – 36

(iii) If a pole of height of 6 m casts a shadow $2\sqrt{3}$ m long on the ground, then the sun's elevation is:
(a) 30°
(b) 60°
(c) 45°
(d) 90°

(iv) The unknown length x in the following figure:
(a) 3 cm
(b) 2 cm
(c) 2.5 cm
(d) 4 cm

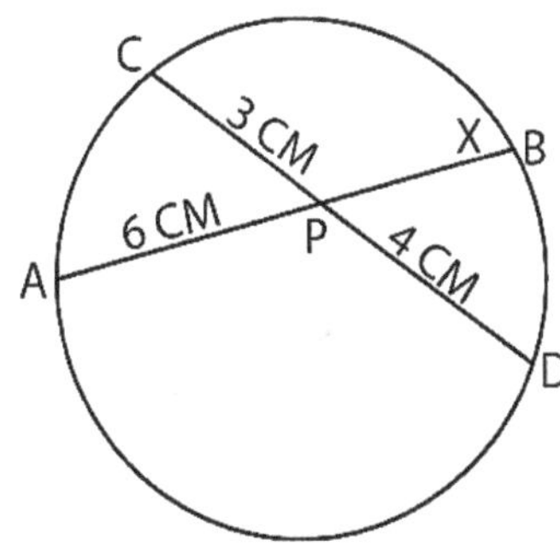

(v) The total surface area of a right circular cone of radius 5 cm is 90π cm^2. Its slant height is:
(a) 13 cm
(b) 14 cm

(c) 12 cm
(d) 11 cm

(vi) M is the mid – point of the line segment joining the points A (0, 4) and B (6, 0). Co- ordinates of M.
(a) (– 3, 2)
(b) (3, 2)
(c) (4, 2)
(d) (3, 4)

(vii) The value of $(1 - \tan A)^2 + (1 + \tan A)^2$ is
(a) $2 \tan^2 A$
(b) $2 \sec^2 A$
(c) $2 \sin^2 A$
(d) $\sec^2 A$

(viii) A game of chance consists of an arrow which comes to rest, pointing at one of the regions 1, 2 or 3. O is the centre of the circle. Find the probability that the arrow is not resting on 2.

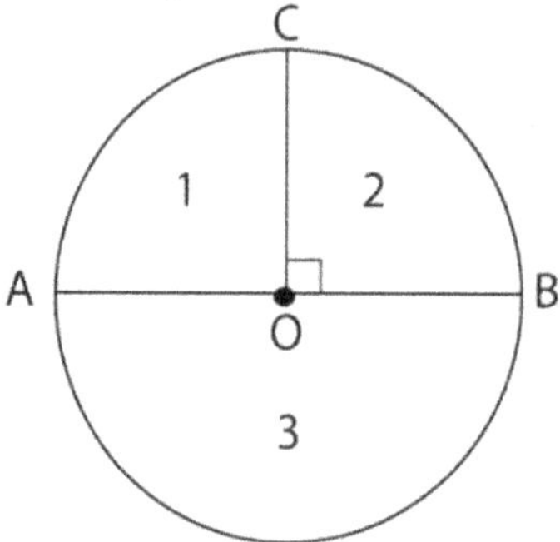

(a) $\frac{1}{2}$
(b) $\frac{3}{4}$
(c) $\frac{2}{3}$
(d) $\frac{3}{2}$

(ix) Find the mean of the following distribution.

X	4	6	9	10	15
F	5	10	10	7	8

(a) 10
(b) 9
(c) 8
(d) 8.5

(x) Find the equation of the line passing through (–5, 7) and parallel to $x-axis$.
(a) $y = -5$
(b) $y = 7$
(c) $x = 7$
(d) $y = -7$

Section B (30 Marks)
(Attempt any three questions from this section)

Question 2

(i) Prove the identity: $\tan A + \cot A = \sec A \cdot \operatorname{cosec} A$

(ii) In the figure given, alongside, line segment AB meets $X - axis$ at A and $Y - axis$ at B. The point P (–3, 4) on AB divides it in the ratio 2: 3. Find the coordinates of A and B.

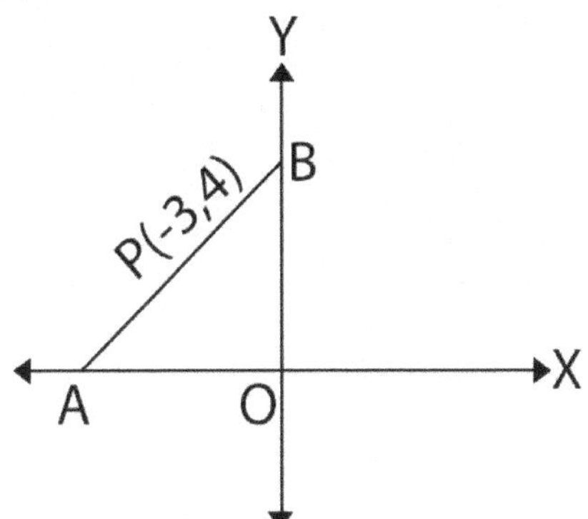

(iii) The marks obtained by a set of students in an examination are given below:

Marks	5	10	15	20	25	30
No.of students	6	4	6	12	x	4

Given that the mean mark of the set is 18, calculate the numerical value of x.

(iv) In the given figure, ABCDE is a pentagon inscribed in a circle such that Acis a diameter and side BC || AE. If angle BAC = 50°, find giving reasons:

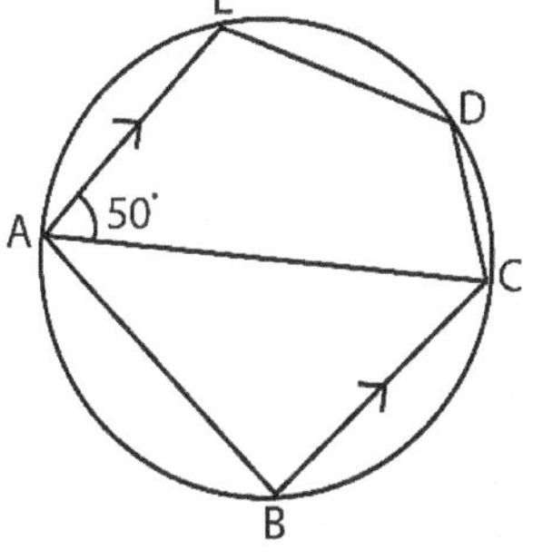

(a) $\angle EDC$
(b) $\angle ACB$
(c) $\angle BEC$

Hence prove that BE is also a diameter.

Question 3

(i) In the given figure O is the centre of the circle and AB is a tangent at B. If AB = 15 cm & AC=7.5 cm. Calculate the radius of the circle.

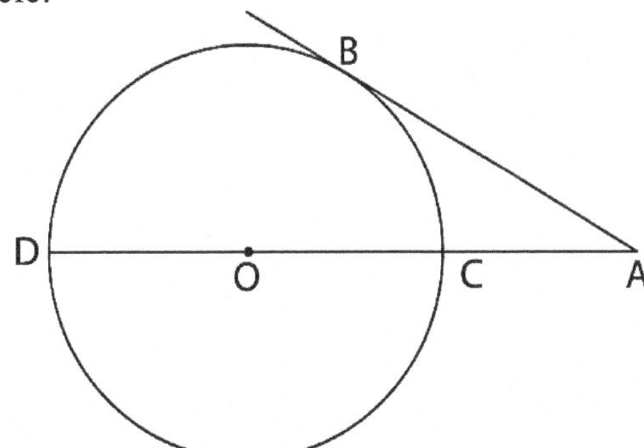

(ii) A (5, 4), B(-3, -2) and C (1, -8) are the vertices of a triangle ABC. Find the slope of the median AD.

(iii) The heights (in nearest cm) of 60 students of a certain school are given in the following frequency distribution table:

Height (in cm)	151	152	153	154	155	156	157
No of students	6	4	11	9	16	12	2

Find:

(a) median
(b) lower quartile
(c) upper quartile
(d) inter quartile-range

(iv) A ladder rests against a vertical wall such that the top of the ladder reaches the top of the wall. The ladder is inclined at 60° with the ground, and the bottom of the ladder is 1.5 m away from the foot of the wall. Find:

(a) The length of the ladder and
(b) The height of the wall.

Question 4

(i) A farmer connects a pipe of internal diameter 20 cm from a canal into a cylindrical tank in his field, which is 10 m in diameter and 2 m deep. If water flows through the pipe at the rate of 3 km/hour, in how much time will the tank be filled?

(ii) In the given figure, O is the centre of the circle. The tangents at B and D intersect each other at point P. If AB parallel to CD and ∠ABC = 55°, find:

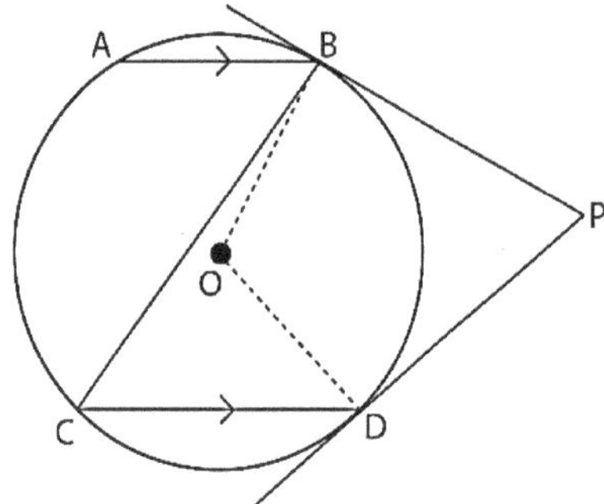

(a) ∠BOD
(b) ∠BPD
(c) Prove the identity: $\frac{1+\cos A}{1-\cos A} = \frac{\tan^2 A}{(\sec A-1)^2}$

(iii) Use a graph sheet for this question. Take 1 cm = 1 unit along both x and y *axis*.

(a) Plot the following points: A (0, 5), B (3, 0), C (1, 0) and D (1, –5)
(b) Reflect the points B, C and D on the y *axis* and name them as B′, C′ and D′ respectively.
(c) Write down the coordinates of B′, C′ and D′.
(d) Join the points A, B, C, D, D′, C′, B′, A in order and give a name to the closed figure ABCDD'C'B'.

Question 5

(i) Find the probability of having 5 Sundays in the month of March in a leap year.

(ii) In the given figure AB is a diameter of the circle APBR, APQ and RBQ are straight lines. A = 35° and Q = 25°

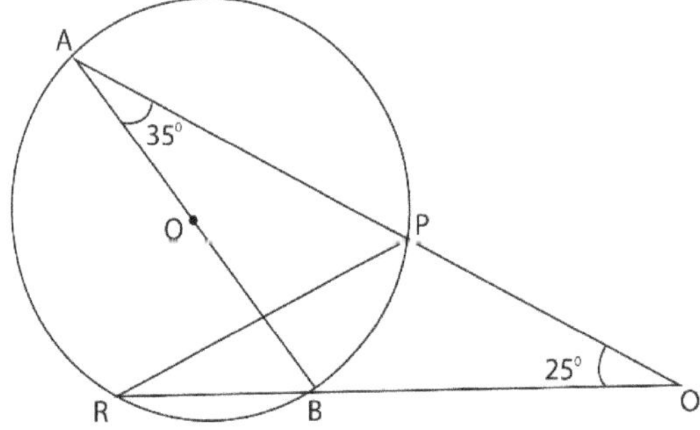

find: (i) angle PRB (iii) angle BPR.

(iii) Find the equation of the line passing through the point of intersection of $7x + 6y = 71$ and $5x - 8y = -23$; and perpendicular to the line $4x - 2y = 1$.

(iv) A vessel in the form of an inverted cone is filled with water to the brim. Its height is 20 cm and diameter is 16.8 cm. Two equal solid cones are dropped in it so that they are fully submerged. As a result, one third of the water in the original cone overflows. What is the volume of each of the solid cones submerged?

Question 6

(i) The mid points of three sides of a triangle are (1, 1), (2, –3) and (3, 4). Find the centroid of the triangle and the co-ordinates of the vertices.

(ii) Find the probability of having 53 Sunday in

(a) a non-leap year (b) a leap year.

(iii) A Mathematics aptitude test of 50 students was recorded as follows:

Marks	50 - 60	60 - 70	70 - 80	80 - 90	90 - 100
No. of Students	4	8	14	19	5

Draw a histogram for the above data using a graph paper and locate the mode.

(iv) A vertical tower stands on a horizontal plane and is surmounted by a vertical flagstaff of height h meter. At a point on the plane, the angle of elevation of the bottom of the flagstaff is $\alpha$and that of the top of flagstaff is β.Prove that the height of the tower is:

$$\frac{h \tan \alpha}{\tan \beta - \tan \alpha}$$